If it ain't broke... BREAK IT!

and Other Unconventional Wisdom for a Changing Business World

ROBERT J. KRIEGEL
and LOUIS PATLER

WARNER BOOKS

A Time Warner Inc. Company

To Edith Kraskin Kriegel, a courageous woman, whose passion, perseverance, and love have taught me that anything is possible.

RJK

In memory of my mother, Connie Patler

LP

Warner Books, Inc., 1271 Avenue of the Americas, New York, NY 10020

W A Time Warner Company

Printed in the United States of America

First trade printing: March 1992

10 9 8 7 6 5 4

Library of Congress Cataloging-in-Publication Data

Kriegel, Robert J.
    If it ain't broke, break it / Robert J. Kriegel.
      p.   cm.
    Includes bibliographical references and index.
    ISBN 0-446-39359-2
    1. Success in business. 2. Job stress. 3. Organizational
change. I. Title.
HF5386.K855 1991
658.4'063—dc20   90-50533
                                          CIP

Book design by Richard Oriolo
Cover design by Mike Stromberg
Cover photo by Art Rogers

What Do These Boardroom Mavericks, Sports Innovators, and Community Leaders Have in Common?

They know that the path to obsolescence is paved with good plans gone bad. They know that you can't get to the top while you're looking at the bottom line. And they know that what you need to make it in this unpredictable market is a double dose of "Break-It" Thinking!

If it ain't broke . . .
BREAK IT!

"In sports or business you can't keep doing what you have always been doing and expect to win in these dynamic times. . . . This book will not only enable you to succeed in the nineties but to have repeated successes."
—**Tony LaRussa,**
manager, Oakland Athletics

◆

"Will make you want to become a 'Break-It' Thinker."
—**Pat Riley, coach, New York Knicks,**
NBC-TV commentator

◆

"Great book! Not the old methods, 'better, quicker, cheaper,' but different and fun."
—**Lois A. Hodg-peth,**
vice president, AT&T

◆

"Shows us how to put innovative energy back into our people."
—**Peter L. Thigpen, senior vice president,**
Levi-Strauss & Co.-U.S.

◆

more . . .

"Change is reality these days. The winners of tomorrow will be those who have the 'Break-It' thinking attitude described by the author. I enjoyed reading it."
—Glen Arnold, president and CEO,
Ameritech Applied Technologies

◆

"The logic of this thesis, i.e., change is a permanent state, is irrefutable. If we don't want to go the way of the dinosaur, we'd better listen."
—Rabbi Joseph B. Glaser, executive vice president,
Central Conference of American Rabbis

◆

"Insightful! Inspiring! A book that will motivate people and give them usable strategies for succeeding in these exciting times."
—Kenneth J. Casey, president,
Professional Investors Security Fund

◆

"Must reading for anyone interested in doubling their mental horsepower. I got more great ideas on how to improve my business and interpersonal skills from this book than the last 50 books I have read—combined."
—Ken Dychwald, Ph.D., author of *The Age Wave*,
chairman, Age Wave, Inc.

◆

". . . New tools to challenge our thinking. . . . May well prepare us to reach new levels of accomplishment."
—Robert W. O'Leary, president and CEO,
American Medical International

◆

"Stimulating, motivating and capped with humor and hidden wisdom, a must for the people leaders of the '90s."
—Alex Sozonoff, general manager,
Europe Hewlett-Packard

"This book not only inspired me and gave me dozens of ideas I have already put into practice but it was fun to read. It is a book for everyone."
—Huey Johnson, former director of Nature Conservatory and secretary of resources for the State of California

◆

"This book makes incredibly good sense. You find yourself thinking with new enthusiasm and direction."
—Michael Creedman, founding host, "Marketplace," National Public Radio

◆

"An unconventional road map for addressing the myriad personal challenges confronting us all in today's dynamic environment. The 'Break-It' Thinking techniques are critical for anyone who wants to excel in these high-pressure times."
—William D. Hanisch, president and CEO, Keystone Resort, Colorado

◆

"A uniquely modern management philosophy. It should be must reading for all of us as we head into the '90s. I thoroughly enjoyed it."
—David Dombrowski, V.P., general manager, Montreal Expos

◆

"*If It Ain't Broke . . . BREAK IT!* prepares everyone for the '90s. I consider this must reading."
—Bob Siegel, president, Levi-Strauss Menswear Division

◆

"An irreverent, punchy, socks-off look at the contemporary corporate mind containing enough new ideas to turn around a dozen new companies and start ten more."
—Paul Hawken, author of *How to Grow a Business*, member, *Inc.* magazine Entrepreneur's Hall of Fame

ALSO BY ROBERT J. KRIEGEL

Inner Skiing (WITH TIMOTHY GALLWEY)
The C Zone: Peak Performance Under Pressure
(WITH MARILYN HARRIS KRIEGEL)

ALSO BY LOUIS PATLER

An American Ensemble

Contents

For several centuries, down through many dynasties, a village was known for its exquisite and fragile porcelain.

Especially striking were its urns: High as tables, wide as chairs, they were admired around the globe for their strong form and delicate beauty.

Legend has it that when each urn was finished, there was one final step. The artist broke it—and then put it back together with gold filigree.

An ordinary urn was then transformed into a priceless work of art. What seemed finished wasn't . . . until it was broken.

A "Break-It" Team—Acknowledgments

Bob Kriegel

Because of all the people who participate in the finished product, a book, like a magazine, needs a masthead. Here is mine:

—Marilyn Kriegel, my wife, lover, and best friend, was in on the project since its inception and was an invaluable aid. Her input can be found on just about every page. I can't catalog all the ways she helped, giving straight feedback on the material; she was an emotional and spiritual guide as well.

—Sue Johnson, my assistant, is also a critically important member of our team. Unselfishly giving her time and feedback, as well as her unfailingly positive nature and good humor, she helped in innumerable ways to make the process a winning experience for all.

—Myrtle Harris, my mother-in-law, was also a major player on our team who came through working long and late hours when the finish line was upon us.

—My son, Otis, for providing love and joy and being a great coach.

—Gary Friedman for being a great friend and advisor in some very tough times.

—My editor, Susan Suffes, who became a good friend as well as a vital team player, for her sense of humor as well as important feedback, encouragement and support throughout the project.

—And many thanks to my agents and friends John Brockman and Katinka Matson for their tough but honest feedback and constant cheering throughout the years.

—Kristin Shannon, chair of Pacific Rim Research in Sausalito, who generously shared her time and experience.

I want also to thank all of the people who took hours out of their busy schedules to be interviewed. And all of my friends who, on hikes, runs, bike rides, and over dinners, supplied endless amounts of encouragement and advice. Among these are Trish McCall, David and Laurie Brandt, Carole Levine, Alan Becker, Huey Johnson, John Rutter, Mark Rosenblatt, Doug Kriegel, Gail Kriegel, Barry Mallin, David Smith, Suki Miller, Stuart Miller, John Syer, Chris Conolly, Ann Geddes, Michael Creedman, Chuck and Judy Nichols, Hillary Maddox and Judy Simpson.

Equally important in this team effort are the thousands of people who have attended my speeches and seminars and shared their ideas and energy.

Acknowledgments

Louis Patler

I want to thank Bob Kriegel for asking me to collaborate with him on this book and for the tremendous opportunity for me to work closely with . . . an endangered species: a best-selling author who is also receptive to new ideas! The future, Bob and I agree, doesn't just "happen"—we dream it, we shape it, we sculpt it.

To my children—Kale, Elina, Caitlin, Johana and Kellin—go my thanks for reminding me daily of the challenges they face. They taught me that if our planet is to survive, and they are to *thrive*, we all must question the conventional mind set and change our thinking, our values, and our priorities.

Special thanks go to Marilyn Kriegel, who readily shared her unconventional wisdom and keen writerly eye. Susan Johnson showed personal and professional grace as we moved from hunches to ideas to manuscript to book. I would also like to thank those who offered time, encouragement and (most importantly) honest feedback: Carl Atkinson, Sara Nolan, Brian Lantier, Doug Huneke, Debbie Ward, The Hon. Elaine McCoy, Miriam Hall, Allen Loren, Max Shapiro, Karen

Gideon, Carole Whitley, and Pat Yount. Kristin Shannon, chair of
Pacific Rim Research, provided both wisdom and humor in full
measure.

I thank my co-creators at The New Games Foundation for teaching
me the value of cooperation, innovation, flexibility, integrity, interde-
pendence and balance in life, and for the realization that he who laughs,
lasts.

More than anyone else, to my wife Catherine goes my utmost
thanks for uplifting my spirit day in and day out, and for sharing her
ideas, creativity and values with me.

While twenty years of experience creating businesses, foundations
and a college offers a fertile source of anecdotes, vignettes and tall
tales, some of the best insights come from my mother Connie, who
died shortly before writing began. She was curious, courageous,
intuitive, and *very* funny. When she laughed, the room filled. She would
have enjoyed this book.

Author's Note

The reader of a book written by two people deserves an explanation of how the authors combined their efforts. Because the material in the book is based on my experience in the field of human and team performance, the first person refers to me. I would dictate the first draft, Louis would then rewrite it. We would keep changing it and reaching further. The collaboration was a true example of "Break-It Thinking" which enabled us to go beyond what I brought to the subject. The final product resulted from our combined commitment, communication, and cooperation.

Progress was only possible when we were able to let go of our attachments to "mine" and to allow our talents to cooperate creatively. In writing this book we had to practice its precepts. We tried "easy" and didn't stick to our plans. Some of our best ideas came on long walks and shooting baskets.

Additionally, because the English language does not have a word for third-person singular that does not connote gender, we attempted to use "he" and "she" equally.

RJK

Introduction

On October 17, 1989, an event occurred that foreshadowed the 1990s. I was watching my son's high school soccer game in Golden Gate Park, San Francisco, when the big earthquake hit. For me, it made explicit the implicit state of the world. It shook everything up. Within a short period of time the Berlin Wall came down, Russia's political and economic environment radically changed, much of Eastern Europe did a 180-degree turn, and the Middle East blew up. The dust has not settled—nor will it.

Welcome to the 1990s: a time of rapid, unpredictable, nerve-shattering change.

The one thing we can count on as we approach the twenty-first century is the certainty that rip-roaring change will challenge our understanding and shake up the basic foundations of the world around us, in every area. Whatever we do, and wherever we do it, everything—workstyles, economic conditions, technology, corporate structures, global communications, lifestyles, environmental responsibilities—everything is changing at a dizzying rate.

In the past, change occurred incrementally, at a slower pace. We had the luxury of making long-range projections and doing strategic planning with some degree of certainty. But today, the rate of change is accelerating *exponentially*, shifting so fast it is tough to make even short-term predictions accurately.

In the future, exponential change will continue to occur everywhere. Consider these few projections as we enter the twenty-first century:

- In 10 years, at least one fourth of all current "knowledge" and accepted "practice" will be obsolete. The life span of new technologies is now down to eighteen months . . . and decreasing.[1]

- Within 10 years, 20 times as many people will be working at home.

- Two-career families will multiply; currently one half of all families have two paychecks; this will become three quarters.

- If you are under 25, you can expect to change careers every decade and jobs every four years, partly because you choose to and partly because entire industries will disappear and be replaced by others we haven't heard of yet.[2]

- Women now own more than 3 million businesses, and will own more than half of all businesses by the year 2000.[3]

- The 40-hour work week will become a dinosaur. We will work 20 percent more and sleep 20 percent less than we did a decade ago.

This is a new and unpredictable world. Any resemblance to the past is purely coincidental. We haven't played in this arena before. The rules are different. The game itself is changing. Everything is moving faster. And what we need to know and how we need to act in order to win has changed as well.

The old ways that worked in a slower paced world are no longer effective. Recycling, revamping, or revising the Conventional Wisdom no longer works. To face these challenges we cannot rely on the "tried and true," because what was tried yesterday is no longer true today.

To keep ahead of the changes, increased competition, and complexity of these times requires a whole new way of thinking, one that is a radical departure from the past. Leaders who stick with conventional formulas will not only miss great opportunities but find their organizations struggling in the backwash.

A fundamental change in thinking is needed that is as radical as the scope, scale, and pace of today's change. In this book the Conventional Wisdom that worked in the past, as well as many traditional assumptions, beliefs, and habits, will be challenged. In their place guidelines will be offered for an *Unconventional Wisdom—UW—*for these uncertain times.

1

Surf's Up! . . . Embrace the Unexpected

LIFE IN THE FAST LANE

"I feel threatened by the new college grads," an engineer at Hewlett-Packard told me. "The half-life of knowledge around here is less than three years. So I'm a veritable antique, and I'm not even thirty yet!"

Today's skills, knowledge, and products live fast, get old before their time, and die young. We are all being asked to learn, do and produce more with less money, fewer resources, and no time to spare.

And this laser-fast pace of change will continue. "Mankind's cumulative knowledge had doubled in the last decade—and will double again every five years," says billion-dollar SPX Corporation CEO Robert D. Tuttle. "It is not an exaggeration to say that more scientific and technical advances will happen in the next year than happened in the *entire* decade of the 70s!"[1]

"On a scale of 1 to 10, I would rate the changes that we have gone through since divestiture as a 4," an AT&T division vice president recently told a thousand of his beleaguered managers. "Using that same scale," he warned, "I see the changes coming at us as an 8." His estimate may actually be too low!

Change is happening faster than we can keep tabs on and threatens to "shake the foundations of the most secure American business,"[2] warned a recent study by the U.S. Congress's Office of Technology. No industry will escape, no one is exempt.

Pardon the grammar, but even if it "ain't broke" today, it will be tomorrow. Today's innovations are tomorrow's antiques.

LEARNING TO PLAY ALICE'S CROQUET

Best-selling author and Harvard Business School professor Rosabeth Moss Kanter likens the constant changes happening today to the croquet game in *Alice in Wonderland*, a game in which "nothing remains stable for very long, because everything is alive and changing."[3]

Today in every aspect of life we are confronted with far-reaching, dramatic changes. Like Alice, every time we turn around the game has changed. No sooner are the rules established than they become obsolete. By the time we notice that a $75,000 house is a deal, it costs $300,000. And as my secretary pointed out, the overnight letter, which was the speed innovation of the eighties, is now used only when you are not in a hurry.

DODGING CULTURE SHOCK

"People are going through an unbelievable culture shock," says a prominent management consultant. "Jobs are vanishing in mergers, takeovers, and restructurings . . . traditional roles are being radically altered. People are being asked to learn . . . entirely new and different ways of thinking, behaving, communicating, and motivating. Their survival in the job, not to mention their success, will depend on their ability or willingness to do something adults hate to do . . . change. The pressures can be intense."

Even those who are doing well feel stretched to the breaking point.

In terms of energy, creativity, and motivation many of us have hit the wall . . . and it hurts.

"Seven A.M. meetings, fourteen-hour days, six-day work weeks . . . and I still can't keep up," a Pacific Telesis marketing executive told me. "How much more can we do? I'm being pushed to—no, *beyond*—the limit."

"We are inundated . . . my mind can't handle it," says Manhattan architect James Truzo. "The pace is so fast I sometimes feel like a gunfighter dodging bullets."[4]

"I never have my head above water for long," a manager of a large electronics company told me. "I feel like all I do is just come up for air. And even when I catch my breath, I know that it's just a momentary lull before the next storm will hit."

CHANGING OUTMODED ATTITUDES

You don't have to be a Nobel laureate economist to see the effects of today's newer, faster game on American business. We are playing a desperate game of catch-up in industries we pioneered. We were world leaders, and now we trail behind.

How did this happen? How did we go from being the leader to being behind in the pack? An MIT productivity study sees the problem largely attributable to *"a deep reservoir of outmoded attitudes and policies."*[5]

"It's no wonder we managed our way to economic decline," writes management consultant Stanley Davis, author of the highly acclaimed book *Future Perfect*. "Our managerial models don't suit today's business. We are still using the model GM founder Alfred Sloan developed for organizing corporate America back in the twenties. As a result we have industrially modeled organizations running post-industrial businesses."[6]

In the face of accelerating change in every area of our lives, the conventional thinking that guided us in past decades is outdated. It's clear that the Conventional Wisdom that worked in the calm seas of the past won't work in today's turbulent environment.

THE PASSING GAME

A vivid example of the pitfalls of sticking to the conventional game plan in times of change occurred in football just after the turn of this century. In 1905, football was a low-scoring game of running and kicking. Guys in leather helmets and a smattering of padding plodded down the field toward the goal line. The offense consisted of formations like the "flying wedge," in which seven players ran together into the middle of the opposition in the hope of gaining three or four yards at a time. It was a tough, gritty game.

Then, in 1906, the forward pass was legalized, making it possible to gain 40 yards with the flick of a wrist. During the first season, however, most teams stayed almost entirely with their conventional, tried and true running game.

Recognizing that they were entering a new era in which the old strategy of "three yards and a cloud of dust" would fast become obsolete, St. Louis University's coaches adapted quickly, switching to an offense that used the forward pass extensively. That season *they outscored their opponents 402–11!*

SEEKING A NEW WAY TO THINK

Each day we face change as challenging as the introduction of the forward pass to football. Every time we turn around, our "game" has changed. The rules are no sooner established than they become obsolete.

In these uncertain times we can no longer recycle, modify, or revise the Conventional Wisdom that worked in a bygone era. That's like trying to win a football game in 1906 with a better running game while the competition throws passes over your head. We need to take bold, fresh steps.

NO PICNIC

"The pace of change in the nineties," says GE chairman Jack Welch, "will make the eighties look like a picnic, a walk in the park. Simply doing what worked in the eighties . . . will be too slow."[7] As Iacocca says, "I have to take risks every day. I'd rather not, but the world doesn't give me that option."[8] In this revved-up, more volatile world, the old, tried and true ways of thinking about (and responding to) change that worked in the past, won't work in the future.

"To keep ahead in this dynamic environment in which the rules are constantly changing," says Bank of America senior vice president K. Shelly Porges, "requires more than a change in structure, it requires a *whole new way of thinking*."[9] She's right, and she's in good company.

The distinguished MIT Productivity Panel is calling on U.S. executives to *fundamentally rethink* their assumptions and habits in this era of exponential change and uncertainty. "We cannot fix things simply by trying harder to do the same things that have failed to work in the past," the report concluded. "The international business environment has changed and we must change too."[10]

RIDING THE WAVE OF CHANGE

"The time to change is when you don't have to; when you're on the crest of the wave, not when you're in the trough," an enlightened executive told me. In an environment where waves of change are coming at us, seemingly from all directions, his choice of a metaphor—as well as its content—couldn't be better. As the events of the last decade have clearly demonstrated, SURF'S UP!

Many years ago while a lifeguard at Rockaway Beach, New York, I became an ardent body surfer. The most fun was a day or two after the annual late summer hurricane, when we'd close the beach and hit the surf to ride the huge rollers. The best surfers usually weren't the greatest swimmers. But they had a certain mind-set. This mind-set and the rules we used for riding those hurricane-driven waves are very similar to those needed today for riding the turbulent waves of change in the business world.

Below are some of the rules for catching any wave you decide to ride.

PASSION RULES

The rules for catching and riding a wave are fairly simple. The challenge is to turn them into action. As in the business world there were always those who are great at "lip service." They look the part, act the part and talk the part but never go where the action is, in the water. These types are called "hodads." They have fancy equipment, the right clothes, the right jargon. To hear them tell it, they are the heir apparent to Duke Kahanamoku, Mickey Dora or Tom Curren. But you'll never catch them in the water. As they say in Texas, "they're all hat and no cattle."

The best surfers don't spend a lot of time on the beach, talking about surfing. They love the water and no matter how rough or calm it is, they are out there looking for a wave. They are totally committed, body, mind, and spirit. "Passion Rules" is a bumper sticker that I have seen on many surfer's cars today. Not a bad bottom line for any of us in whatever we do.

NO DARE/NO FLAIR

Good surfers, like top performers everywhere, are constantly pushing their limits. Combining skill and preparation with boldness and daring, they are continually trying new moves and going for bigger waves and longer rides. Knowing that no two waves are ever the same, they try and ride each one a little differently. Staying ahead of a wave demands taking risks and constantly challenging yourself and those around you.

EXPECT TO WIPE OUT

Good surfers understand the power of the waves and embrace the risks of the sport. As such they are prepared to eat some sand before lunch every day. They know that for every ride there may be two or three times as many wipeouts.

Changing, uncertain conditions are not a source of fear; rather they are seen as an ally, an opportunity to test their strength and agility, mentally and physically. Top performers welcome the unexpected, thrive in the big waves, and learn from their wipeouts. They know, in fact, that if they are not wiping out they are playing it too safe and won't keep improving.

DON'T TURN YOUR BACK ON THE OCEAN

Understanding the nature of the environment, surfers know that they are dealing with forces beyond their control. They realize that uncertainty and unpredictability are the name of the game, just as it is in our world. They respect the power and they appreciate the grandeur of the ocean. Consequently, they never take it for granted. They never turn their back on the ocean.

KEEP LOOKING "OUTSIDE"

In surfing lingo, "outside" refers to the waves coming in on the horizon. Surfers know that you have to pay attention to the wave closest to you, the one you are about to ride and—simultaneously—to what's coming.

There are two reasons to look "outside." First, there may be a bigger and better wave just behind the one in front of you. And second, if you haven't noticed what's on the horizon, that next big wave may break on top of you just as you are coming up for air, after riding this one.

MOVE BEFORE IT MOVES YOU

To catch a wave, you have to begin moving well before it comes to you. A big wave, like change itself, moves so fast, that if you wait too long it will pass you by and leave you struggling in the backwash.

Looking outside enables you to prepare for the future. Just as in the outside world, the surfer must know what is coming on the horizon and move before it arrives. Learning to look outside and move before the wave reaches us teaches us a vital lesson for staying ahead in any turbulent environment.

NEVER SURF ALONE

In a complex society no one tackles life all by him or herself. No smart person tries to do everything or be everything to everybody all the time. Surfers, knowing this full-well, have one final rule: Never surf alone!

They know that it's important to have the security of a good backup should an emergency arise. They also know that by pooling their knowledge and resources they can learn about and get to more exotic spots. They can also trade tips about the latest equipment, hot spots and techniques.

It's also a lot more fun having a friend along. You have someone who can "talkstory" with you while you wait for the next set of waves, someone with whom you can share hopes, dreams and joys. In a world in which most of us are becoming increasingly isolated, we can all experience more joy, creativity and effectiveness with a little help from our friends.

The Surfer's Rules

1. Passion rules.

2. No Dare/No Flair.

3. Expect to wipe out.

4. Never turn your back on the ocean.

5. Keep looking "outside."

6. Move before it moves you.

7. Never surf alone.

SURF'S UP! GET YOUR BALANCE

Applying the surfer's mind-set to your own life and work is exhilarating. Knowing the rules for riding waves in the ocean can teach us how to ride the waves of change whether they are rolling into New York, Illinois and Arizona or Hong Kong, Paris and Moscow.

The future—unpredictable and uncertain—is coming toward us like enormous waves of change. Set after set after set they are getting bigger and coming faster. The surf is up from California to Calgary to Calcutta. But how we respond is a matter of choice. We can stay on the beach or get out into the water.

The future belongs to those who decide to ride; to those who have the courage to paddle out where the big ones are breaking; to those who welcome the unexpected.

This book describes a type of thinking that will enable you to embrace the waves of change, seeing them as exciting and challenging rather than intimidating and threatening. It will teach unconventional rules for breaking out of old modes and mind-sets so that we can take effective risks, constantly innovate and continually be on our edge. Following some of this simple yet effective Unconventional Wisdom will make your work and your life richer, more rewarding and fulfilling. You'll find that riding the wave of change is the most exciting and exhilarating way to live your life.

UW *says:*
Ride the wave of change.

2

Put Fire
in Your Heart

Our culture is in love with numbers and data. We are told that having the right *information* is the key to getting ahead. Success, we are led to believe, will be based on instant recall of sharp and timely facts. This is, after all, the "information age" and we are supposed to stay on top of it! But is this really the key to success? Or are we missing something essential?

GETTING BEYOND THE NUMBERS GAME

Let's look at some of the numbers that Conventional Wisdom says are all important.

This attitude shows up everywhere. For example, success in our educational system is tied to the ability to memorize and apply information. Top grades in school go to the students with the megabyte memory and laserlike ability to recall stored information. Conventional Wisdom says that future success and classroom grades go hand in hand: students with the best grades are called "the most likely to succeed."

THE LOWER-HALF CLUB

Conventional Wisdom has convinced us that "the numbers don't lie." We believe in the numbers, in this case, grade point averages. We strive for the best numbers. We are convinced, and we convey the idea to our children, that their future depends upon high grade points. But if numbers are the barometer of success, and the figures don't lie, then how do we explain the following contradictory evidence?

- Over 50 percent of all the CEOs of *Fortune* 500 companies had C or C− averages in college.

- 65 percent of all U.S. senators come from the bottom half of their school classes.

- 75 percent of U.S. presidents were in "the Lower-Half Club" in school.

- Over 50 percent of millionaire entrepreneurs never finished college!

THE POOR MAN'S AND WOMAN'S *WHO'S WHO*

I could easily compile a *Who's Who* solely of successful people who didn't finish college or were in the Lower-Half Club. Inductees would include Gen. Colin Powell, chairman of the Joint Chiefs of Staff; NBC television superstar Bryant Gumbel; entrepreneur and best-selling author Paul Hawken; Yvon Chouinard, founder of the Patagonia outdoor wear company; and Huey Johnson, cofounder of the Trust for Public Land and a director of the Nature Conservancy, to name a few.

The "Poor Person's" *Who's Who* would certainly also include Donald Cram, whose grades in his major, chemistry, were so lackluster in college that a professor urged him to change fields. Cram persisted because he loved the subject and in 1989 won the Nobel Prize for Chemistry.[1] And Irving Wallace was a college dropout who wrote incredibly detailed and well-researched books that sold over 120 million copies.

Let us not forget all those millionaire and billionaire entrepreneurs who had no degrees, but lots of dreams . . . like J. B. Fuqua, whose Fuqua Industries recently topped $1 billion in sales; John Johnson, the founder of *Ebony* magazine, as well as a whole enterprise of businesses, who never went past the third grade; or 36-year-old Lars-Erik Magnusson, the Swedish real estate magnate who dropped out of school at 16[2]; and, of course, the teenage enfants terribles Steve Jobs and Steve Wozniak, who founded Apple Computers; or world-renowned sports illustrator Brian Robley, who had to beg his art teacher to give him a D instead of an F so he could continue as an art major[3]; and the many, many other peak performers who were seen as *least* likely to succeed by classmates and teachers.

If you went strictly by the "numbers," every one of these people would have been firehosed long ago.

WHAT IS NOT THE BREAKFAST OF CHAMPIONS?

Athletic performance, like academic ability, is also assumed to be a "numbers" game. Conventional Wisdom says that those individuals with a god-given natural ability to run faster, jump higher, or throw farther will be the champions.

If this is so, how do we account for the myriad number of successful underdogs, such as the U.S. Olympic hockey team that defeated the Russians in the 1980 Winter Olympics? The Russians had all the numbers going for them—they were vastly more talented, more experienced, more skilled, as well as being stronger and faster skaters. On every empirical criterion the U.S. players were out of their league. But they won anyway.

Many athletes whose "numbers" would place them in the Lower-Half Club have been incredibly successful in sports.

- Basketball's Larry Bird can't run as fast or jump as high as most NBA players.

- Football's Joe Montana can't throw as hard or as far as most NFL quarterbacks.

Bird and Montana are in the tradition of Ty Cobb, Billie Jean King, Johnny Unitas, and Chris Evert, none of whom was an exceptional natural talent. Yet all were legendary champions. Obviously, raw natural ability alone is *not* the breakfast of champions.

THE HEART BEHIND THE NUMBERS

Describing the qualities that make San Francisco 49er Joe Montana, twice the Super Bowl MVP, one of the greatest quarterbacks to play the game, Pro Bowl teammate Ronnie Lott said, "You can't measure the size of his heart with a tape measure or stopwatch."

Walt Frazier, a teammate of basketball Hall-of-Famer Willis Reed, who was captain of the champion New York Knicks teams of the early seventies, has said, "No one ever outhustled Willis—at practice, during a game, or even at a kids' clinic. What did it for him was desire. As a player and a man, he was always on fire."[4]

PASSION!

When I was researching my book *The C Zone: Peak Performance Under Pressure,* I interviewed over 500 top performers from all areas of work, the arts, and sports. No two were alike, but the one quality they had in common was *passion!* It was their drive, their enthusiasm, their desire that distinguished them. They were passionate and excited about what they were doing.

A top executive headhunter, when asked about the qualities he looked for in a leader, said, "The thing that makes the difference between a good manager and an inspiring, dynamic leader goes beyond competence. It's *passion.* That is the single quality that is going to lift a person head and shoulders above the rest in these tough times."

Passion: a burning commitment brings your whole being into play—body, mind, and spirit—making you feel more vital and fully alive and enabling you to tap inner strengths, resources, abilities, and energies that you didn't know existed. Passion kindles a spark that inspires you and others around you to greater heights.

A Harvard Business School professor Dr. Abraham Zaleznik says that he "clamors" for the return of strong leadership that is imaginative and bold: "Leaders [who] get excited about their work and, by contagion, stimulate their subordinates. [Such] excitement builds strong relationships and high morale throughout an organization." Inspired leaders, he says, "move a business beyond problems into opportunities."[5]

FIRE IN THE HEART

It's not only "leaders" and "champions" who need passion—we all do. It doesn't matter what your field is, or the position you hold, or your age.

After a presentation, Michael Liacko, the vice president of sales for Bell & Howell, was asked, "What individuals make the best salespeople?" Walking up to his flip chart, Liacko drew a vertical line down the length of the page. On the left side, he listed basic skills and competencies: product knowledge, being well informed about client competition and the industry, good track record, background in electronics, success in previous jobs. All the usual requirements.

On the right side of the chart, he wrote one thing: *"Fire in the Heart!"* He looked at both sides of the chart, pointed to it, and said, "If I *had* to make a choice, I'd choose someone with fire over someone with the background, the education . . . the works. People with fire are more motivated, more resilient, will work harder, and are more resourceful. I can show them the ropes and give them the sales manuals. But if people don't have fire in their heart they won't go anywhere."

A PASSIONATE MOVE

A wonderful example of fire in the heart is Debi Coleman, who in a brief period of five years went from being a finance manager for Apple's Macintosh division, to VP of manufacturing worldwide.

Speaking about this unconventional jump from finance to manufacturing, Coleman said, "The move I made was not intuitively obvious . . . except if you knew how passionately I cared about manufacturing."

A formidable task facing Coleman when she took this job was to improve the performance of the Fremont manufacturing plant, one of the most innovative personal-computer factories in the world. Under her leadership, the factory yield went from 30 percent to 70 percent in nine months, incoming materials acceptance went from 80 percent to approximately 98 percent, and they turned over their entire inventory thirty times in one year.

Coleman, who had always wanted to work in the factory, says, "I don't think you should ever manage something that you don't care passionately about."[6]

Echoing the Liacko's and Coleman's of the world, Charles Wang, founder of the billion-dollar Computer Associates International, says he hires his sales force on "drive and enthusiasm, not technical expertise. If you have it in your heart," he says, "we can put what you need in your head."[7]

UW *says: Light a fire in your heart.*

PASSION INDEX

Participants in a Hewlett-Packard management training program I organized each chose a "change project"—some specific area they wanted to improve, such as productivity, efficiency, or innovation. The initial focus of the program was to set objectives for the project and develop strategies that were specific, measurable, and time-related.

I then asked them to intuitively rate their project from 1 to 10 on a Passion Index, with 10 indicating burning desire and 1, smoldering ashes. I told them, "If your passion for the project is lower than a 7, either change, get yourself more fired up, or forget it. It's too tough out there and there's too much on your plate already to take on something you are not genuinely excited about. A project under a 7 will become a burden to you and your people, and you'll only go through the motions with it."

Some ignored my advice and continued working on their projects as planned. Those whose passion index was 7 or above were more motivated and excited than the others and were the first to launch their ideas into action.

Taking a lesson from this example, rate your passion for what you are currently doing on a scale of 1 to 10. Whatever your score, there's a lot of Unconventional Wisdom throughout this book that'll help to light your fire or to turn a small ember into a blaze.

FROM GOOD TO OUTSTANDING

I do not want to downplay the importance of information, skills, and experience. Everyone needs to be competent at work, at school, at home. We all need to know the basics. If you don't know the material, haven't practiced and done your homework, you don't belong in today's game, and you certainly won't last long anyway. That's a given.

But information, skills, and competence only take you to "good." And everyone playing the game is at least good. The bottom line is that "good" isn't good enough these days. Passion, fire, burning commitment, and desire—these are the qualities that will take you from "good" to "outstanding."

Fire in your heart will give you that extra boost, making you more curious, more persistent, more resourceful in your quest for information. Having passion for what you are doing will prevent you from being stopped by failure and the unexpected roadblocks that are the present-day norm. Passion will make you more motivated to take risks and give you the extra "juice" to keep growing, learning, innovating, and confronting challenges.

"I NEVER GIVE UP"

Passion is critical for the perseverance needed to excel at any endeavor. After becoming the youngest player to win Wimbledon, 17-year-old Boris Becker was asked what he thought was the secret of his success. After talking about his passion for tennis and his burning desire to win, he looked at the reporter and said that the *most* important thing is that "I *never* give up! I never give up in a match, in a game, or when going after a shot."

Becker's daring style of play is often attributed to his never-say-die mentality. With dirty knees and bloody elbows, he leaps and races after shots that many others would give up on.

Perseverance is especially important when obstacles emerge unexpectedly, when nothing is predictable, and when the competition is fierce. We need to persevere in order to handle adversity, to bounce back from failure.

Edward Beauvais's journey to start America West Airline is a testament to persistence and passionate belief. To start the company, Beauvais and eight other partners took out second mortgages and used the credit line on their many different credit cards—and they still came up $18 million short! Deciding to make a public offering of stock, Beauvais made forty trips to Wall Street. "Every major investment banking firm turned us down."

After *two years* he hit paydirt, and since then American West has raised $250 million from stocks and debentures. "You have to be willing to hear 'no' a thousand times. You have to be tenacious . . . determined to get it."[8]

"You have to hang in there and do whatever it takes," says Curtis Strange, the first man in over 35 years to win the U.S. Open twice in a row. "Fortitude and guts, whatever you want to call it . . . you have to have persistence."[9]

PERSEVERANCE MADE EASY

Conventional Wisdom associates perseverance with doggedness, mulishness, and hammering away over and over again. The little voice inside your head says, "Grit your teeth, tighten your jaw, and push yourself" and you can do something that is difficult or undesirable, like checking a report one more time or calling up someone who has repeatedly said no.

But football great O. J. Simpson tells us, "When you're excited about what you are doing, you'll practice more, and you won't see it as work at all . . . it's all part of the game."[10]

As O. J. points out, true perseverance is *not* forced. People who are fired up don't have to push themselves to persevere. When you are excited about what you are doing, you don't have to convince yourself to "stick to it," you have to convince yourself *not* to. It's not something you *have* to do, it's something you *want* to do. *With passion as a base, perseverance comes naturally.*

Anyone who has ever started a business or pursued a project they were excited about is a living example that when you are passionate about what you are doing, perseverance comes with the territory. You don't have to push yourself to start—you have to force yourself to stop.

HEAD SWEEPS FLOOR

When you have fire in your heart, nothing is too much trouble or too demeaning. You do what needs doing. When Howard Head, the brilliant innovator who revolutionized two sports (with the invention of the metal ski and the metal and midsize tennis racket), started his business, he literally did anything and everything. "When the floor needed sweeping, I swept it," he said. "When the sales force needed a rousing speech, I gave it. I did whatever needed to be done."[11]

"You do whatever it takes," George "Papa Bear" Halas used to say about his founding of the Chicago Bears. Halas, a Hall-of-Famer as a football player as well as a coach, and who has more wins than any other man in professional football history, would do virtually anything for his team. He was known to fix the showers, chalk the field, collect wet towels after practice, tape his players' ankles, and clean the mud off their cleats.

"YOUR BLOOD HAS THAT PARTICULAR THING IN IT"

I remember reading about Bill Cosby's early days as a starving comedian. When he dropped out of Temple University in his junior year and made a commitment to his career in comedy, he threw himself into it completely. He'd stay up till all hours talking to old comics, working on new material. That was his education and training as a comedian.

"Anyone can dabble," he commented, "but once you've made that commitment, then your blood has that particular thing in it, and it's very hard for people to stop you."[12]

Cosby, Head, and Halas didn't have to force themselves to stick to it, to do the extra work it took to be successful, to go the extra mile. In fact, you would have had to force them *not* to. That's what passion does to you. It fosters commitment. It excites and exhilarates. It's not that you have to *try* to persevere or *try* to stick to it. Passion sweeps you away. The thought of giving up or hedging your bets never enters your mind. When your blood has "that particular thing in it," nothing can stop you.

PASSION IS CONTAGIOUS

Passion isn't restricted to the world of sports or entertainment, nor to the world of work. Passion in any one area of your life affects every area. When you are passionate about something—*anything*—it gives you more vitality, more energy, more purpose, and it transfers to the rest of your life as well.

A salesman for one of the largest manufacturers of building supplies told me, "I was a runner until I hurt my hip and had to have an operation on my fifty-seventh birthday. While I was recuperating, my doctor suggested that I find another form of exercise that was easier on my legs. I took up sculling.

"After about a year of training I realized I was only thirty seconds off the time needed to qualify for the world master's championships. It was like a fire was lit inside of me. I started getting up at four in the morning. I'd skull before work. I'd skull after work, and that excitement carried over into my job. I went from being in the middle of our sales force to being in the top five percent! I've been skulling for five years and I'm *still* fired up. My life is just in-*cred*-i-ble."

When you have fire in the heart, it lifts your entire life. Days go faster. Life's chores become more interesting. You have more stamina, more resiliency, and more buoyancy. And when you are excited, it radiates to everyone around you.

KNOWLEDGE ON FIRE

Passion sets knowledge on fire; as an executive told me. "In the knowledge business you need your heart engaged to keep your brain at its best. Passion gives you the edge."

Passion and commitment take you from being merely competent and skilled, to outstanding. Fueling the fire in your heart is a first and critical step for being more motivated and creative, and confronting the many challenges necessary for keeping ahead of the wave of change.

"Fire in the heart" plays a crucial role in differentiating the "outstanding" from the "good."

- A recent nationwide cross-industry study found that the most significant factor, the one that distinguished "top" from "good" sales performers, was *enthusiasm.*

- TV sports analyst extraordinaire John Madden, a Super Bowl winning coach himself, says the difference between the guys who make the Pro Bowl and those who don't is *enthusiasm.*

- The prestigious *Endicott Report* confirmed that one of the three most important qualities in on-the-job success is *"enthusiasm . . . passion . . . intense excitement!"*[13]

- "If you don't have enthusiasm," says Kemmons Wilson, Sr., founder of Holiday Inns, "you don't have anything."[14] *Enthusiasm* is a very old word used to describe those who are spirited and passionate. The root meaning, "infused with spirit," characterizes people who are excited about life and have fire in their heart.

Maybe you are excited about backpacking or softball or gardening or riding a mountain bike, or protecting the environment. Maybe your family makes everything worthwhile. The important thing is that you *have* a passion and *find* the fire in your heart. With fire in your heart, nothing is insurmountable. With fire in your heart, you'll find that nothing is too hard, no peak too high, no dream impossible. And you'll enjoy the climb as much as reaching the summit.

UW *says:*
Put fire in your heart.

3

Stoke It . . . Don't Soak It

PROTECT THE FLAME

We all agree that the world is changing and that we need to respond effectively. Key to that response is the determination to keep the fire in your heart burning.

BEWARE THE FIREHOSE

Yet the most common reaction to change is resistance. Here's a familiar story. Maggie, a merchandising manager for a large supermarket chain is excited about a new idea that would change and expand the chain's marketing approach to appeal to the increasing number of double-paycheck families. Her boss listens to her enthusiastic and well-prepared presentation and from time to time interrupts, saying things such as:

"It's not in the budget. Where's the money going to come from?"

"Who'll do all the extra work to set it up?"

"It's going to decrease our quarterly numbers."

"It'll never work."

"It's not practical."

"Why change? Things are working the way they are."

"Yeah, but . . ."

"We've never tried anything like that before."

"That's not the way we do things around here."

In an attempt to cling to the familiar and stay on safe ground, Maggie's boss responded like a fireman hosing down a fire. He effectively "firehosed" her, dousing her ideas, enthusiasm, and spirit.

TRYING TO CONTROL THE UNCONTROLLABLE

Leaders in every field emphasize the importance of embracing change. Yet the only people who really welcome change are babies with wet diapers and busy cashiers. No matter how positive the change, most people, like Maggie's boss, try to avoid or resist it.

Let's face it, change *is* disturbing. The natural tendency is to stick with what we know, play it safe, and gravitate toward the familiar. Overtly and covertly, we resist.

Firehosing is a common way we undermine or dismiss the daring strategy, the new idea, and even the simplest suggestion for improvement. What's worse, though, is how often we firehose *our own* dreams and creative ideas, without knowing it.

It's easy to understand why firehosing happens. In the face of change and uncertainty, Conventional Wisdom is cautious, exhorting us to "pull in the reins," "dig in our heels," and "batten down the hatches." Conventional Wisdom is the fireman's best friend and our own worst enemy.

Firehosing can *seem* prudent, as it is tied to the "lessons" of the past. It appears to inject a little control into an otherwise uncontrollable world. But these attempts to stay in a comfort zone are not without their costs: they extinguish the sparks of innovation, enthusiasm, and creativity that are so necessary for progress. Maggie left her boss's office disappointed and dispirited. Unwittingly, by firehosing her idea, he had also dampened her enthusiasm. It will be a long time before she regains her motivation and makes another suggestion.

Below are examples of some classic firehoses:

THE SUPERRATIONALISTS

Firehosing, which occurs at all levels of an organization—top to bottom, leader to staff, boardroom to mailroom—can initially seem quite logical and rational. For instance, several years ago I was leading a management seminar at Hewlett-Packard with the objective of envisioning a new financial control system for the midnineties. Every time someone would come up with a new idea, one manager, sitting in the back row, would point his pipe toward the person, snicker in a supercilious way, and firehose the idea, saying, "We can't do that"; "Systems people would never buy it"; "That'll never work"; "We'll never get the software to do that."

After about twenty minutes, Bob Wayman, Hewlett-Packard's chief financial officer, rose from his chair. Pointing at a diagram differentiating the functions of the imaginative, creative right hemisphere of the brain and the rational, logical left brain, he glanced back at the man with the pipe, smiled, and asked, "Is it ever possible for somebody to have two left brains?!!!" Unfortunately, in most companies today, the answer is a resounding YES!

The rational objections of the Firehosers seem appropriate and logical because they are based on old "truths." However, in today's world, yesterday's truths are obsolete by tomorrow.

BOTTOM-LINERS

In their dogged and myopic pursuit of the bottom line, rational and logical, left-brain thinkers have firehosed innumerable good ideas, good people, and good companies. "We don't have passion anymore," says Russell Baker, best-selling author and syndicated columnist for the *New York Times*. "In business, instead of passion we have the bottom line. This means that bookkeepers, accountants, lawyers and tax experts have replaced entrepreneurs."[1]

Conventional Wisdom has it that we need more bottom-line thinking in these tough times: "Trim the fat, cut the costs, get lean and mean." Seen in terms of "the numbers," new ideas are viewed by bottom-liners as potential problems, rather than as pragmatic opportunities.

"We have such a bottom-line mentality around here," a division manager of a large manufacturing plant told me, "that someone's always got a reason why something new *won't* work, a reason to shoot it down. It's gotten to the point that my people are unwilling to initiate anything. It's not worth the flack they have to go through. Our new product reviews are like gunfights. What we need to get out of the bind we're in are some more *top*-liners."

The dampened spirit and lack of innovation caused by bottom-line Firehosers often end up costing an organization far more than trying the ideas that were firehosed. Baker comments, "You'd think that these types that constantly thump themselves on the chest about being 'bottom-line guys' would be ashamed of it."[2] Bottom-liners are shortsighted if they fail to weigh the long-term costs of demotivating people, hindering innovation, and dousing the fires of the entrepreneurial spirit.

THE SEASONED VETERAN

Often firehosing is well intentioned. We've all run into the seasoned veterans who have "seen it all." Before you finish a sentence they firehose your great idea or shatter your bold dream without realizing it. Their vast experience, they believe, will rescue you from sure disaster. Recalling someone who failed miserably trying a similar idea, these "rescuers" will try to prevent you from wasting a lot of time, energy, and anguish, not to mention money, on any new idea or exciting new development. With the "benefit" of their experience, these Firehosers will give you a perfectly reasonable explanation why you can't do it, why you shouldn't even try it, why it won't work.

Bo Jackson, the wondrous athlete who excels in both professional baseball and football, had to contend with truckloads of seasoned veterans who "knew" from experience that no one could succeed in two sports. "Remember Gene Conley and Danny Ainge and Dave De Busschere?" they would remind Bo. "They tried two professional sports and had to drop one."

Bo's response? "There are always people out there who are trying to assess your life for you, and tell you what you can and can't do. And that's not right. You just have to do what you can do and don't worry about what people say."[3] Bo has proved the vets wrong by excelling in both football and baseball.

If you're not as passionate as Bo and don't have a lot of fire and confidence sustaining your dreams and ideas, rest assured that the so-called seasoned veterans will douse *your* fire with *their* experience every time.

YEAH, BUT!

A pervasive yet subtle Firehose is contained in the word *but*. As in the person who seems to be *agreeing* with you and going along with your suggestion, and then adds *but!*: "Great idea, *but* it's not in the budget" or "Terrific suggestion, *but* no one's ever done that before. . . ."

Fritz Perls, the developer of Gestalt therapy, once said to discount everything before the *but*; the real response comes after.

UW *warns that everything before the **but** is bull.*

To avoid disappointment, we often firehose ourselves with **Yeah, but's.** We use them as a disclaimer: "Yeah, that was a great deal, *but* I'll believe it when the check clears . . ." This kind of firehosing may prevent disappointment, *but* it also prevents you from feeling good about your accomplishments and douses your enthusiasm and confidence.

THE NAY SAYERS

Firehosers always focus on what's wrong with an idea rather than what's right. They always have their reasons why something won't work, always a "Yeah, but" skeptical quality to what they say.

Approaching investors about his new idea, which turned into the Sharper Image, an incredibly successful catalog and retail chain, Richard Thalheimer recalls how at first he "got the usual flack from the status quo society. I found out," he says, "that the world is definitely filled with nay sayers. Everybody can find something wrong with an idea."[4]

Another example. David Bobert had to put up with more than his share of firehosing when he began developing a coin-operated vending machine that dispensed . . . *air*, for filling tires. It was just the kind of off-the-wall, oddball idea that friends and associates loved hosing down. "What," they'd say to him, "you're going to sell *air!?*" Undaunted, Bobert stuck it out and had the last laugh. He built his company, Air-Vend, into a $5 million enterprise.

There is nothing new about people having bold ideas firehosed. Imagine how strong the passion and persistence of the great inventors, discoverers, and visionaries must have been, enabling them to avoid getting their ideas dampened or extinguished prematurely.

"THINGS WILL GET BACK TO NORMAL"

Watch out for the Firehosers who resist change by saying, "This, too, will pass"; "It's only a passing fancy"; "Things will get back to normal if you just leave well enough alone." They would lead you to believe that everything moves from instability to stability, from upheaval to normalcy.

Conventional Wisdom assures us that everything happens in cycles. No matter what is going on now, the assumption is that things will cycle back. The operational word is "back," meaning back to "normal," back to the "good old days." Firehose axioms that encourage you to stick with the old and recapture the past are comforting but delusionary.

Things will never get back to "normal" because unpredictability and change *are* normal. There is no going back. Get used to it. Change will be followed by more change. That's one thing that *isn't* going to change. The waves in this ocean won't flatten out, they're only going to get bigger and come at us faster.

"WAIT AND SEE"

Holding still and doing nothing is another way to firehose change. At a hospital undergoing drastic changes and major restructuring, one seasoned veteran manager told me, "This new CEO has only been on the job for eight months. The last one tried lots of new things too, but nothing much changed. I'm not going to rush to reorganize or change what we're doing. I'll just wait and see what happens."

There is nothing quite as lethal as doing nothing. Adopting a "wait and see" attitude in these fast times is like dropping the anchor for your sailboat while waiting for a strong wind. While you wait, other boats will tack with any breeze they can and leave you in their wake.

A RED SEAT IN A BLUE CAR

As a corollary, when change arrives by edict from the *top*, with no input or choice, it is not uncommon to have it firehosed by those *below*. People resist change when they feel they are not *in* control or are *being* controlled. When people are pushed, resentments flare, and they push back one way or another.

"Here's the thing," says Roger Smith, chairman of General Motors. "You can't push people . . . you can't drag them. If they don't want to do something . . . they will stand there and smile at you, but there goes a red seat in a blue car."[5]

The "red-seat-in-a-blue-car" syndrome is unbelievably costly, too. In a *New York Times* report, Kate Ludeman cited a staggering estimate of resistance in the workplace: "The deliberate and persistent waste of paid time costs American business $170 billion [yes, BILLION] annually—12 percent of the payroll of businesses."[6]

Noncompliance has been fatal to many a great idea and strategic plan. It is natural to firehose decisions that we haven't been asked about, or don't agree with, or feel no "ownership" of. If you don't involve the people in the decisions affecting their lives, expect to have those decisions firehosed.

YOU CAN'T TEACH AN OLD DOG NEW TRICKS

Firehosing also occurs when people are afraid they can't learn a new skill or won't be able to keep up with the changes required of them. For example, an auto dealership was restructuring its sales and service strategy. As a result, the customer service people, who up to that point had been expected only to solve problems and repair cars, now had to sell the service contracts as well.

The backlash was immediate. "Hey! we're not salesmen," one mechanic yelled, "we're in service. Most of us have been here over five years. You can't teach an old dog new tricks. Let the guys that know how to sell, sell. And let us keep doing what we've been doing and what we're good at. We don't know contracts from quiche."

This giant Firehose from the customer service people was responsible for dousing management's plans and delayed the implementation of the change for several months.

INNER FIREHOSING

It's bad enough when someone turns the hose on us, but an even more insidious type of firehosing occurs when we turn it on ourselves. One way we firehose ourself is by assuming that our ideas will be firehosed by others. We beat them to the draw, telling ourselves, "The boss will never buy this"; "They won't let me do it"; "They'll never approve"; or "She'll never say yes!"

Jan Carlzon, the chairman of Scandinavian Airlines, who has been an enormously successful leader, understands the damage inner firehosing can do. "Many times people say, 'I want to go through this wall,' and they start walking toward the wall and they are two meters away when they tell themselves, 'It will not work, the authorities will not let us, the management will not let us.' Consequently, they turn away. . . ."[7]

Firehosing yourself puts an end to dreams, ideas, and enthusiasm and leaves you with a bad case of "the Five D's"—discouraged, disappointed, disgruntled, defeated, and depressed. Worse still, in self-defense, after hosing ourselves, we then complain about the lack of support. The truth is, we rejected ourselves.

BETTER THE DEVIL YOU KNOW . . .

Many of us firehose change even when things are *not* going well, fearing that the change will only make matters worse. The sales manager of a management training company was very dissatisfied with his job. He felt that his contributions weren't being recognized and that he wasn't having enough say in the decisions affecting his group. Furthermore, he felt that his company's programs hadn't kept up with the times and that management wasn't interested in developing new ones.

When I asked him why he didn't leave or at the very least start looking for a new job, he shrugged his shoulders, saying, "I'd probably run into the same type of thing somewhere else. At least here I know the pitfalls and who the bad guys are."

Many of us suffer from this type of Firehose. Dissatisfied with our jobs or relationships, we "stick it out" because of the fear of the unknown, saying to ourselves, "Sure, it's not working out, but it pays the bills. Things could be worse. Here, at least I know the ropes." We stay with what we know and have, even though we're miserable.

GROUCHO'S COUNTRY CLUB

Self-doubt is another Firehose that douses the fires of new ideas. Have you ever had a great invention, project, or dream you thought about pursuing? You know the idea is original, but you wonder, "If it's so good, why hasn't somebody else come up with it before?" or "Can I ever get this off the ground?" or "No one's ever done this before, who am I to suggest it?" or "It's so obvious, *some*body must have thought about this before I did!"

As the spray from this Firehose builds in intensity, your enthusiasm dwindles. Finally, the spark goes out and you go back to what you were doing before, but with markedly less enthusiasm. You have then joined Groucho's Country Club, whose motto is: "I wouldn't join any club that would have me as a member!"

HEDGING YOUR BETS

"I think deep down all of us know what we want to do," Eddie Murphy told Arsenio Hall, "but the thing is, most people say, *'Before* I do *that* I'd better do *this* in case *that* doesn't happen, so I'll have something to fall back on.'"[8]

We firehose ourselves by labeling our dream a "fantasy." We then hedge our bets, until finally, like a malignant self-fulfilling prophecy, the *hedge* takes up more and more time and we spend less and less time on the *bet.* As with the would-be novelist who has no energy left after a day spent teaching high-school English, the hedge wins.

The son of a friend of mine dreamed of becoming a sports announcer, but because he didn't think there were many of these jobs available, he hedged his bet and began selling advertising for a TV station. His plan was to learn about sportscasting in his spare time from the announcers at the station. It never happened. He had to spend all his time doing his own job. Several years later he became the sales manager, and though his career was on the upswing, his dream had struck out. To this day, although he regrets his caution, he still continues to firehose himself by saying, "I'm forty-one, it's too late to start."

DODGING THE SPRAY

One of the questions I am invariably asked after talking about Firehoses is: "What can I do to avoid them?" When the hose is pointed at you or when you aim it at others, the first step is to *recognize* it, to know a Firehose when you see one. It is then much easier to protect yourself or, better still, to turn the water off completely.

Not long ago, at a new products brainstorming meeting for a major health-care organization, I placed a squirt gun at the center of the table. I explained to the group about firehosing and said, "Anyone who hears someone firehose an idea, open fire." After about 15 minutes a vice president made a self-deprecating remark, stopped himself in the middle of a sentence, smiled, grabbed the gun, and squirted himself right between the eyes! The floodgates opened and pretty soon every time someone firehosed an idea, people lined up to spray them.

This lasted about 25 minutes when a strange thing happened. People actually changed their expectations and their behavior! They began fueling other people's ideas and suggestions rather than dousing them. It was one of the most rapid and amazing transformations I have seen.

The result of that session was the development of a line of products that is now the bellwether of the organization. An ancillary—but no less important—result is that the experience enhanced teamwork, camaraderie, and a spirit of fun, too. The organization now puts squirt guns out at all meetings . . . just in case!

KEEPING THE FIRE HOT

To keep confronting the challenges in our changing environment demands passion, boldness, and the courage to challenge convention. More than anything else, this spark or inner fire is essential to performing at peak levels in these high-pressure times. Firehosing, if unchecked, will douse your inner flame, dampen your enthusiasm, and smother your dreams and creativity. But with a modicum of UW, firehosing can be (pardon the pun) extinguished.

In fact, many of the techniques and tips discussed throughout this book will help you to recognize a Firehose more easily and dodge its spray. Then the time and energy previously spent stifling passion and enthusiasm can be put to better use stoking fires, supporting ideas, and encouraging dreams and innovations that are vital.

UW *says:*
Stoke it, don't soak it!

4

Dreams Are
Goals with Wings

Too often the fire in our heart gets extinguished by overly rigid plans, and short-term quotas and goals. I witnessed this recently when a Fortune 100 computer company let a major opportunity slip away because of company policies that firehosed potential contracts.

In this instance, the defense department wanted to develop a better computer system for one of its jet fighters. A relatively minor investment in research and development was necessary, but since the contract represented about $90 million a year—and they had a good chance of getting it—everyone was excited. Top management's last word regarding the request was "Go ahead with it . . . ." And then the Firehose hit: ". . . as long as it doesn't impact next quarter's numbers." It did. They didn't get the contract.

SHORT-TERM AND SHORTSIGHTED

Is this a true story? Unfortunately it is and it illustrates the mind-set that prevails in many companies in this country. As a culture, on both the individual and the organizational level we have developed a fast-food mentality: we want instant gratification, instant recognition, and instant profit.

One of the things Victor Kiam hated when he was president and chairman of Benrus Watch Co. was the focus on short-term results and having to answer to the stockholders about them. "We were constantly saying, 'If we do this now, what's it going to do to our earnings in this quarter?'"[1]

In the dogged pursuit of short-term goals and the bottom line we have developed cultural myopia. All of our hopes and aspirations are related to making next quarter's numbers. With this foreshortened field of vision, we live by the quarter and die by the quarter.

"We need to break out of this linear short-term thinking that assumes you set goals at the beginning of a period, manage your company around those goals, then evaluate performance and reward people when, presumably, the goals are achieved," says Bank of America senior vice president K. Shelly Porges. "It's too constricting. We need to enlarge ourselves and our perspectives and recognize that goals may change during the period in pursuit of vision. "[2]

RIGID GOALS, FRIGID RESULTS

One year Chris Evert's goal was to win Wimbledon and be ranked first in the world. She did both and experienced that great feeling of accomplishment that you get when you achieve a hard-won victory. But, she said, it lasted only about 25 minutes. Then it was back to reality and on to the next goal.

Many of us have had a similar experience of living for a goal and, upon reaching it, feeling let down. You work hard all year to "make the numbers," and at year's end you have a bittersweet realization: next year the goals or quotas will be upped and last year's record-breaking performance will be as exciting as yesterday's news, its accomplishment taken for granted. "And this," a friend of mine said, "gets old really fast."

I have a friend who has his own small insurance company. He has seven agents working for him, and each year they set aside time to establish the goals for the following year. "I gotta tell you," he confided, "each year it gets harder and harder to get them pumped up. We usually make our goals, and everyone makes good money. We celebrate, have a little party, a dinner, everyone gets a bonus . . . and then it starts all over again."

It's no wonder that, according to research by Dr. Ron Lippitt, "during the course of goal-setting meetings, participants become more and more depressed. This discouragement occurs in part because [the process] reinforces the belief that the future will be no different from the past."[3]

"GOALS ONLY LIMIT YOU"

In the relentless pursuit of the next quarter's bottom line, we fail to see anything that doesn't have a linear relation to making the numbers. Such tunnel vision blinds us to opportunities for innovation and creativity. It prevents us from seeing other possibilities and options— alternative routes that may appear as a consequence of change, new technologies, or an unpredicted circumstance.

When we live and die by the short-term numbers, it's easy to lose perspective. Everything is exaggerated. Small victories are cause for celebration and small setbacks become huge catastrophes. Minor annoyances take on major importance.

As a result, the mad-dash rat race to make the short-term numbers hinders our creativity, our motivation, our spirit.

Summing up this fixation on short-term goals and objectives, Scott McNeally, founder and CEO of Sun Microsystems, said that the motto at their company—the second-fastest-growing company in economic history—is "Goals only limit you."

UW *says: Goals create limitations on the imagination and inhibit innovation.*

GOALS ARE SECONDARY

Having goals is not the problem. What gets us into trouble is the importance we attach to them. Goals have their place . . . second place, following dreams. They do serve a purpose. They give us something specific to shoot at and provide feedback to tell us how we are doing. They are a way of keeping score. But if goals are to be beneficial for enhancing performance, productivity, and motivation, they must be guided by something larger and more encompassing, something that inspires us and infuses us with passion, creativity, and courage.

OLYMPIC STARTING BLOCKS

Many years ago I was talking about goal setting to John Naber, the TV broadcaster who had won four gold medals and one silver for swimming in the 1976 Olympics. He said he used goal setting extensively during his training. He set very specific goals for each event, including daily, weekly, monthly, and quarterly objectives, some of which involved improving his time by thousandths of a second.

He told me that having specific goals really helped him measure his progress. But those goals were just a step toward achieving a larger dream, a means to an end. There was one thing that was much more exciting to him, without which he felt he wouldn't have accomplished nearly as much. The dream of winning the gold medal and being the world champion kept him going through all the days and years of hard practice.

Not a day went by when Naber didn't *see* himself on top of the victory stand with a gold medal around his neck and the flag going up. He could *hear* the National Anthem playing and the crowd cheering. Without that, all of the goal setting in the world wouldn't have helped.

Successful people in all walks of life echo Naber. The key to sustained peak performance is finding something larger than a goal, something bigger to shoot for. Something that moves you. A dream you can chase. A vision that inspires.

LBV: LEADERSHIP BY VISION

"My thinking has really been turned on its head," says Donald Povejsil, former vice president of corporate planning for Westinghouse. "Ten years ago I believed the key [to success] was tightly reasoned analysis of markets and competitors." Yet at the small and very successful business units Westinghouse created, Povejsil saw people making decisions based on a vision rather than a narrow set of goals.

"I could detect a distinct correlation between this vision and the performance of these 20 or so business units. The good ones had a vision. As for the bad ones, it was hard to tell why they came to work in the morning. . . . Vision is the linchpin of strategic management; there's no other conclusion you can reach after a while."[4]

Povejsil's realization was confirmed by a poll of *Fortune* 500 CEOs. When asked what will characterize top leadership traits in the decade to come, number one on the list was vision.[5] Organizations need a vision to fire people up, engage the spirit, and provide direction. Leadership by vision—LBV—will be to the nineties what management by objectives (MBO) was to the seventies.

Like an organization, we each need a personal vision or dream to fuel the fire in our heart, provide more meaning to our efforts, and encourage us to confront the challenges that lie ahead.

WE DID THE IMPOSSIBLE

Dreams can empower people as nothing else. A wonderful example is the now famous story of Eugene Lang, millionaire entrepreneur from the South Bronx. In his late sixties he was asked to talk to students at the junior high school from which he had graduated. The years had taken their toll on the South Bronx and it little resembled the Central European, immigrant community of Lang's childhood. Now it was a battlefield of poverty, drugs, and gangs, and a breeding ground of despair and hopelessness.

Lang had prepared a speech for the graduating eighth-graders designed to "motivate them" with the conventional wisdom, "If I can do it, you can, too." After looking out at an audience that clearly wasn't interested in him, Lang threw away his prepared speech and said one thing, "If you graduate from high school"—typically about 20 percent of the youth of the South Bronx would earn a high school diploma—"I will send you to college."

Four years later, the result was phenomenal. All but two of the 60 kids finished high school and many have gone on to the best colleges. When they were asked by the media about their success, they said, "He gave us hope, he gave us a chance to dream, he gave us a golden opportunity." One of the students, upon meeting Lang later, rightly said, "Mr. Lang, we did the impossible."

When we have a dream and pursue it, nothing is impossible. We tap into power, personal resources, and creativity that we never thought we had. We can accomplish what had previously been considered impossible. In the process we discover that the biggest limit is our mind telling us what our limits are.

BURGER KING UNIVERSITY

The owner of a mid-Atlantic Burger King franchise was constantly faced with the industry dilemmas of language problems, high employee turnover (40 percent per year), and consequent high training costs ($40,000 per year).

Taking heart from Lang's example, and with a generous dash of courage, he found a solution. He offered to pay college tuition for employees who stayed with him for four years. That's the only thing he changed. "You stay with me, I'll pay tuition for you." Two years into the new "fringe benefit" program, his turnover is down to 9 percent and his training costs have been reduced by 75 percent.

DREAMS ARE GOALS WITH WINGS

Like most creative functions, dreams are housed in the right hemisphere of the brain, along with passion, imagination, and emotions. Goals, on the other hand, are formed in the left hemisphere. They are rational, linear, and measurable. The dream is an ideal state and the goal is a real state. The dream supplies the vigor, vision, and direction; the goal, a specific, short-term target and the strategies for hitting it. The goal is a step toward the dream. *The dream is a goal with wings!*

A dream supplies meaning and intrinsic value. It is our deepest expression of what we want, a declaration of a desired future. A dream is an ideal involving a sense of possibilities rather than probabilities, of potential rather than limits. Goals that are set without a dream utilize literally only half of our brain power. The passion is missing when we work with only our rational left brain. Without passion there is little enthusiasm and vitality. Without passion there is no fire in the heart.

A dream is the wellspring of passion, giving us direction and pointing us to lofty heights. It is an expression of optimism, hope, and values lofty enough to capture the imagination and engage the spirit. Dreams grab us and move us. They are capable of lifting us to new heights and overcoming self-imposed limitations.

Dreams, unlike goals, aren't limited by what you think can or cannot be done, or by what your rational mind tells you is or isn't possible. It represents something that you really want, as opposed to something you think you can get. Goals are tangible, but dreams are intangible.

Dr. Martin Luther King, Jr., said, "I Have a Dream"—he did not say "I have a strategic plan." The dream of racial equality Dr. King talked about was an elusive, desired state but one that touched people's hearts and evoked a response that altered the history of an entire nation.

The key today is to have both dreams *and* goals, passion *and* "ration." The starting point of any journey is a dream, a vision of some far-off possibilities. It must be exciting and moving. Once you are enthusiastic about where you are heading, *then* you set some goals and bench marks that will help you to get there. When short-term goals become an end in themselves, passion fizzles out. Similarly, rational steps work best in the service of passion. UW alerts us that dreams are goals with wings.

ORDINARY PEOPLE, EXTRAORDINARY DREAMS

This country was (and is) built on the dreams of ordinary people who, by following their dreams, accomplished extraordinary things. In the

1930s, for example, A. G. Giannini, although very bright, left school at 14 to take care of his two younger brothers on a small family farm. Later he got a job working for a bank and had a dream about starting one of his own that would serve "the little guy." He believed that on the strength of many little guys, a national bank could be built. By having the courage to make then unheard-of loans for automobiles and appliances, his dream was realized by the time of his death in 1949. The bank he founded is called the Bank of America.

Or consider Pete Seibert's story. A ski instructor and former ski trooper in World War II, since the age of 12 Seibert had wanted nothing more in his life than to start a ski area. One day, after an exhausting seven-hour climb in deep snow, he reached the summit of a mountain in the Gore Range in Colorado. Staring down at the vast bowls below and at the stunning peaks beyond, Seibert said to himself it was "as good as any mountain I've seen."

Compared to the hard work that followed, the seven-hour trek was like a leisurely stroll. Seibert had to climb mountains of red tape, meet the U.S. Forest Service's stiff leasing requirements, and raise large amounts of capital "from frugal friends and suspicious strangers" in order to buy land from ranchers and build a village.

"Everybody else thought we were crazy," says Seibert, "but we thought we could do any damn thing we pleased." . . . Seibert's dream is now a reality called Vail.[6]

Pip-squeak meat-slicer company

After being fired from a job he'd held for 14 years, Tom Watson joined a company that manufactured scales, meat slicers, time clocks, and punch cards to sort data; he envisioned that these simple punch cards could start a revolution in information storage. He borrowed enough money to rescue the company when it fell on hard times and he gave it a new name. "What a big name for a pip-squeak company that makes meat grinders," his son said. It was 1924, and International Business Machines had just been born.

DREAM MACHINE

A dream can become a magnificent obsession. It can begin in childhood and refuse to go away. We've all had them, but not all of us have had the courage or encouragement to chase our dreams. A fortunate few, captured by their dream early on, have.

Samuel Roger Horchow remembered spending many of his most pleasant days as a child opening mail-order catalogs at random. "Those catalogs were simply dream machines for me, endlessly capable of taking me far away. That's when I decided that I wanted to be part of that magic world."[7]

The fact that there were hundreds and hundreds of catalogs to compete with never caused a moment's pause to Horchow. He created his catalog on the basis of his tastes and his vision. Horchow's "dream machine" catalogs are whimsical and farfetched and passionately personal. You can order a six-foot-long plywood Holstein cow, a Haitian effigy of a clarinet player, or a blown Waterford ship's decanter of full-lead crystal. And with each purchase, the customer is getting a small piece of a big dream.

DREAMS COME IN ALL SIZES AND SHAPES

Your dream doesn't have to revolutionize an industry, win the Olympics, or make a million dollars. It doesn't even have to be about business or something that makes a buck.

Dreams can be general and abstract, such as wanting to make a difference in people's lives, own your own business, be renowned for your work, or have a loving relationship. Tony Tiano, president of KQED-TV, the San Francisco public television station, says his vision is "elusive, like an abstract painting far off in the distance. I can just barely see it. It's something I want. It moves me."[8]

In other instances your dream can be more specific—like John Naber's dream of winning the gold medal, or a dream of becoming president of the corporation you work for or of writing a novel. Our dreams come in all shapes and sizes. The key is to have a dream that inspires us to go beyond our limits. Dreams ignite a fire in us and give us "genius and magic." Consider some of the following varied dreams:

- Peter Brown, a housecleaner, dreams of opening his own restaurant.

- Catherine Partman, mother of five, dreams of starting a business, writing a book, and producing a videotape to educate expectant mothers and new parents.

- Tim and Tina Frederick, financial analysts, dream of opening a bed and breakfast in Northern California.

- Trish McCall dreams of spending a year in Italy with her family.

- Charlene Modena, a teacher, dreams of living on the sales of her art.

Having a dream—whether it is personal or professional, big or small, realistic or crazy—and *pursuing* it, adds meaning to your life. It gives your everyday activities a larger sense of purpose. And when your dream is shared by those you work or live with, it's doubly exciting.

Myrtle Harris, a senior citizen, dreams of speaking to seniors groups around the country about all the resources available to them. Taking advantage of one such resource (discounted airfares), she fulfilled one of her dreams, to go to the Kentucky Derby. As she says, "Just getting there was a thrill. My horse didn't win, but I did!"

PEOPLE'S JOBS ARE TOO SMALL FOR THEIR SPIRIT

If you walk into the headquarters of Patagonia, the outerwear manufacturer located in Ventura, California, you will see employees in T-shirts and bare feet, and walls with surfboards leaning against them. "You'd think this was some kind of laid-back California company," says Yvon Chouinard, the former mountain climber who is the founder and head of the company. "But these people are comfortable here. They never want to go home. They work till all hours. They love it here because they know what we are about, that we are dedicated to something more than selling clothes and being financially successful.

"Sure we make great products . . . but our vision is much larger. The vision at Patagonia is about saving the environment. It's about paying rent on the planet. So we give a substantial percentage of our profits to environmental organizations. It's a compelling vision for our people, one that grabs them. They feel they are contributing to something more than just to the bottom line, and they feel proud of it."

Today, *people's jobs are too small for their spirit.* As Chouinard says, "They don't want to work for a *company*, they want to work for a *movement*, something that has a larger meaning and gives them a sense of purpose about what they are doing."

A compelling corporate vision that resonates with its employees' dreams and aspirations and touches their hearts as well as their pocketbooks will be the model for the nineties. These organizations will have inspired, highly motivated people working for them. They will have little attrition; at Patagonia, "People are lining up to work here."[9]

People want more from life than just to go to work and pick up a paycheck. There is a desire for more meaning and purpose. They want their lives and consequently their work to matter, to be a part of a larger vision and to feel they are contributing to it. Companies need to create visions that go beyond the notion of being "number one" if they want to attract and retain a spirited work force.

ONE PERSON, ONE COMPUTER

The growth of Apple Computer, which during the eighties was one of the most spirited companies around, and the impact of its products and technology on all of us, was the direct result of the inspiring "one person, one computer" vision of its founders, Steve Jobs and Steve Wozniak, two teenagers who founded Apple Computer in a garage.

Says John Sculley, chairman of Apple, their vision carried a double resonance: "It spoke to the individual and to society. It articulated our new vision of society—an egalitarian vision of an affordable, highly powered information tool."

"I bought the dream," says Bill Atkinson, who headed Apple's MacPaint technology team. "I bought the dream of making a dent. Not only did I buy it, I tasted it and knew it was right."

Sculley adds, "At Apple . . . a clear vision, a set of values, and directions are the forces that bind us together. . . . The dreams of all that is possible become our unifying force."[10]

DON'T BE REALISTIC

In the "real world," dreams are not taken seriously, and often they are squelched. A manager for a major printing company told me of a talk he had had with one of his bookkeepers. Although she hadn't finished high school and English was her second language, she was undaunted. Her dream was either to have her own company or become the comptroller of his company.

Out came the *Firehose*! The manager, representing "reality and experience" and ignoring her "passion" cautioned, "You do have good bookkeeping skills, but with your education you ought to set your sights on something that's more within your reach, something a little more realistic." Angered by this, a month later she quit the company . . . to pursue her dream.

What did she do? She started a bookkeeping service for small companies owned by people who spoke English as a second language! Restaurants, laundries, tailors, retail stores, and gas stations were her niche. Today, her business has expanded and she has five offices in Northern California.

This experience taught her manager that "sometimes we're better off if we *aren't* realistic." *The truth is,* we don't know what is realistic or unrealistic, or what someone is capable of if they are passionate about fulfilling their dream.

CREATING LIMITS

I was talking to a group of bankers recently, and afterward a vice president posed a typical question: "What if I'm a coach of an Olympic hopeful whose dream is to become an Edwin Moses, but I know that he hasn't got the ability to achieve that dream? Isn't my job as a coach to prevent him from having expectations that are clearly beyond him? Shouldn't I help him have a clear sense of his own limitations?"

What if you'd said that to a Larry Bird or J. B. Fuqua or any peak performer who clearly didn't have the "natural talent," education, or gifts to get them to the levels that they achieved? "You're just thinking with your rational mind," I responded pointedly. "You don't have any idea of what someone else's limitations are!"

It's true. We don't have a clue as to what people's limits are. All the tests, stopwatches, and finish lines in the world can't measure human potential. When someone is pursuing their dream, they'll go far beyond what seem to be their limitations. The potential that exists within us is limitless and largely untapped.

UW *says: When you think of limits, you create them.*

"One of the most important things in life," Norman Cousins reminds us, "is the need NOT to accept downside predictions from experts. It's true in interpersonal relationships just as it is true in business. No one knows enough to make a pronouncement of doom."[11]

Yet Firehoses abound and they must be overcome. "The most important thing when you're just starting out is not let the nay-sayers steal your dreams," says Denver entrepreneur Barbara Grogan. "The world is chock-full of negative people. . . . They have a thousand reasons why your dreams won't work, and they're ready to share them with you at the drop of a hat. Well, this sounds trite, but you just have to believe in yourself and in your ability to make your dreams come true."[12]

DREAMS ARE THE FIRST CASUALTY

"I'm a big fan of dreams," says acting superstar Kevin Costner. "Unfortunately, dreams are our first casualty in life—people seem to give them up, quicker than anything, for a 'reality.'"[13]

In the workplace, personal dreams are disregarded in deference to corporate goals; in our personal lives, dreams fade as we get older and become more realistic. We think we know "from experience" what can and what can't be done, what we are and are not capable of, what is possible and what isn't. We then proceed to firehose our own dreams with what we think is a dose of "reality."

UW believes that the tone is set by the person in charge. But **UW**

affirms that you are the person in charge of your own dream. Dreams are often the first casualty because we willingly abandon our own hopes and aspirations in favor of the boss's.

When I talk to audiences about the importance of having dreams, there is always a sympathetic reaction. It touches something in people. They get quiet . . . and pay close attention. So many of us have lost our dreams that when I talk about it directly, people tell me it is a reminder of something missing.

SAVING YOURSELF FROM DISAPPOINTMENT

Whenever I bring up the subject of dreams, someone always says defensively, "Dreams? Ha! If I don't make my quota at work, it's going to be a nightmare. Dream? I haven't slept in a week, how am I going to dream? My dream is to make it through the day."

Conventional Wisdom has firehosed many a dream. "Don't get too big for your britches"; "Don't bite off more than you can chew"; and "Get your head out of the clouds" are only a few of the ways dreams are laid to rest.

I was on *The Oprah Winfrey Show* just after the 1988 Seoul Olympics with five young athletes who had barely missed making the U.S. Olympic team. One woman had been leading in the trials and accidently ran out of her lane, another had lost by one one-hundredth of a second, and another by two centimeters.

Talking about the disappointment and frustration of coming so close, Oprah asked, "Now, seriously, might not it have been better to save yourself from the disappointment, to have lowered your sights a little?" It was an interesting question, considering the source—a woman who is one of the greatest success stories in TV history, who by chasing her dreams has accomplished incredible things.

"What do you think?" I asked the studio audience. "Would it be better not to chase your dream and avoid disappointment, or to have a dream, go for it, and not make it?" To a person, everyone agreed that to have a dream and go after it was the far better choice.

Each of the athletes confirmed this. They talked about how they wouldn't trade the experience of going for their dream for anything. Giving their all in pursuit of making the Olympics gave them purpose and meaning, it had literally opened the world to them. Chasing their dream helped them discover something in themselves that, if they hadn't aimed high, they would never have known existed.

WHAT IF YOU DON'T HAVE A DREAM?

I am often asked, "What if you don't have a dream?" I answer, "No one is without a dream." We all have hopes, aspirations, visions, and dreams, but we're so busy racing around that we don't take time to notice them. We lose our dreams in the frenzy of day-to-day activities.

Bank of America's K. Shelly Porges told me she thinks that "the problem is not that people are working so hard they don't look up, it's that they are working so hard because they don't *want* to look up. They're afraid," she says, "that there is nothing there . . . no meaning, no purpose, no vision . . . that they're running on empty."[14]

Remember, when you lose your dream you lose a little of your potential in the process. As your dream fades, so does your fire. Life gets a little paler. You lose your vigor, confidence, passion, and vitality.

The good news is that even if you have been "running on empty," there are many ways to find your dream, refuel, and begin again.

STARTING THE JOURNEY

Here are several techniques by which you can find or recapture your dream. Deciding to focus on finding your dreams begins a process that can yield amazing results. Take a moment to answer each of the following questions. Let your imagination soar. No holds barred. Don't try to make sense or be realistic. Think about what you *really* want, what adds meaning and purpose and passion to your life. Just thinking about it starts the journey. Write down your responses and read them back to yourself out loud.

1. Someday I'd like to_____.

2. I've always wanted to _____.

3. I'd really love to _____.

4. Wouldn't it be great if I could _____.

5. If it were a perfect world, I would _____.

Your responses to these five questions will prepare the way for you to utilize many of the following dream-finding exercises. As you read them, insert yourself into each example, be your own guinea pig, and think as freely as you can . . . and BEWARE of Firehoses!

The personal videotape

Close your eyes and imagine you're in your home watching a videotape. As the tape begins, you see your own name on the screen and it is dated five years from now. You have accomplished everything you set out to do and are in an ideal situation, living out your dream.

Just watch the tape run. As you view it, don't edit or firehose anything. Let the tape play itself out unencumbered by your rational mind. Don't analyze it or think about it or firehose it. Where are you? What are you doing? How does it feel?

After you have viewed your video, while it is still fresh in your mind, write down a few key words that capture the essence of how you felt watching it, not what you were doing in the tape. These "seed" words are the point of departure. Some typical examples are "proud," "independent," "courageous," and "creative." Keep a card on your desk with the seed words on it to trigger your memory of the video and to remind you of your dream.

Reverse visioning

Imagine you are 85 and looking back over the years. You have lived an active and fulfilling life. You realize that you have gone far beyond what you ever expected you would do or be. As you look back from age 85, ask yourself these questions:

1. What did you do with your life?

2. What were the significant milestones at age 30, 40, . . . 80?

3. What qualities did you exhibit?

4. How do other people describe your life?

5. Do you have any regrets? If so, what are they?

6. What would you have done differently?

Heroes and heroines

Write down the names of your heroes and heroines on a large piece of paper. Don't worry about the strange bedfellows that might turn up. I've seen such a range, you wouldn't believe it: John F. Kennedy, Eleanor Roosevelt, a high school English teacher, Gorbachev, Nelson Mandela, a cousin in the Peace Corps, Madonna, Satchel Paige, Michael Jordan, and Katharine Hepburn.

K. Shelly Porges tells of a heroine she found while attending a tea hosted by the dean of the Cornell School of Hotel Administration. The teas almost always featured successful speakers from the business world, almost all of whom were males. One day the speaker was a woman who was the sales manager of a major hotel chain. Porges, a graduate student, was sitting in the audience and saw in the speaker everything she wanted to be: articulate, successful, attractive, visionary.

While Porges was listening to the speech, she began daydreaming, putting herself in the speaker's place and thinking, "What would I say if I were speaking to this group?" Years later Porges was invited to the dean's tea as the honored guest and began by saying, "You won't believe this, but I began preparing for this speech seven years ago."[15]

What are the *qualities* that your heroes and heroines share? What is it about them that attracts you to them? Which of their qualities have you developed in yourself? Which have lain dormant waiting to be awakened?

Visualize yourself having these qualities. How do you look? What are you doing? What would you do differently right now in order to exhibit those qualities?

Remember that you don't have to do what *they* did to embody their qualities. If your heroes are Mick Jagger or Steffi Graf, you don't have to be a rock singer or a tennis player. Maybe Jagger's swagger, or Steffi's determination, are the traits you admire. After all, a determined, brash dreamer would go pretty far in life!

The magazine cover

Imagine yourself as *Time* magazine's Man or Woman of the Year five years from now. What did you accomplish that got you on the cover? Write out the quotes of the people describing you on the cover. What are some of the key adjectives they use? How many of these key qualities have you already developed?

Find three adjectives *Time* used to describe you. Write them down, then think about what you will have to do to make those terms accurately describe you now.

REKINDLING YOUR DREAMS

Many of us have faced temporary setbacks or felt discouraged in pursuit of our dreams. Yet it always amazes me how quickly we can rediscover our dream and get back into the chase.

"I'm burned out," building contractor Mike Stanley said to me. "I used to love the people part of my work with clients and now every little request or change annoys me. I'm not enjoying it anymore.

"I wanted to move up North and build houses," he continued. "It's growing like crazy so there's lots of potential. It's a better environment to bring up my kids, a lot less crowded and materialistic. But I lost a bid on a big parcel of land last year, and I got discouraged. That just seemed to take all the steam out of me. I haven't had a lot of energy since. It's getting tougher and tougher to pull myself out of bed in the morning. I don't know why I keep doing this, but I don't know what else to do."

I steered him back onto the subject of building houses "up North" and living a quieter life. It was amazing. Just talking about it renewed his energy. I could feel his excitement build as he talked not only of the possibilities of working there but also of the quality of life. "Why don't you make another trip up there to scout out the area again?" I suggested. He smiled and nodded in agreement. A few weeks later he was at my door. "I'm moving north! I found an even better piece of property than I saw last year."[16]

Fortunately for the rest of us, Mike's experience is common. Old dreams require just a little attention to begin working their magic back into our lives, especially after a setback. Like blowing on an ember, our dreams can flare up and ignite our hearts at any time.

KEEP YOUR DREAMS ALIVE

Once you have found your dream or rekindled one you thought was gone forever, the real work is *keeping the dream alive*. One way to accomplish this is to have reminders of it all around you. These will help you remember why you are doing what you are doing, rekindle your fire, and rejuvenate your spirit. Remembering your dreams will put your everyday activities into a larger perspective.

A regional sales manager for Hewlett-Packard had a dream of having H-P dethrone IBM in his area, with himself at the helm. The problem was, as he looked out his office window he faced a large building with three letters on it, I-B-M!

So, to keep reminding himself of his dream, he took a picture of the IBM building, sent it to an art studio, and had the "IBM" airbrushed away and "H-P" put in its place. He enlarged the photo to poster size and put it on his wall. On the new "H-P Building" he outlined the penthouse suite in yellow pen and wrote "my office." Every day it graphically reminded him of where he wanted to go and what his dream was.

There are small reminders in every walk of life:

- The salesman who kept a picture of his dream car, an old reconditioned Corvette, at the top of his sample case, so it was the first thing he saw whenever he opened it.

- The schoolteacher who began collecting maps of bike routes across the country to serve as a daily reminder of her dream of cycling from coast to coast.

- Arnold Schwarzenegger, seven-time Mr. Universe, who would go into the corner of the gym every hour on the hour and visualize himself winning the Mr. Universe contest again.

All these reminders help to keep dreams alive. They add kindling to the fire in our hearts every day. They keep us moving forward and give us more vitality.

Jesse Jackson's son said it eloquently in nominating his father at the 1988 Democratic Convention: *"The shame in life is not to fail to reach your dream, but to fail to have a dream to reach."*

UW *says:*
Dreams are goals with wings.

5
Try Easy

TIME POVERTY

One of the biggest limits we impose on our own goals and dreams is believing that faster is better. The pace of life has increased and more and more things have gotten out of control. We try to keep up by living our lives at a faster pace.

Conventional Wisdom tells us that to keep ahead we have to speed up—"Pedal to the metal." And in spite of admonitions to work smarter, not harder, we continue playing the desperate games of "hurry up" and "catch up." That's the reality today.

Today's most precious commodity is time. And most of us feel impoverished—we just don't seem to have enough of it. It's no wonder that the cry heard from every corner of our lives is: "Too much to do in too little time."

THE GOTTA'S CAN RUN YOUR LIFE

I call this response the Gotta's, as in:

I *gotta* make this deadline.

I *gotta* be great in this presentation.

I *gotta* finish this paperwork, make three phone calls, and get to this meeting, and I'm late already.

I *gotta* make a decision.

I *gotta* read all this material before tomorrow's meeting.

I *gotta* cut costs.

I *gotta* make my quota.

I *gotta* pick up my kid at child care, do the shopping, make dinner, and finish that report.

I *gotta* catch that plane.

(Fill in your own.)_____

CHAPLIN'S SPEEDING CAKES

A classic example of the Gotta's is Charlie Chaplin's cake-decorating scene in the film *Modern Times*. Standing next to a conveyor belt as beautiful creamy white cakes roll by, Chaplin sprays on the frosting, adds a rose or two, puts the cake in the box, and puts the box on a shelf. Everything is working fine and he is enjoying himself immensely.

Then the belt speeds up. In his haste to keep up, he begins moving with the famous Chaplin hyperspeed. As the cakes fly by him, the icing gets sprayed all over, the roses look like Rorschach's ink blots, and the cakes go *ker-plop*! on top of each other, forming a sweet white mound on the bakery floor. Chaplin foreshadowed our current "modern times." We used to laugh at this scene; now we live it—and it's not as funny.

GOTTA'S CHECK LIST

When I mention the Gotta's in my speeches, it always elicits a response of laughter and understanding. It's so familiar. The Gotta's have become the primary conventional response for anyone trying to get ahead in today's fast-paced environment.

It doesn't matter what you do or where you do it, the Gotta's are everywhere. You've got the Gotta's if:

- You're working harder but wondering if you are accomplishing that much more.

- You always feel behind . . . running a little late.

- You are more irritable, critical, or short-tempered with the people around you.

- You see less and less of your friends and family.

- You get more headaches, backaches, stomachaches.

- You have a tough time relaxing.

- You feel guilty if you aren't working.

- It's all work and no play.

- You're married to your job.

- You put off routine things (such as returning phone calls, writing letters, reading reports, and paying the monthly bills).

- You tire easily and feel fatigued.

- You sometimes feel depressed or sad without any apparent cause.

- You need to be continually busy.

Consider a story Bette Midler told about preparing a birthday party for her two-year-old daughter. "I'm just flying by the seat of my pants," she said. "I'm obsessed. I went nuts. I just went nuts. Baking cookies. Hanging decorations. All I could think of was 'I gotta, I gotta, I gotta.' "[1]

HURRY SICKNESS

When you have the Gotta's, you walk, talk, eat, write, think and do everything else too fast. You are always racing and yet feel a little behind. This "Type A" response has been called "hurry sickness." It is a state of barely contained panic.

Hurry sickness mimics the symptoms of the White Rabbit in *Alice in Wonderland*, who sings, "I'm late, I'm late, for a very important date. No time to say hello—goodbye—I'm late! I'm late! I'm late!" Only this is no fairy tale. One manager told me it's like a "chronic state of overwhelm, a feeling of constantly being in over your head and out of control."

THE ULTIMATE FRINGE DEFICIT: *KAROSHI*

Not surprisingly, research has found that the Type A life- and workstyle is incredibly stressful. Dr. Ken Pelletier, a leading authority on stress in the workplace, says that it "leaves the person frustrated, nervous and hostile."[2]

You are much more inflexible, impatient, irritable, and anxious when you've got the Gotta's, which in turn make you much more at risk of a heart attack or high blood pressure, to say nothing of your not being much fun at home or with friends—if you have any left. In fact, the Gotta's can literally kill you, and the phenomenon has become of such concern in Japan that they have a word for it. "To the millions of Japanese who operate in perpetual overdrive this phenomenon has long been known as *karoshi*, or death from overwork,"[3] said a news report. It is certainly as Louis Patler says, "the ultimate fringe *deficit*" for the employee, but it also takes its toll on companies that are being sued by the dependents of the deceased for negligence and related acts.

SPEED KILLS QUALITY AND SERVICE

Not only the Japanese are suffering the physical effects of stress. Stress-related claims by white-collar workers in California, for example, soared 700 percent during the eighties. But the real totals "may be nearly four times higher," says the California Workers' Compensation Institute, which estimated the cost to industry of stress-related work losses at $460 million in 1988.[4] And if California is supposed to be the place where people are more "mellow," imagine what these figures would be for New York City?

For most, the Gotta's get going when people are trying to be conscientious and perform better. Ironically, the evidence is mounting that you actually perform *less* effectively when you are in a high-speed, rush-rush mode.

For example, two of the most important goals in business today are improving quality and service. But when you have the Gotta's, you're in too much of a hurry to give the effort that would result in superior quality and/or excellent service. You don't have the time to dot the Is and cross the Ts," to perfect your designs, to follow up with your customers. The refinements that make for top quality are usually missing, and the little extras that make the difference between good and outstanding service are absent as well.

You also can't concentrate or think clearly when you're rushing around madly. With the Gotta's, your mind is racing and darting from one thought to another, causing careless mistakes:

- You miss an important point in a presentation because your mind is thinking of the next point.

- You forget to include the date or place of a meeting in your memo and have to do it over.

- You leave an important document on your desk in the rush to get to an appointment.

- You give a wrong price quote or delivery date in your haste to respond to a client.

Only recently have companies begun to understand the high price of working at high speed. A major Japanese bank estimated that careless mistakes due to "rushing" *added 25 percent to its expense budget!* Simply speeding up doesn't guarantee that productivity and efficiency will go up, too. In fact, it is typically quite the contrary.

SPEED KILLS CREATIVITY AND INNOVATION

When we are in a rush, we end up doing things in a rote manner, exactly the same way we've done them before, only faster. Working as fast as we can in order to get on to the next thing that's gotta get done, we don't take the time needed for incubation, contemplation, or experimentation, which is necessary for innovation and creative problem solving. As a result of our time famine, we go for early closure on important issues, grabbing at the first "solution" and running with it. Before we know it, rote responses become routines, and routines lead to ruts, which kill creativity and motivation as well.

SPEED SABOTAGES TEAM WORK AND COMMUNICATION

The Gotta's not only sabotage performance, they also undermine human relationships. As our world becomes more of a McLuhanesque "global village," individuals, companies, and countries become increasingly interdependent. Consequently, the days of the individual working in a vacuum are over.

The trouble is, if you have the Gotta's and are besieged with work, you're in too much of a rush to communicate clearly and to develop and cultivate relationships. Most research tells us that the key to communication—whether you are selling, managing, or working together on a team—is listening. But even though we acknowledge this, who has time to listen when you're racing a mile a minute? Not only do you not listen or concentrate well when you have the Gotta's, but to add insult to injury, you become brusque and pushy: you are more impatient and ill-tempered than usual, and you cut people off, treating every suggestion or phone call as a nagging interruption.

"When I am racing and have stacks of proposals on my desk, all demanding instant attention, I know I really turn people off," the director of a private foundation told me. "I don't listen or help people solve problems; I just tell them something expedient so I can get on to the next thing. Ugh! I'd hate to be on the other end of the phone with me when I am like that. The problem is, with all that I have to do, I'm finding that I'm more like that every day."

GOTTA SAY YES

In the desire for increased productivity and decreased costs, many corporations encourage and institutionalize this harder-faster-longer mind-set. These Gotta companies and Gotta bosses make you feel as though you gotta say yes to the increases in work load, quotas, or travel. If you say no to a new project—even though you are already overcommitted, overloaded, and overwhelmed—you're afraid of being seen as disloyal or as not having "the right stuff," not being a "team player," or not willing to give 110 percent.

An executive of a leading Western bank recently told me that members of management were coming to realize that their valued and loyal employees were burning out in the face of their corporation's high-stress culture. "Because of our 'gotta-say-yes' work ethic, my staff overpromise and overcommit," she said. "As a result, they also *under*perform.

"My people are exhausted," she told me. "We have been asking an awful lot of them. At this rate, we are going to have wholesale burnout. We're starting to see lots of careless errors. Morale is at an all-time low. Forget innovation. And that is at every level," she continued, "from me on down. Even the people who are doing very well won't last at the rate they are going."

ADRENALINE JUNKIES

For some, facing the challenge of rapid change with the Gotta's seems to get the juices flowing. "I love the rush, the pace," one ad agency executive told me. "I thrive on the excitement. I love pressure and always being on the go." But how long can that last? When you constantly have the Gotta's, if the adrenaline is on all the time, how long will it be before the juices *over*flow:

You may be able to channel the adrenaline for a while. But the pressure and speed become a habit. That's why many Japanese bank workers stayed until late into the evening during the work week when the government encouraged banks to close on Saturdays. They needed their work "fix" for the week. The Gotta's had become addictive.

Unfortunately, as with any addiction, it is easier to get the Gotta's than to get rid of them. The Gotta's become too much to manage physically and/or mentally, and we become members of a workaholic society. And if our inner fire is constantly roaring at full blast, eventually we will burn out.

UW *says: Speed kills!* . . . *(slowly).*

SNEAKING UP ON YOU

If you are not careful, the Gotta's will get you and you won't even know it. The Gotta's are as subtle as they are insidious. And like Chaplin at the conveyor belt, before you know it you're out of control.

Sometimes the Gotta's start with increased demands for more productivity and/or cost cutting. Conventional Wisdom urges us to meet the challenge of change by speeding up to keep up. Then additional resources and support systems are pulled out. Now you are forced to do more with less and you are expected to go even faster. More demands. More speed. All of a sudden you are in over your head, working far into the night, on the weekends, and still feeling behind.

The truth is that most of us are going as fast as we can. We can't go any faster, any longer, or any harder. We're *at* the limit, hitting the wall, mentally and physically. We have to find alternatives to speeding up. Longer, harder, and faster won't open the gates to the future; you have to take an alternate, unconventional route.

DECREASE SPEED, INCREASE PROFITS

The smartest people make different choices. They use an unconventional thinking that turns the "speed-up-to-keep-up" ethic on its ear.

Heinz Foods chairman Tony O'Reilly was the epitome of the eighties speed king. One of the leaders in the "lean 'n' mean" movement, he kept Heinz profitable throughout the decade by closing factories, cutting staff, and speeding up production lines.

Entering the nineties, O'Reilly realized that his red-pencil–speed-it-up approach, may have been successful in the short run, but it had alienated workers, decreased the quality of the products, and left the company wasting millions of dollars a year. Dramatically shifting his tactics, Reilly said, "We want to secure our cost reductions from something we never concentrated on before—*the price of nonconformance* [by overworked workers]. . . . We've begun to question our entire manufacturing processes right across the spectrum. . . ."

At Heinz's StarKist tuna plants, where the company had laid off fish cutters and sped up the production line, O'Reilly discovered that the remaining employees were so overworked they were leaving tons of meat on the bones every day. The solution was to slow down the production lines, hire more hourly workers, and retrain the entire work force. As a result, StarKist's labor costs increased by $5 million, but they also eliminated $15 million dollars worth of waste from unused tuna. Those two simple and unconventional moves—*adding* workers and *slowing down* production—yielded *annual net savings of over $10 million.*[5]

At Heinz's Ore-Ida potato-processing plants, managers realized that years of "take no prisoners" cost cutting and speeding up had contributed to a decline in sales by actually changing the taste and texture of the company's popular Tater Tots. New high-speed slicing machines were so fast they were pulverizing the spuds, making the Tots mushy instead of chunky.

The solution? Slow the machines down and you get more uniform Tots. Of course, decreasing the speed also decreased productivity, but more importantly it brought back the taste and quality for which Tater Tots were known. The result was double-digit increases in sales for three years, which more than paid for the cost of slowing down, and the increase in morale was incalculable.

TRY EASY, DON'T TRY HARDER

An example of this arises out of my experience working with a group of world-class sprinters, ten of whom were trying out for three remaining qualifying places for the Olympic trials. In the first practice heat, just about all of the athletes had a bad case of the Gotta's and were tense and tight. They had worked very hard for a very long time on their dream of making the Olympic team. This meet represented their chance, so the stakes were high.

After writing down their times, I told them we were going to time them again in 15 minutes. But this time I said, "Don't run flat out, go at about nine tenths."

The results were amazing! To everyone's surprise, each ran faster the second time, when they were trying "easy." And one runner's time set an unofficial world record.

The same is true elsewhere: trying easy will help you in any area of your life. Conventional Wisdom tells us we have to have no less than 110 percent to keep ahead. Yet conversely, I have found that giving 90 percent is usually more effective. The Gotta's force us to try too hard, to tighten up, and to push ourselves past our peak performance zone and into the panic zone. Contrary to Conventional Wisdom, therefore, the next time you are faced with a difficult task, remember a passionate 90 percent is better than a panicked 110 percent.

UW *says: Try easy!*

LESS IS MORE

Another Gotta that is rampant in organizations is: "Gotta communicate *as much information* as possible, preferably everything I know, *in the least amount of time.*" We've all been on the receiving end of these well-intended but overloaded efforts. We have been at meetings where presenters try to deliver more material than anyone can possibly digest, talking a mile a minute, using overheads so crowded with numbers that you can't see the white space. We've received memos, recommendations, and reports encumbered with enough facts, figures, rationale, and backup material that it would take seven-league boots to wade through to find what is really important.

To communicate effectively, **UW** offers you a simple alternative: less is more. Adding to this point, Winston Churchill, one of the great Break-It Thinkers, demanded that correspondence to him be limited to one page. If you can't say it in one page, Churchill reasoned, you don't know it well enough. Not a bad piece of Unconventional Wisdom.

GETTING RID OF THE GOTTA'S

Slowing down, doing less, and trying "easy" are three unconventional strategies for getting rid of the Gotta's. But as with any addiction, if you really want to get rid of them, first you have to recognize them and admit you've "got 'em."

Learning to recognize the Gotta's will minimize their scope and their magnitude—and the sooner, the better. The awareness itself helps to decrease the debilitating long-term effects. Simply recognizing that you have the Gotta's helps to distance you from their insidious effects.

I learned from Fritz Perls, the father of Gestalt Therapy, that "awareness in itself is curative." Once aware of the Gotta's, you will no longer be a victim but will begin to take control.

Throughout this book you will find many unconventional examples, tips, and techniques that will enable you to conquer the Gotta's. You'll learn how to do more in less time—with more quality and creativity—by breaking the rules, changing the game, and challenging the status quo.

UW *says:*
Try easy.

6

Always Mess with Success

IF IT AIN'T BROKE, BREAK IT!

When things are going well, Conventional Wisdom warns us, "Leave well enough alone." "If it ain't broke," the advice goes, "don't fix it." But how well does this advice hold up as we confront the challenge of uncertain times?

It is easy to succumb to the idea that we'll enjoy the sweet smell of success indefinitely if we don't mess with it. Practically speaking, however, this is bad advice. In our highly competitive world, following these old axioms will leave you, and your company, in the dust.

DOWN THE YELLOW BRICK ROAD . . . INTO A WALL

"Over the years, we've become the victims of our own success," said John Young, chairman and CEO of Hewlett-Packard.[1] What Young is talking about are the big and little companies, with the best and brightest leaders, who are blinded by short-term success and encouraged by the Conventional Wisdom, "Don't mess with success." Instead, they go headlong down the yellow brick road . . . straight into a brick wall.

Barry Diller, chairman of the entertainment conglomerate Fox Inc., says, "You can put a $22 trillion company together, and . . . heaven help the company that rests on its laurels . . . because there will be some fool standing on the corner outside who will have a better idea than you will. Head-to-head he'll succeed, and you will fail."[2]

UW *says*: *If you don't mess with your success, someone else will.*

COMPLACENCY BREEDS FAILURE

Once they are making a lot of money, many salespeople, for instance, tend to get complacent. They get lazy and sloppy and stop attending to the basics. One salesman told me that when he was first starting out he did a lot of prospecting for new clients and would "prepare, prepare, prepare" for every sales call. "I would be up at the crack of dawn calling prospective clients; and before any call I would learn everything I could about the account, the competition, the market-place, everything. Then I would rehearse my presentation—asking all the right questions, anticipating anything that could arise—and have responses ready.

"But when I started making a six-figure income I began to take my success for granted. I got complacent and took shortcuts. I stopped prospecting and relied on the accounts I had. I also prepared less for each call. I figured I knew my stuff. All of a sudden my numbers were way down and I didn't know why. At first I thought it was just bad luck or timing. Now I realize that I forgot to do what got me there. I have to get back to thinking like a hungry salesman."[3]

The same thing happens in many different areas when people or teams are successful. Success, conventionally speaking, is the goal, the finale, the reward, the finish line. Because it is viewed as the end and not the means, there is a tendency to think we've "got it made" when we achieve our goal. We think we know the basics, have the skills and drills "down," and start taking success for granted. The result is, we get lulled into complacency and slack off.

In sports, where results are so visible, complacency undercuts performance. Look what happened when Mike Tyson started "believing his press clippings," which heralded him as one of the greatest heavyweight champions ever and suggested he was unbeatable. He didn't bother to train rigorously for his fight with the previously unheard of "Buster" Douglas. And got knocked out.

Similarly, in the 1988 Olympics, swimmer Matt Biondi, thinking victory was assured in the 200 butterfly, glided home and didn't take the last stroke—he was touched out by .001 of a second.

THE LAKERS LOSE THEIR EDGE

Comparing the attitude of the team that won the NBA championship in 1984 with the team that reported to the 1985 training camp, I recall Los Angeles basketball coach Pat Riley saying that they took their success for granted: "Hey, we're the best," players were thinking. "We beat *Boston*. We beat Boston *in* Boston. We beat Boston in Boston with *Bird*."

The signs of creeping complacency, Riley explained, were very subtle at first: players weren't diving for balls, they weren't running as hard, and some players were coming to practice late and leaving a bit early.

It's no wonder they began the 1985 season by nosediving in the standings. The showdown came, Riley said, on the night they were being awarded their 1984 Championship rings, playing lowly regarded Cleveland. At "showtime," in front of the hometown fans, they lost by 34 points!

BRINGING THE CUP DOWN UNDER . . . AND BACK AGAIN

A great example of a dynamic innovative individual who fell into the "don't mess with success" trap is the Australian Alan Bond and his experience in the America's Cup races. In 1983, the Australians challenged the United States for the America's Cup—the Americans had hung on to it for 134 years! Assuming that the traditional design was "broken" and needed "fixing," Bond, the head of the Australian syndicate, questioned every aspect of past boat designs. Out of this bold, no-holds-barred process came an innovative and revolutionary double-keel design. It gave the Aussies a distinct advantage. In a major upset, Bond's boat, *Australia III*, beat Dennis Conners's American entry in four straight races.

In preparing for the America's Cup rematch in Freemantle, Australia, four years later, Bond made a fatal mistake. He assumed he had a "finished product" and stuck to it. Forgetting the innovative "break it" thinking process with which he had developed his winning boat, he used essentially the same boat he had used to win the cup four years before. He didn't even make the finals.

Whether in a boat or in business, "don't mess with success" thinking gets you stuck in an eddy. It focuses energy and materials on maintaining the status quo rather than growth, on conservation rather than innovation, and on playing not-to-lose rather than to win. Here are some cautionary tales of the high price paid by companies that failed to mess with their success.

"IT AIN'T BROKE SO LET'S MAKE IT BIGGER"

Remember when no fun-loving cook would be caught dead without the shredding, chopping, slicing, grating gizmo that revolutionized home cooking, the Cuisinart? Its creator, Carl Sontheimer, showed he understood the American appetite for powerful, time-saving kitchen gadgets. The Cuisinart filled a market niche . . . and the company's cash registers as well.

Amazingly, 15 years after the Cuisinart food processor's introduction, 85 percent of the company's revenues still came from the original product. Cuisinart had managed to stay profitable for a long time by doing almost nothing differently. "It's still selling, it ain't broke, so let's not fix it."

The problem was that Sontheimer forgot his formula for success—innovation and anticipating the needs of the market. Paying little attention to the changing eating habits and increasing time famine of Americans (as well as to the newer, faster, cheaper guns in town—like Presto Salad Shooter), Sontheimer stuck with what he thought was a winning hand. In fact, when sales began to drop dramatically, he decided to make a bigger, more expensive model. Thinking "It ain't broke, so let's just make it bigger," Cuisinart nearly went broke and eventually filed for bankruptcy! "Cuisinart," wrote *Forbes* magazine's punsters, "got chopped up by far hungrier, less complacent companies."[3]

ACT ONE: DEC DECKS IBM

In the early eighties, IBM was caught not practicing the kind of thinking that had made them leaders in the first place. Big Blue was paying too much attention to its successful products and too little attention to its own customers' changing needs. "Hey, we're Big Blue," they seemed to say, "no one can beat us at our own game."

"For years we've been telling IBM what we want, and they never gave it to us," a computer manager at a large Southern bank complained. "Now we're listening to what DEC has to offer."[4] While IBM rested on its laurels, DEC (Digital Equipment Corporation) stepped in and with an innovative strategy captured a big slice of IBM's midrange computer pie. They pounded IBM from 1984 to 1988, during which time their sales doubled and their earnings quadrupled.

ACT TWO: DEC DECKS DEC

By 1987, DEC had itself become a giant, and at the annual stockholders' meeting, founder Kenneth H. Olsen was basking in the overwhelming success of what the annual report referred to as a "brilliant strategy": one computer design (VAX) and a single set of software, made in different sizes and capable of sharing information with any other DEC computer.

A year later it was a different story! Customers were shifting to low-cost desktop networks, reducing the need for large minicomputers. They were also demanding hardware and software that would connect to many different sizes and brands. DEC had followed IBM's lead and gotten complacent. "We forgot to watch what was going on outside," DEC's Pier-Carlo Falotti, head of European operations, said. The result was a complete reversal of the success of the year before. In one year DEC had a 17 percent drop in profits and discovered the hard way that "it can't live by VAX alone."[5] Like IBM, DEC tried to coast and discovered that in a rapidly changing environment, resting on your laurels can lull you to sleep, and you wake up to find yourself far behind.

Zenith learned this lesson, too. As the largest manufacturer of laptop computers, Zenith, like DEC, was on a roll. But while NEC and Toshiba were pushing for a lighter, faster machine, Zenith rested on its laurels. Their early lead wasn't sufficient for them to retain their place in the market. Ultimately they had to abandon the market entirely— selling their laptop division to a French firm.

"NUMERO DOS" AND RISING

The "Beer Wars" serve as an interesting example of taking much too much for granted. "Corona is the Johnny-come-lately that is bringing in Mexican soda pop," said Leo Van Munching, Jr., president of the U.S. company that distributes Heineken, the number one imported beer. Seriously underestimating both the competition and the changes in the marketplace in the last few years, Heineken cut media spending by 78 percent.[6] During the same period, Corona upped its ad budget 245 percent.

The result was that Heineken's sales dropped by 15 percent in the imported beer market, while Corona's rose 15 percent. Corona is now *numero dos* and continues to munch away on Van Munching's market share.

FROGS IN HOT WATER

Stories of corporate complacency, arrogance, and lethargy can be told for business sectors such as pharmaceuticals and factories, building supplies, bicycles, telephones, and tools. Then there is what happened to the American automotive industry as the Japanese and Germans passed our road hogs in sporty little cars.

If you fail to constantly improve, if you assume "it ain't broke yet," someone else *will* build on your idea, will make it better, and *you'll* soon be broke.

"It ain't broke, don't fix it" thinking breeds a false sense of satisfaction. It causes you to behave like the old story of the well-fed frogs soaking in pots filled with the warm, soothing waters of success. Like these frogs, by the time you realize the environment has changed, the water is boiling and you're too weak to climb out.

UW *says: Mess with success or your success will mess with you.*

THERE IS NO SUCH THING AS A "FINISHED" PRODUCT

"It ain't broke, don't fix it" thinking assumes that there is such a thing as a "finished" product. This static, conservative, conventional attitude is contrary to nature. In billing systems, nothing is ever finished. The natural tendency for all living things, says Nobel Prize laureate Albert Szent-Györgyi, is to keep growing, changing, and evolving.

Everything around us is constantly changing. Thinking that you can stay ahead by repeating the past is folly. Everything is in process. Everything. Animal, vegetable, technology, your lifestyles, and the map of the world . . . everything. No exceptions.

Not only is everything changing, but everything exists in relationship to something else that is changing: a service to a need, a product to a consumer, a leader to a constituency, manufacturing to the environment, a coach to a team. If you or your products don't grow, improve and evolve, as in nature—they (and you) will face extinction.

UW *says: Treat your product as if it's alive and it will stay that way.*

KAIZEN

The Japanese are clear on the concept that "finished never is." In fact, they even have a word for it, *kaizen*, meaning "continuous improvement." *Kaizen* is the basis for the corporate culture of most successful Japanese businesses. "The spirit of *kaizen*," comments international management consultant Kiyoshi Suzaki, "begins with the acceptance that the status quo is not perfect."[7]

Toyota, the most profitable car company in the world, keeps getting better. Extensive interviews with Toyota executives in the U.S. demonstrate the company's total dedication to continuous improvement. It is simultaneously restructuring its management, refining its already elegant manufacturing process, planning its global strategy for the twenty-first century, tinkering with its corporate culture and even becoming a fashion leader. Says Iwao Isomura, chief of personnel, "Our current success is the best reason to change things."[8]

PEPSICO: NOT IN TRIVIAL PURSUIT

PepsiCo is an organization that not only believes in continuous improvement but practices it. Pepsi-Cola is the largest-selling food product of any type in the U.S. market and is a $13 billion brand worldwide. Pepsi's Doritos, Kentucky Fried Chicken, and Pizza Hut operations are well known around the globe.

"Some might argue that we should not tamper with these brands in either image or substance," says PepsiCo chairman Wayne Calloway. "We don't agree. We know that in a fast-paced world, today's popular brand could be tomorrow's trivia question."[9]

BELIEVE IN THE PROCESS, NOT JUST THE PRODUCT

Many successful people and organizations start to believe it is the product that brings success. A premier product, however, is the result of a process—studying the market, listening to the customer, experimenting, innovating, taking risks, and working your tail off. That is what created and sold the product.

The common mistake is to cling to the product, rather than recognize the process. The product and the producer then become stagnant while the market and the competition are changing. While you are holding your product up to the limelight, somewhere, someone is about to pass you by. If you stop focusing on the process, learning, change, and innovation stop, too.

PLATEAUING

The direct result of conventional wisdom such as "Don't mess with success" and the accompanying complacency is *plateauing*, which happens when the individual or the organization stops growing and moving upward. The performance curve flattens out as do the innovations and new product development. Companies like IBM, DEC, Cuisinart, and Heineken, as well as many others who have tried resting on their laurels, have found that plateauing is quickly followed by *plunging*.

Successful people as well as organizations run the risk of becoming complacent. For instance, I see many people in middle management who have lost their fire and "retired" on the job. Fearing that there is no room to advance and being unwilling to take chances in these uncertain times, they feel trapped and become resigned to staying where they are.

As a result they "settle in," doing just enough to get by. They retire on the job. Going through the motions, they actively resist change or any new challenges. The last thing they want to do is to take any risks or do anything that might rock the boat. This attitude, which I see in many large corporations, is incredibly counterproductive. One result is that these managers lose the very thing they have been desperately trying to keep—their job.

This is a very boring, lifeless, and lackluster way to spend eight to ten hours a day. There is no spark, no juice, no fun when you are just going through the motions. When the individual has given up, there is no joy. Everything is drab and dull and tedious when there is no fire. Gone is the enthusiasm that adds so much to work and life. Even minor tasks take major effort when you have no energy and drive. This workstyle, which also has profound effects on the individual's life outside work, becomes a vicious cycle.

STARTING A VITAL CYCLE

Even if there isn't any more room at the top, it is still possible to feel more vital and alive at work and regain the old spark. Contrary to Conventional Wisdom, the key to keeping the spark alive is to *stop focusing on the goal,* whether it is getting ahead or, as it is for many these days, just keeping a job.

UW *says: Focus on the process, not the goal.*

I know this will sound like heresy, but stick with me. Rather than have people concentrate on a rigid idea of success, I have them think about how they could revitalize themselves on the job, what they could do that would make them more enthusiastic. In other words, rather than making numbers or achievement or survival the goal, strive to recharge yourself.

A typical reaction is that people at first laugh and make remarks like: "The best thing I could do to recharge myself would be to stay home." Yet when we get down to a serious discussion, their response always amazes me.

When formerly sullen and "turned-off" people start thinking about how to revitalize themselves, their attitude changes. The head of human resources for a management consulting firm told me, "I am in charge of recruiting, and I keep going to the same colleges and graduate schools and interviewing and eventually hiring the same type of kids year after year. Not only do I feel we are missing out on some good possibilities, but I am so BORED I could 'phone' it in. But these are the types that are being asked for, and I"—she saluted—"am great at following orders."

"I think I'm going to shake things up a little," she said with a smile. "I'm going to start going to some schools that are out of the mainstream and talking to different types of students. I think we could get some good new blood this way, and I certainly would have more fun."

We all get stale at times. Although you can do this exercise when you are feeling lethargic, you don't have to wait until then. Doing it can prevent you from getting stale.

Try it now. Answer the following questions as candidly and imaginatively as possible. Beware of potential Firehoses.

1. What could you do to recharge yourself on the job, to feel more alive and vital?

2. What would you be doing, and how would you be thinking, differently than you are now?

3. See yourself thinking that way and doing it.

Recharging yourself increases energy and enthusiasm. Getting back some of the spark not only makes you feel better, it enables you to do your job better, too. When energy and skill are combined, you are more productive, more creative, and certainly more motivated and energetic. In other words, when you are more energized, you perform better and that makes you feel better . . . *and* you have started a very vital cycle.

"FIX IT" ALL THE TIME

Whether you think you have reached the top, have plateaued, or are still climbing, you can't stay still. "You have to keep changing to match current challenges," says J. B. Fuqua, chairman of the billion-dollar-a-year conglomerate that sells sporting goods, gardening products and financial services. "You know the old saying 'Don't fix it if it ain't broke.' The fact is, if you don't fix it *all the time*, it will break."[10]

Syndicated columnist John Heilborn reports that in the computer industry things are "moving so quickly that by the time a product has been brought to market, a newer model is generally already being moved out of someone's engineering lab to replace it."[11] If a product or idea has been out in the marketplace for a year without any changes, rest assured that it's already broken, whether you know it or not.

Staying with what's working today, in a world where tomorrow is coming at an ever-increasing rate, is a very risky business. UCLA's Ichak Adizes, professor of management and the author of *Corporate Lifecycles*, says that when an organization is at the peak of success it "does not mean it has arrived. . . . If it does not refuel . . . keep . . . nourishing itself, it will lose the rate of growth and eventually its vitality will level off."[12]

LIFE IMITATES ART

When it comes to a commitment to messing with success, our lives should imitate art much more than they do. Consider the following:

- James Michener was asked to name his favorite book among those he had authored. "My preference, among the thirty-five books I've written," he said after a long pause, "is always the next one. I'm an old pro. And the job of an old pro is to move on to the next task."[13]

- David Harrington, violinist with the avant-garde Kronos Quartet, echoes Michener's sentiments: "To me . . . being an artist is a source of perpetual renewal, because it is a task that has no real ending point."[14]

- Medical researcher J. William Langston made great advances in our understanding of the causes of Parkinson's disease and attributed much of his success to Picasso. "One thing I remember about Picasso," he said, "was that he was always changing, always trying something new. That's just as important in science."[15]

- Jessica Tandy, Oscar winner for her role in *Driving Miss Daisy*, was asked if any of her performances have left her unsatisfied. "All of them," came her instant reply. "I've never come off the stage at the end of a performance and said, 'Tonight, everything was perfect.' There'll always be some little thing that I'll have to get right tomorrow."[16]

THE BEST ARE NEVER SATISFIED

Like great artists and athletes, all top performers know they cannot stand still for long. They always look for ways to improve. Tony Gwynn, the first player since Stan Musial to win three consecutive batting championships, says, "I really don't think I'll ever be satisfied. . . . Once you think you're where you want to be, you're not there any more."[17]

Echoing Gwynn, K. Shelly Porges, Bank of America senior vice president, observed, "The greatest challenge we have as we become successful is never to rest on our laurels, never to feel like we've done it. The minute you feel like you've done it, that's the beginning of the end."[18]

Two of the best basketball players of the eighties, Larry Bird and Magic Johnson, are great examples of the "never finished, never satisfied" mind-set. In their off-season, each works to keep upping the level of his skills. One summer, for example, Bird lifted weights; another he ran more; and another, he laid out a regulation court, glass backboards and all, on his mother's front lawn, just "to learn some new moves."[19]

"Once you're labeled 'the best' . . . you want to stay up there, and you can't do it by loafing around," he said. "In basketball, the guys are getting bigger, stronger, and faster, the game is faster and more sophisticated. . . . If I don't keep changing, I'm history."[20]

Magic spent one summer learning a "back-to-the-basket post-up game and a 'junior, junior' skyhook."[21] "My game," says Magic, "is not really shooting hook shots, *[it's wanting] to learn something new.* . . . The point is, I want to constantly be adding new tricks to my game."[22] The metagame for Magic and Bird, as with all top performers, is to keep learning, day in and day out, rain or shine.

SUCCESS AS A SPRINGBOARD NOT A PEDESTAL

Learning from IBM's problems of the early eighties, Chairman John Akers is not letting IBM rest on its laurels anymore. Jacques Maisonrouge, former head of IBM's European operations, gives some keen insight into Akers's thinking. Citing a recent *Fortune* survey of most-admired companies where IBM ranked number one (with scores in the top five, in five out of eight indicators), Maisonrouge pointed out that "any other company would have broken out the Dom Perignon. John Akers immediately commissioned task forces to find out how we could do better on the other factors."[23] (The only thing Akers could have done better, I think, is break out the champagne *and* commission the task force!)

UW *says: Use success as a springboard, not as a pedestal.*

A pedestal is static and presents a big stationary target, which makes it easy for someone to knock you off it. A springboard keeps you in motion, continually reaching for greater heights.

A great example of using success as a springboard is writer Frank Deford, whose accolades and achievements are staggering. By the age of 50 he had covered all the major sports stories many times over. He had won the Sportswriter of the Year Award six times, had been a writer for *Sports Illustrated* for 27 years, and had written ten books, two of which became movies.

In April 1989, Deford, called the most celebrated sportswriter of this generation, pushed back his old Olympia typewriter, got up from his desk, and walked away from the most idyllic job in sports journalism.[24] Feeling the challenge was not there anymore and being willing to mess with success, he accepted the high risk post of editor-in-chief of the *National*, whose goal was to become the first U.S. daily sports newspaper.

CHANGE WHEN YOU DON'T HAVE TO

Most organizations don't change until they have to. They wait until things are going poorly and then desperately try to find a quick fix, changing strategies, products, services—anything to try to catch up. The problem is that you don't think clearly with a gun at your head. The poor decision making, lack of innovation, and low morale characteristic of organizations playing catch-up create a vicious cycle that keeps them significantly behind.

Innovative thinking and the resulting quality and service so necessary today don't come from a struggling organization that's "gotta" make some changes fast to keep its head above water.

UW *says: The best time to change is when you don't have to.*

Initiating change when you are out front will keep you there. Contrary to Conventional Wisdom, the best time for pioneering and innovation is when you are on top. Confidence is high.

"We reorganize for good business reasons," IBM chairman John Akers says. "One of the good business reasons is that we haven't reorganized in a while."[25] That's the type of thinking that will prevent complacency.

A WELCOME RECEPTION

"Becoming complacent or satisfied with the status quo is a death knell," says Paul Viviano, president and CEO of Saint Jude's Hospital, an extremely profitable and innovative healthcare facility in Southern California. "When things are going well is the time to keep thinking ahead. People are feeling positive and the spirit is high, which is a good environment to breed innovation."[26]

At a workshop I did on innovation for Saint Jude's, one of the problems identified for improvement was their admissions area, which in hospitals is traditionally cold and bureaucratic, time consuming, and humiliating to the patient. Although better than most, the managers realized that parking at Saint Jude's was far from admissions, which meant long walks for people often carrying bags. Patients had to wait a long time to be admitted, and then they were confused about where to go when they got inside.

Showing the creative and innovative spirit that Viviano talked about, the managers got the bright idea that they could learn from the real pros on admissions, the hotel industry. Out of the workshop came plans for a doorman, a bellman to carry bags, a concierge to advise about the hospital, and computerized admissions. Bigger, clearer signs; a new cheerful paint job; and music in the lobby were also part of the plan.

"The attitude of most hospitals, especially at admissions, when the patient is usually the most afraid and disoriented, is, 'We are doing you a favor,'" said one manager. "We want people to feel more well cared for and cared about. After all, that is what hospitals are supposed to be about—healing, health, and well-being. We should reflect that from the moment of admittance."

BREAK THE MOLD AND BREAK IT AGAIN

Everything around you is in a chronic state of flux. A Hewlett-Packard senior manager, who was also an engineer, not so jokingly gave me a key bit of his wisdom: "If your product is successful, it's already outdated."

Keep looking at new technology, new materials, new delivery systems, new information. Keep checking with the customer. Keep your eye on the competition. Keep changing to meet the changes in the world around you. Like the surfers do, keep looking "outside" to see what's coming on the horizon. If you don't, the next wave will leave you flailing in the backwash.

"Success is never final," says John Wooden, the "wizard of Westwood," who led more UCLA teams to NCAA championship than any other coach in basketball history.[27] Great performers in all areas can benefit from the **UW** that is contained in the poem Coach Wooden tells all his athletes:

> *And failure waits for all who stay*
> *With some success made yesterday.*

Those who subscribe to the Conventional Wisdom, "If it ain't broke, don't fix it," will be ill-equipped in the days to come. As the rate and intensity of change escalates, the temptation will be to look for a safe harbor. Yet, as we shall see, the constant search for safety, predictability, and security comes at a very high price.

UW *says:*
If it ain't broke, BREAK IT!

An Aboriginal tribe made a practice of moving on when the harvest was lush and food plentiful. When life was too easy they knew there was a danger of becoming fat, lazy, and unprepared for the inevitable seasons of scarcity when their survival skills would be needed.

7

Playing It Safe
. . . Is Dangerous!

When things get tough, Conventional Wisdom offers us a lot of free—and useless—advice, including such favorites as "Don't make waves"; "Play it safe"; "Pull in your horns." Consequently, rather than performing at our potential, we concentrate on cutting our losses.

During the mideighties, when IBM was experiencing tough times, I was invited to speak at several of IBM's management conferences. Prior to the programs, John Steuri, a division general manager, told me, "Talk to them about the importance of taking risks. It's tough out there. We've got to be more entrepreneurial. Nobody is taking risks, they're all playing it safe. We're not going to get the lead back that way. Playing it safe is dangerous."

PLAYING "NOT TO LOSE"

Sports provides a great arena for seeing how people play it safe and play not-to-lose when under pressure. The golfer worried about missing will putt too tentatively and the ball rolls short. Wanting to make sure the second serve goes in the box, the tennis player aims it carefully and serves it too softly—*plink*, right into the net.

I often saw this play-it-safe strategy in my Inner Skiing programs. Afraid of falling, skiers would be "too careful." They would ski tentatively, leaning back, up the hill. But when your weight is back on the tail of the skis, they jet out from under and you lose control. *Whammo*! Your worst fear gets realized. Playing it safe is *dangerous*.

After winning an NCAA-record 29 games in a row, Ray Meyer, coach of the De Paul University basketball team, was actually relieved when his team finally lost. Why? Because Meyer saw that the team was so worried about not ending their winning streak that they weren't playing their game, the fast-break, run-and-gun style that had gotten the streak going. They were too tentative, too intent on protecting their record. Finally, when they lost, a somewhat relaxed Coach Meyer told the press, "Now we can get back to playing to win instead of playing not to lose."

PLAYING TO WIN VERSUS PLAYING NOT TO LOSE

A very visible contrast between playing to win and playing not to lose occurred in the semifinals of the 1990 Wimbledon tournament.

On one side of the net was Monica Seles. Her opponent was Zina Garrison. As the match proceeded, though, it became increasingly clear that Seles's most formidable opponent was not Garrison but herself.

"The match was so close," said a crestfallen Seles afterward. "I was going for the safety shots. I found it hard to really pound the ball, and even on her second serve, I was scared to hit it for winners."

Garrison, on the other hand, didn't play it safe. "I just told myself to go for it," says Garrison. "None of this tentative stuff. If I'd missed, at least I'd know that this time I went for it."[1] Advantage, game, set, and match to Garrison.

STANDOFF

Games are a great learning vehicle. One of my favorites is called Standoff. In this game two people stand facing each other, about an arm's length apart. The object of the game is to get the other player off balance by slapping or dodging palms. Size or strength alone offer little or no advantage, whereas timing, quickness, and strategy make the difference.

Initially I tell people, "Play with only one goal in mind: *Don't lose.* Don't get knocked off balance, play it safe. The object is to be a survivor. Assume that if you are knocked off balance you have just lost your job."

After the game I ask for key words that describe the attitudes and the strategies the players used to ensure they didn't lose during the game. Below are responses typical of those cited by thousands of Standoff players:

Playing "Standoff" not to lose

Hesitant
Cautious
Defensive
Tentative
No risks
Back on my heels
Reactive
Anxious
Focused on losing
Tight
Hold back
Tense
Boring

Playing not to lose at work

We then transfer the discussion to how we play not to lose at work. Below is a representative list from one group:

Don't make any decisions
Call a lot of meetings
Tell people what they want to hear
Sell price rather than value
Establish a committee
Maintain the status quo
Maintain the account base rather than calling on new accounts
Cut everything
Compromise, don't confront
Send lots of memos and copies to everyone
Paralysis by analysis
Try nothing new—stick with what you know

Playing Standoff quickly reveals that playing not to lose is a no-win game. When you play it safe, you don't take the risks, innovate or confront the challenges necessary to win. When you play not to lose, you don't utilize skills and strategies that would get you ahead. Worrying about losing, failing, or making a mistake gets you tense, anxious, and apprehensive, which prevents you from being at your best and from enjoying the game. And when you aren't enjoying what you are doing, you won't do it well.

GOOD ISN'T GOOD ENOUGH

Occasionally when you play it safe you may play a pretty good game. But in our action-packed culture, we are surrounded by "good enough" performances. What is becoming apparent is that being "good" isn't "good enough." Simply doing a "good" job won't give you the edge you need in today's incredibly pressure-packed marketplace. "Good enough" only puts you in with the rest of the pack.

In sports, the difference between a good performance and a great one is measured often in hundredths of a second. The same fine line is true in business and in school. The factor that differentiates peak performers from good performers is not usually their level of skill. It is how they think and act under pressure. And as the pressure increases, so does the importance of the mental game. Peak performers are bold and daring; they don't play it safe, they don't play not to lose.

BLIND SPOTS AND PANIC BUTTONS

Everybody plays not to lose in some areas of life and in some situations. To perform at peak levels, you need to be able to recognize your own blind spots and understand where, when, and how you aren't taking risks or confronting personal challenges.

Playing not to lose is so deeply ingrained that many of us do so automatically. When faced with what seems to be an imposing challenge or a tough situation, "play it safe" becomes the subliminal message.

We all have our blind spots, old habits, and panic buttons, especially when we're under pressure. Becoming aware of them is the first step in breaking the pattern and avoiding getting tripped up by them in the future. Just as when you are traveling, if you are aware of the roadblocks, obstacles, and detours that could surprise you, slow you down, or stop you in your tracks, you can change your route and avoid them completely. Understanding *yourself* and the way *you* think under pressure is critical for thriving.

Here are some examples of the most common ways people and organizations play not to lose. See which of them you can identify with.

M&M: THE CORPORATE JUNK FOOD DIET

When Harry Truman was president, he had a sign on his desk that said, THE BUCK STOPS HERE—the final responsibility was his. With the play-it-safe mentality, the prevailing attitude is, "Pass the buck."

In a fast-paced world, making decisions can appear to be risky. People don't want to go out on a limb and risk having the finger of blame pointed at them. One way to avoid responsibility for making a decision is to try to get everyone "on board" by utilizing a "meetings and memos strategy"—the M&Ms of business. Call meetings, form committees, do more research, get a focus group going—anything to avoid making a choice, taking a stance, or reaching a decision. Consequently, rather than generating business, they generate reams of paper; and instead of taking action, they hold endless meetings.

A high price is paid for all those committees and meetings, both by the company and the "meet-ees." Many studies have estimated that the average manager spends about 40 percent of his or her time in meetings. In fact, when I mention that figure, most people scoff at it, saying they wish it were that *low*. "I go to so many meetings," one marketing manager told me, "that the only time I can get some work done is after five, when the meetings stop and I can get to my desk." And at the end of a long day of meetings, when tired and rushed, people do not do their most creative or quality work. It's tough to think clearly when your mind is buzzing from a day of meetings and you are bushed.

CYA-c.c.

Millions of memos are sent out every day. That's bad enough. But adding insult to injury is the fact that every memo has 10 CYA (cover your ass) copies sent. The combination of the memo and the CYA mentality takes an enormous toll of time, energy, and resources. Think of how much time you spend in a day or a week reading, talking, filing, and doing "damage control" of memos that have nothing directly to do with you but that somebody copied you to cover themselves.

"I have more garbage to read, more expertise I'm expected to have, more hedging that I'm exposed to. I get so many memos you'd think my initials were 'c.c.,'" the chief counsel for a major energy company, told me. "Finally I had to write a memo and c.c. it to everybody in the office telling them not to c.c. me anymore. Period!"

DECISIONS, DECISIONS, DECISIONS

Lee Iacocca extends the scope of the problem when he points out that many people won't act until they have all the information. But by the time they get 75 percent of what they thought was needed, the first 15 percent is usually outdated. The key to decision making is that at some point you have to rely on your gut instincts, which causes lots of sleepless nights for people who like to play it safe.

Steven Bochco, creator of such megahit TV shows as *Hill Street Blues* and *L.A. Law*, said that most people in the TV industry test, test, test, relying on mountains of market research and data before making a decision about a new show. He relies on one thing: "instinct."

Unfortunately, research shows that the overwhelming majority of Americans (85 percent) are reactive and static, not action- or dynamic- or instinct-oriented. They wait and they meet, meet and wait. With a ready arsenal of conservative, Conventional Wisdom at their disposal, they try to control outcomes in an out-of-control world. Their impulse is to lower the sails and wait out the storm.

Regarding the danger of playing it safe and waiting to make decisions, Thomas Watson, Jr., founder and former chairman of IBM, said, "I never varied from the managerial rule that the worst possible thing we could do would be to lie dead in the water with any problem. Solve it, solve it quickly, solve it right or wrong. Lying dead in the water and doing nothing is a comfortable alternative because it is without immediate risk, but it is an absolutely fatal way to manage a business."[2]

CONSENSUS LEADS TO COMPROMISE

Play-it-safe decision making seeks consensus and is usually done by committee. In this sense it is a lot like the classic definition of the camel as a "horse put together by a committee." Although consensus has a great deal of merit, it can also be a subconscious ruse for playing it safe, for no one taking responsibility.

Seeking a "win/win" decision by consensus can result in compromise by identifying the lowest, rather than the highest, common demoninator—a no-win for everyone. The hottest innovative idea can become lukewarm when watered down by every committee member and every possible consideration.

In many companies, decision by committee is anathema. "In [PepsiCo's] freewheeling culture, a committee is defined as 'a dark alley down which ideas are led . . . to be strangled.'"[3]

TEST, TEST, TEST

The conservative mentality at Procter & Gamble, one of the advertising accounts I worked on in the sixties, was a great example of playing it safe. If we had a new idea for a product, a promotion, a new package, new ad copy, first it would be tested in focus groups, then in three or four test cities around the country, then in a region. Test, test, test . . . research, research, research—even down to, would you believe, which frame the package or promotion would first appear in the commercial footage. Consequently, if the idea was any good, the competition would know about it before you could roll it out and would beat you to the draw.

Recently, however, Procter & Gamble has made some major changes. Reexamining their play-it-safe strategy, they are altering their centralized structure. Demonstrating a new nimbleness, Procter & Gamble now puts products into national distribution after much less market testing than before. This is a big step for a company where in my experience, for years, everyone had to approve ad copy on every brand. With new daring, P&G has been able to reassert itself as the market leader over archrival Colgate-Palmolive.

"IT'S NOT IN THE BUDGET"

One of the most common ways managers and executives play it safe is by rigidly adhering to the "numbers." The words, "It's not in the budget," have probably squelched more innovation than we can count. Relying on the budget to guide decisions, managers don't have to put themselves on the line, don't have to take chances.

One reason that organizations run "by the numbers" will stagnate in a fast-moving environment is that budgets are usually drawn up far in advance of the period they cover. An annual budget, for instance, is usually finished at least three months before the fiscal year starts, and the planning that created those numbers was done much earlier than that. In a world that is changing by the second, with some products having half lives of less than six months, these numbers and budget forecasts can quickly become outdated and meaningless in the face of unpredictable changes in the marketplace, new competition, or a technological advance. The budget then acts like handcuffs preventing quick responses to these unforeseen changes.

Not only are budget numbers quickly outdated, but the thinking behind it is as well. Jean-Marie Descarpentries, who runs the multibillion-dollar Franco-British CMB Packaging, which has been growing at a rate of 26 percent a year, says, "If your budget is the basis of your plan, you content yourself with an extrapolation of the past."[4]

UNDERSPENT DOES NOT MEAN WELL SPENT

Donald A. Curtis, a senior partner at a major financial services firm, Deloitte & Touche, goes further. "Reliance on the budget," he says, "is the fundamental flaw in American management." That's because managers assume that you can manage the business by managing the money. "Wrong," Curtis argues. "Just because a budget was not overspent doesn't mean it was well spent."

Budgets are fine for keeping score, but decisions are being made not on the merit of a new idea or service to the customer but on whether it fits into the budget. And some managers will go to any lengths to make budget, especially if incentive pay is at stake; marginal customers are wooed, prices are cut too deeply, distributors are overloaded with goods.

Playing it safe and relying solely on the numbers (many of which are outdated by the time they are used) may seem safe and even pragamatic, but it will prevent you from reacting quickly to the incredibly rapid changes in the marketplace. As 3M CEO Alan

Jacobsen says, "I never want to hear anyone put down a project because it isn't in the budget."[5]

CUTTING AND CHOPPING

Here's another version of playing not to lose: When the going gets tough, cut your losses! Cut budgets, cut costs, cut overhead, cut R & D, cut inventory. Cut, cut, cut. From Apple to Zenith, very few companies were exempt from the cut-and-chop mind-set of the eighties.

As a result of this, euphemisms like "downsizing" and "restructuring" crept into the vocabulary of American business. As providence would have it, I picked up my morning paper and saw the following headlines on the front of the business page:

- RAYCHEM WILL TRIM WORKFORCE BY 900—LAYOFFS PART OF RESTRUCTURING EFFORT

- BIG HOSPITAL SUPPLIER TO LAY OFF 6,400

- NEW ENGLAND BANK TO AX 5,600 JOBS

While it seems reasonable to get "leaner and meaner" in more competitive, fast-changing times, remember, you pay a high price for cutting costs. Despite all the layoffs of the past decade, despite increased automation and just-in-time inventory systems, U.S. productivity "crept up by a scant 1.2% a year on average in the eighties. . . . That's virtually no improvement from the seventies." All that downsizing did little to up productivity.

You want further evidence? Think about this: More than half the 1,468 restructured companies surveyed by the Society for Human Resource Management reported that employee productivity either stayed the same or deteriorated after layoffs.

If you want employees to love the customer and provide great service, to really make quality job number one, if you want them to be more productive, assume more responsibility, take more risks, and make faster decisions, be wary of the lean-and-mean approach. Seventy-four percent of managers at downsized companies said their workers had lower morale and distrusted management.[6]

The "cut-and-chop" mentality creates an environment that "cuts" quality, innovation, and motivation as well. Performance is replaced by conformity, innovation by maintenance of the status quo. Spirit and morale plummet. People are scared and constantly look over their shoulders. The motivation is to keep a job, not to keep improving, to play not to lose rather than to play to win. As a result, though you may have cut your costs, you've often cut your lifeline as well.

Bell & Howell, buffeted by takeover skirmishes and rumors of layoffs, became aware that the resulting "nervousness and gloom cost money."[7] Rumors were spreading faster than voice mail. Their sales reps reportedly spent as much time on the phone, seeking updates of the rumors, as they did in the field selling. Studying sales performance during this period, B&H determined that at least 11 percent of profits—millions of dollars—were lost to the "lean-and-mean blues" of their *retained* employees.

R&D: THE SOUND OF (NO) MUSIC

Robert S. Miller, Jr., executive vice president of Chrysler Corporation, tells an outlandish but true story that illustrates another down side of downsizing.

"A foreign cinema owner decided the movie he was showing was too long, so he decided to cut out what he considered irrelevant. Well, the movie was *The Sound of Music*. And you know what he did? He cut out all the songs. So help me God, believe it or not, he actually shortened *The Sound of Music* by cutting out the songs! I figure his version of the movie must have started with the Nazis chasing the von Trapp family up a mountain. And it must have lasted about fifteen minutes.

"It was of course an absurd, shortsighted, and unpopular decision, and to you and me, it sounds flat-out, world-class crazy," says Miller. Then he goes on to make a world-class point: "But when you get right down to it, is cutting the songs out of that musical really all that different from, say, cutting R&D out of a company by crippling it with staggering debt in the name of 'improving shareholder value'?"[8]

THE MUTANT ALIEN ROBOT THAT ATE TOKYO

The great director Akira Kirosawa made a series of high-budget box office smashes in the 1950s, the so-called Golden Age of Japanese cinema.

But in the 1960s, with the advent of television, audiences decreased. Reacting to the dwindling audiences the Japanese film studios began to play it safe. They cut budgets and began cranking out cheap formulaic pictures with titles like *The Mutant Alien Robot That Ate Tokyo* (that was made up, but you get the picture). The audiences dwindled further, leading to more cuts, more bad films, and more diminishing audiences. And the downhill spiral continued. The industry has only recently turned away from its play-not-to-lose budgeting practices.[9]

The cut-cut-cut mind-set is a defensive strategy that stops forward motion.

UW *says:* By trying to "hold the fort," you often bring the fort down with you.

DEFENSE IS NOT THE BEST OFFENSE

Under pressure, peak performers don't play defensively. When under pressure they take the offensive. "We weren't making money when I came here," says Jan Carlzon, CEO of Scandinavian Airlines Systems, one who understands when UW says there are many hidden costs to cutting costs. "We were in a desperate situation, and *that's the worst time to focus on preventing mistakes and cutting costs.* First we had to increase revenues. . . . Then we could think about cutting costs, because only then would we know which costs could be cut. . . ."[10]

Another example of the attitude it takes to win in a competitive environment is provided by McCormick & Co., the largest producers of spices. Faced with profits in 1986 that were no higher than in 1981, resulting from changes in consumer habits, many companies would have been tempted to play it safe and make the cuts necessary for short-term improvements in the bottom line. Much like Scandinavian's Carlzon CEO "Buzz" McCormick, Jr., played to win rather than not to lose. Rather than cutting back in products or people, the company began pouring money into reconstituting itself. "We revitalized our entire retail line, repackaged it, and repromoted it," said the CEO. Because of this, McCormick profits are expected "to keep growing more than 10 percent annually for the next several years."[11]

To *get* an edge these days demands that you be on your edge. You won't get that edge by being cautious and hesitant. Steffi Graf once said that when the game is on the line, hit harder. In one of my seminars, a manager of a food chain wisely said, "when you play not to lose, you don't win."

PREPARING NOT TO LOSE "THE BIG GAME"

Worrying about losing or making a mistake will often get us to play not to lose. A sales engineer at an IBM conference who had played football for a major collegiate power told me the following story. His team always had the best record in its conference and was usually nationally ranked. But nearly every time they played their conference rival, they lost. "And we always had a better team—on paper at least," he added.

"But the coach would always prepare us for the game by yelling, 'This is the big game! Don't blow it! Use your heads, don't make any stupid mistakes! Don't take any chances! Let's play our game.'

"We'd run out onto the field tense and tight, which is not the way we usually were before a game. We were more concerned about not making mistakes than about winning the game." The coach's play-not-to-lose attitude actually had predisposed the team to lose.

When I was working in advertising, the same type of play-not-to-lose approach often prevailed. "This is a key meeting," the boss would tell us. "Don't screw up. Don't offer any new ideas or say anything that we haven't rehearsed. Just stick to the script." Off we'd go into the meeting, petrified of making a mistake. In fact, we were more concerned about not erring than in performing well and being creative. The resulting tension and stress turned us into robots. We were tentative and hesitant in everything we did; like the football players, by playing not to lose we wouldn't win.

Charles Lynch, the chairman of express delivery company, DHL, and a former international tennis player, once told me that his preparation for a big match or an important meeting would include anticipating all eventualities, including the worst. Thus prepared, before the meeting or match, the thought of losing never entered his mind. He only focused on what he had to do to win.

UW *says: If you are worried about losing, you most likely will.*

THE HIGH PRICE OF LOWBALLING

Combatants in the "cola wars" a few years ago also discovered that lowballing can be a dangerous way to play. Once consumers saw Coke and Pepsi at a "wartime" price, they didn't see why they should have to pay more after the "cease-fire." It has taken years for these companies to recuperate from the wild promotional prices.[12]

UW *says: The price is high for selling low.*

One of the most common complaints from sales management is that many salespeople play not to lose by "lowballing." They sell price rather than emphasizing value, quality, or service.

One owner of a growing business desperately wanted to get the huge Pan Am account for their airline bags and travel kits. As a way to get "in" with the client, she gave them a low price on a lesser item, vinyl passport holders.

It was a sizable order, but she didn't make any profit because her bid was so low. However, she saw it as a "loss leader," a way of getting established as a supplier for Pan Am. When the request for bids for the lucrative airline bag contract were sent out, their company wasn't even contacted. Asking the Pan Am purchasing agent why she was left out, she was told that he was going to use his old suppliers who were "known" and did high-quality work. But he told her that he would certainly consider her as a future supplier for products like the passport holders and ticket wallets.

PLAYING PRUDENTLY

In a speech at the Commonwealth Club in San Francisco, *New York Times* Washington bureau chief Hedrick Smith, author of the best-selling book *The Washington Power Game*, talked about how this play-it-safe strategy affects politics. Because the press makes so much out of scandals, mistakes, and human failings, the prime qualifier for each party, he argues, is a safe candidate—one who is overly cautious and doesn't take bold stances, doesn't speak out about anything controversial, doesn't take a stand. Therefore, what we voters get is mediocrity, "leaders" lacking in courage, vision, and passion. The by-product in the 1988 presidential elections was the lowest voter turnout in 64 years.

YOU CAN'T PLAY WITHOUT HASSLE

Many bosses play not to lose by avoiding confrontations with problem employees, acting as if the problems don't exist and will improve on their own. They don't want any hassles or arguments. Yet by avoiding the problem they implicitly reinforce the negative behavior, which of course causes more trouble.

Waiting for latecomers to arrive before beginning a meeting is a common example of this desire to keep things copacetic. But waiting and not confronting the latecomers actually honors them and gives the message to others that it's okay to come late. People then begin assuming the meeting will start 10 minutes later than the advertised time. Then the latecomer comes even later and the vicious cycle continues. I saw this firsthand at a major corporation. No one knew when they should arrive at meetings. The result? Some people stopped coming, others arrived a half hour late. It was chaos.

A manager talked to me about a problem employee whose performance was slipping but whom he didn't want to confront because, "I might turn her off or even lose her if I call her on the carpet." The employee's behavior was never confronted, but the manager's ostrich approach *did* send a message to her and the other employees nonetheless: "There are no repercussions for poor performance, nothing will happen." Eventually, he fired her.

Not confronting problems when they arise is like letting weeds go unattended. Pretty soon they get out of control and you have to take extreme measures.

PLAYING FOR KEEPS

Tony La Russa, the manager of the world champion Oakland A's baseball team, says the best advice he ever got was, "Don't manage to save your job. Manage to win."

Describing a situation in which the conventional play-it-safe strategy calls for a bunt, La Russa says sometimes you have to let your hitters swing away. If you bunted and failed you could always say, "I called the right play. My players didn't execute. But," he says, "the players are aware of the situation. If they see you trying to cover your ass—if you bunt in that situation—they lose respect for you." The bottom line, says La Russa, is "if you're trying to cover your ass, you won't be successful."[13]

PLAYING IT SAFE

Playing it safe is like body surfing in two feet of water. You may not drown, but you're also not in deep enough to catch any but the most meager of waves.

The most dangerous strategy is to play it safe. In its place, Break-It Thinkers take risks and break rules and challenge convention, making change an ally.

UW *says:*
Playing it safe is dangerous.

8

Don't Compete
. . . Change the
Game

DEFINE YOUR OWN MARKET

Every nation's economy now affects and is affected by events in every
other country. In our global economy, more and more companies are
learning to break away from costly old habits. A particularly bad habit
is letting your competitor define the market.

For example, Levi-Strauss's menswear division was competing
unsuccessfully in a market created by Haggar, the long-established
leader in men's slacks.

ATTACKING MOUNT HAGGAR

The results of this "assault on Mount Haggar," says Bob Siegel,
president of the division, "was a big headache. It seemed that there
was no passage, and indeed there wasn't, not up the face of Mount
Haggar. But what we discovered was that there may be another way

to scale the mountain. Rather than confront Haggar directly, perhaps we could take a flanking route to the top."

Knowing that the baby boomers, lifelong jeans' buyers, were hitting their forties and looking for another type of casual pants, Levi-Strauss's flanking maneuver was to establish a new casuals category, Dockers®.

But that was just the start. Dockers® literally changed the game—the way pants were merchandised, marketed, and sold. First of all, Levi's designers altered the fit, making their pants comfortable, loose, and stylish, with a flattering silhouette.

REDESIGN THE FIELD

Dockers® also created bold, bright, eye-catching mainfloor displays that revitalized the rather dull and drab men's department. To lure customers in, the department stores moved Dockers®, with their visually exciting displays, closer to the main traffic aisles. Levi-Strauss has also provided the bigger stores with merchandising coordinators to keep the faster-moving products in stock and on display.

The result of this is nothing short of incredible. By taking a different route than that of conventional head-on competition, the Dockers® category of the Levi's menswear division went from sales of $1 million in 1986 to $500 million in 1990!

Conventional Wisdom says: To win you must attack the competition head-on, beat them to the punch. Using **UW**, Levi's menswear division changed the game and came out a big winner.[1]

DON'T COMPETE HEAD-ON

Patagonia has continually outflanked the competition and created a new standard for outerwear by practicing this **UW**. "I never compete head-on," says Yvon Chouinard, Patagonia's founder and chairman. "When people copy our product and undersell us, we don't get into that fight. We either change the product or drop it. We are in the business of creating unique products, not competing. I am not interested in getting into another cola war."[2]

Levi-Strauss and Patagonia are not the first to win by not competing directly. In the fifties, Volkswagen changed the game when it introduced the "Bug," which flew in the face of the huge finned monsters rolling off the Detroit assembly lines. By not competing directly with the bigger guys and extolling the virtues of "think small," VW won big. Avis, too, won big by not competing head-on. Avoiding a direct clash with Hertz, they made history by extolling the virtues of being number two and "trying harder."

Battling the competition head-to-head and beating them to the punch is one way to play to win. Contrary to Conventional Wisdom, competing head-on, as we have seen above, can actually limit success and is not necessarily the most effective way to play.

COMPETITION BREEDS CONFORMITY

The person who was most influential in teaching me about the limits of competition was the former head of Columbia University's educational psychology department, Dr. Brian Sutton-Smith, one of the world's leading authorities on games. In the early seventies, Brian was an adviser on my doctoral research when he came to talk to a group of coaches and teachers I directed. Being an experiential educator, he had us start out by playing a number of kids' games like capture the flag, hide 'n' seek, and ringalevio.

A very energetic and joyous individual, not at all the stereotypical academic, Brian played all of the games with us. But he had one annoying peculiarity: he was continually bending the rules, reshaping roles, changing the boundaries, reversing strategies. Everything we took for granted, he challenged.

When we asked him about his methods, he explained that when we compete we implicitly agree to play the game the way it has always been played, to abide by the formal and informal rules and roles, as well as the unspoken rituals. Although competing can be fun and exciting, it is not very creative, and limits the imagination.

UW says: *Competition encourages conformity.*

Kids are always changing the rules, the boundaries, the roles, and the way the game is played. In fact, research shows that kids often spend more time creating and re-creating a game than actually playing it. Rather than playing by a fixed set of rules, they continually attempt to redesign the game so that it fits the needs of the situation and their own desires as well. Kids at play don't just conform, they continually create and re-create.

ME-TOO, ME-TOO

The same is true in the business world. When you compete head-on, you are implicitly agreeing to play the same game, to abide by certain rules and assumptions, which limit creativity. If your thinking is contained within certain parameters, innovation will be rule-bound and therefore restricted to small incremental changes.

Innovation is a change in the way we do things: to innovate is to introduce new methods. Today, what passes for innovation is often not much more than a variation on what you have been doing: a new package design, a faster gizmo, a special promotion, or a new marketing niche.

When you are competing head-to-head there is too much focus on the competition and how to beat the other person. Much of the "innovation" becomes a form of "me-too-ism," where small changes enable you to keep up or provide a minimal advantage for a short period of time. Someone lowers the price and others quickly follow suit with an even lower price. One automobile company gives a three-year, 30,000-mile guarantee, and another raises the ante, giving five years and 50,000 miles. . . .

Look at what has happened with the frequent-flier programs in the airline business. What was a creative idea now has been copied so much that every airline has a program and no one has the advantage. The same is true in the highly competitive world of banking. Bank of the Avenue offers more hours, automated tellers, Saturday banking, or a lower interest rate. Bank of the Boulevard and Bank of the Boardwalk immediately jump on the bandwagon and follow suit. "The trouble with the banking business," says John B. McCoy, chairman of Bank One, "is that when you find something good, 150 people jump into it."[3]

This competitive me-too-ism occurs not just in automobiles, airlines, and banking, it is seen in every industry. One company offers an innovative cost, service, or quality benefit, and everyone tries to one-up the leader. And the game continues.

TV-Too-ism

A visible example of me-too-ism is the morning TV talk shows, which compete fiercely for rating points worth hundreds of thousands of dollars. Yet some morning programs are essentially the same. The conformity in this enormously competitive industry is mind-boggling. The hosts look the same: each show has a blonde woman, a dark man, and a jolly weatherman (not -woman). They all interview the same people, in what looks like the same studio. They take similar trips, and have the same news at the same time.

They all are afraid to try something new and break with tradition. It's no wonder TV ratings are steadily dropping. In their competitive battle, everyone has conformed.

This tendency toward conservatism has been true with the big three networks in almost all areas of programming. While two recent hits, *The Simpsons* and *Twin Peaks*, proved that creative risks are worth taking and rules are worth breaking, basically the 1989–1990 TV season was another one fraught with tired clichés and characterized once again by declining viewership. Slowly, and thanks to scrappy Fox Network, cable TV, and home video, the lumbering big three are learning, as NBC Entertainment president Brandon Tartikoff says, "The tried and true equals dead and buried."[4]

TILTED PLAYING FIELD

"There is a tremendous amount of debate in the United States about a level playing field," says University of Michigan Business School professor C. V. Prahalad. "I think a level playing field is a fundamentally wrong notion. Strategy is not about a level playing field. Strategy is about a differential advantage," says Prahalad. "We must . . . ask the question, 'How do I change the rules of the game in my business so that I hold the high ground on a nonlevel playing field?'"[5]

A good illustration of this process is how a small company like Canon challenged an industry giant like Xerox. Canon's considerable success didn't come from squaring off against Xerox's big machines and centralized copying concept; rather, Canon made a new game and created smaller machines and personalized copying.

DON'T COMPETE

It would be naive and foolish to say, "Don't compete, don't come out with a new benefit, service, or price break that will give you a competitive advantage." Anything that gives you an edge, even a small one-upping of the competition, is important these days. But though you may gain some small incremental advantages by competing head-on and beating your competition to the punch, you won't get the breakthroughs that are needed to really move ahead of the pack.

PLAYING FASTBALL

To drive this point home, I have people play a game I call Fastball. I break volunteers into three teams of about 10 to 15 players each. Each team is given a soccer ball and the players are asked to stand in a circle about an arm's length apart and count off. "The object of this game," I tell them, "is to have everybody on your team touch the ball in order. Time starts with the first touch and ends with the last. On your mark, get set, go!"

Each team passes the ball around the circle as fast as possible, like a hyperactive bucket brigade fighting a fire. The winning team takes just under 45 seconds. "Not bad," I say. "But the record is 5 seconds."

"Five seconds! Impossible!" They respond. I then give them a minute to figure out a faster way to play Fastball, after which they play again. Two teams make adjustments and drop their time to under 35 seconds.

Totally abandoning their old strategy, the winning team finishes in 9 seconds. How? Instead of passing the ball around the circle, they put the ball on the floor in the middle of the circle, reach down and touch it! We don't have to say anything else. The 300 people in the room get the message.

In the "work" sessions that followed this game, the level of creativity and innovative ideas were far beyond anything that had previously transpired. Learning from Fastball, people broke out of their fixed way of solving problems and making decisions. The "way it has always been done," and other Firehoses, no longer smothered their creativity.

MISSION IMPOSSIBLE

Conventional Wisdom tells us to set goals that are challenging but achievable. John Young, CEO of Hewlett-Packard, took a different tack. Rather than setting reasonable goals, he set unreasonable ones.

- He told his employees that he wanted a laser-jet printer that could retail for *less than one-third* the current price.

- He also told his employees that he wanted to *reduce by 50 percent* the time it took to take a product from the idea stage to its implementation in the marketplace.

"Impossible!" was the response of one of the managers. "He's crazy, we're going as fast as we can right now. There's no slack in our operation."

The manager was right. Young's goal was impossible . . . but only if approached in the traditional manner of doing the same thing—faster. To take up the gauntlet that Young had thrown down, people had to break out of the conventional mind-set. Rather than the faster-longer-harder approach, Young's challenge forced people to think of radical new ways to deliver on time. They did. His "unreasonable" goals were met in record time. Conventional thinking, he understood, cannot keep up with exponential change.

BREAK-IT THINKING

If you want to get a real jump on the competition, you can't simply keep playing the same old way, utilizing the same strategies and assumptions that have guided you in the past. To gain a real advantage you have to challenge old ways of thinking and the basic assumptions about how the game is played. You need to break out of your fixed mind-set.

We call this *"Break-It" Thinking.* Break-It Thinkers don't win by conforming to a given set of rules or by competing harder, faster, longer. They *reinvent* the game. They don't play by the rules, they create new ones. They break the rules, not the law. Break-It Thinkers don't go along with the way it has always been done. They question everything. Break-It Thinkers are mavericks whose minds roam outside the traditional fenced-in ways of thinking and acting. That's why some of the best examples of Break-It Thinkers are kids: they don't conform . . . they create; they don't repeat . . . they invent.

None of us can afford to subscribe to the idea that "the way it's always been done" should simply be perpetuated. We must break away from the accepted, the taken-for-granted, the never-questioned, and the conventional. These days we have no choice.

Below are some stories of Break-It Thinkers who have dramatically reshaped the conventional wisdom that has traditionally guided their game. As you will see, most of these innovations didn't require genius, just a willingness to question the way "it" had always been done and to do something to change it. Most Break-It Thinkers are in fact ordinary people who did the extra-ordinary by having the courage, in Robert Frost's words, to take the road less traveled.

Flip the game on its ear

Sports is probably the most visible competitive vehicle in our culture. Everywhere we look we see teams and players going head-to-head in order to win. The emphasis is on playing harder, faster, and longer than your opponent, and "may the best man or woman win."

Given the importance of adhering to a given set of rules in sports, it is ironic that some of the greatest breakthroughs came from people who broke with tradition. These are people who didn't conform to the conventional way but created new ways of "playing," which then changed the game itself.

Going downhill . . . faster

When Jean-Claude Killy made the French national ski team in the sixties, he was prepared to work harder and longer than anyone else to be the best. At the crack of dawn he would run up the slopes with his skis on, an unbelievably grueling activity. In the evening he would lift weights, run sprints, do visualization—anything to get a little extra edge.

Much to his surprise, he discovered that the other members of the team were working as hard and as long as he was. Simply working harder and longer, he realized, would never be enough.

He then began challenging the basic assumptions concerning the existing racing technique, continually experimenting. Each week he would try something different to see if he could find a better, faster way down the mountain.

His Break-It Thinking resulted in the development of a new style, *avalement*, the "jet turn," which became known as the French technique. The basics of *avalement* were almost exactly opposite the technique of the time. *Avalement* involved skiing with your legs *apart* (not together) for better balance, and *sitting back* (not forward) on the skis when you came to the turn, which "jetted" you through the turn.

Killy went on to win three gold medals in the 1968 Olympics, as well as the World Cup and virtually every other major skiing accolade. He is generally considered the greatest ski racer ever. Although he was a great talent and did work very hard, Killy became the greatest because he had the guts to challenge the status quo and the conventional wisdom, and the courage to be a Break-It Thinker.

Fosbury's Flop

Like Killy, high-jumper Dick Fosbury did a 180-degree-er on the traditional thinking of the time. The conventional approach, used by all his rivals, was a feet-first approach called the Western Roll. Fosbury revolutionized high jumping by turning the conventional wisdom literally upside down! He approached the bar at a 45- to 60-degree angle, turned his back to it, jumped in the air, and went over the bar *headfirst!*

Thus was born what the press called "the Fosbury Flop," which secured an Olympic gold medal for Fosbury. "The Flop" became the standard high-jumping technique used today.

Chang-ing your game

Another example of challenging the existing thinking came in the 1989 French Open. The seventeen-year-old American Michael Chang had just defeated the world's top-rank player Ivan Lendl to win the tournament. But it wasn't *that* Chang had defeated Lendl, but *how* he had done it that had the crowd buzzing.

Injured and exhausted near the end of the match, Chang broke two of the most basic commandments of winning tennis. First, in a sport where powerful overhand serving is usually the key to winning, Chang, served *underhand,* and the confused Lendl's returns went into the net.

Second, on match-point, facing Lendl's 125 mph serve, Chang moved *closer* to the net and stood at the line of the server's box. The bewildered Lendl double-faulted, producing one of the most memorable upsets in recent tennis history. That's Break-It Thinking!

Challenging the Conventional Wisdom on these previously sacrosanct aspects of the game—serving and returning serves—Michael Chang radically changed his strategy—and his standing in the tennis world.

SELL, DESIGN, BUILD

After just four years of operation, Connors Peripherals, makers of disk drives, is the fastest growing major manufacturer in America, with revenues surpassing $1 billion. Connors's success has resulted from flipping conventional wisdom around: start by selling, then design what you sold, and then build it.

"Most of our competitors do it the other way around: trying to generate orders for what they have built," said Finis Connors, the company's founder and chairman.

With Connors, the sale comes first! They won't engineer a new product unless a major buyer has spoken for it.[6] "First we conceive products we know we can generate. Then we sell them . . . We talk to the customer about the concept. You have to be prepared to make changes instead of doing what you want. With the specifications in hand, you're ready to work on design."

"If every business conceived its products according to customer specifications, this country would spend a lot less on R&D," says Connors. "I think it would work anywhere. The purpose is very simple: it's so you carry no extra inventory, but you never have to turn down a sale!"[7]

A LAWYER WHO BROKE THE LAW

Gary Friedman, the youngest partner in an East Coast law firm, loved the drama of the courtroom and was very good at it. Well known throughout the area, he was clearly a rising star with a very promising future.

But Friedman felt increasingly cramped by the traditional combative and adversarial legal tactics in which no one ever really seemed to win. He also noticed that his euphoria after a win was very transitory. In fact, in these all-or-nothing verdicts he wasn't even feeling so good about winning anymore.

Following his values, Friedman decided that he couldn't do what was "right" for him and for his clients within the confines of lawyering as he knew it. He began to wonder if there couldn't be an alternative.

As a result of much soul-searching, Friedman started a practice in "mediation" law. Rather than having a combative, alienating environment in which each party was pitted against the other in a bitter battle, Friedman worked with *both* parties, helping them to reach an agreement based on fairness rather than greed. In mediation, the power is with both parties' arriving at a *mutually agreed-upon decision,* a far cry from the traditional setting in which a judge makes the decision and the parties often don't even see, much less talk to, each other. The lawyer-mediator's role was to help *both* parties create solutions that worked for both sides—to bring people together, not separate them.

Today, Friedman's groundbreaking work is widely known and respected. In addition to his successful mediation center in the San Francisco area, he teaches at the Stanford Law School and conducts training programs in mediation for lawyers and judges throughout the United States and Europe. Following his values resulted in Friedman's turning the Conventional Wisdom upside-down, making possible more humane lawyering and litigation. Having the courage to question the rules of a very old game, Friedman created a new one—one that was guided by the values of fairness and provided value for everyone.

PRICE BREAKS THE RULES

In the retail business there are three cardinal rules: (1) Do anything you can to lure in customers; (2) build on the bedrock of "location, location, location"; (3) keep your doors open as long as possible. Tell that to Sol Price, the founder of a billion-dollar retail discount warehouse chain, the Price Club. To give you an idea of the volume they do, a friend quipped that "the express lane at the Price Club is two thousand items or less."

Not only are the Price Club's huge discount warehouses in atypical, *out-of-the-way locations* (breaking rule number two), but people actually *pay* to get in the door (shattering rule number one), and you need an elephant's memory to figure out their hours! (breaking rule number three). With Break-It Thinking, Sol Price found that when value is high, people are willing to spend a small fortune and travel to faraway places.

PIONEERING AT AMEX

Shortly after Sarah Nolan took over as president of AMEX Life Assurance Company, she was determined to extend the boundaries of the game. "The world will change, whether you want it to or not," she said. "The people and businesses that will survive and prosper will not only anticipate that change, they will shape it."[8]

Rather than reorganizing, reshaping, or restrategizing AMEX Life's existing business, Nolan broke off a piece of it and formed a small entrepreneurial unit she called the Pioneer Team. This was no "skunk works," but rather a separate independent business with a small off-site office. Nolan's instructions were designed to change the nature and assumptions of the way they were doing business. "Don't investigate anything we do already, that's the past; assume it's wrong. . . . Re-create this business from scratch and follow two rules: you have to put the customer first, and you have to make a profit."

Nolan's Break-It Thinking was based on the idea that big business moves slowly, laden with old strategies and outdated systems and procedures. The model of the future needs to be small, quick, and flexible. Initiating a truly entrepreneurial venture would, she felt, yield principles and practices that would "migrate" into the larger company.

The results were dramatic. Transferring the "fresh-start" thinking of the Pioneer Group back into the larger organization, says Karen Gideon, vice president of strategic marketing and head of the team, "increased internal and external communication, made us more flexible, and offered truly good service." Nolan and Gideon are now migrating key features of the Pioneer Team throughout AMEX Life's business. And, oh yes, the Pioneer Team was able to cut expenses by 40 percent and increase profit significantly within the first year!

PUTTING YOURSELF OUT OF BUSINESS

The future leaders of commerce must be willing "to transform their businesses," says Harvard Business School professor and author Abraham Zaleznik. These people "don't cook broth from a standard recipe."[9]

Zaleznik must have had Christopher Whittle in mind. *Inc.* magazine says, of Whittle, chairman of Whittle Communications, the $200-million-a-year publishing company, that he "seems to challenge his industry's most sacred rules and conventions."

Whittle has inverted the prevailing thinking about the most basic aspects of the publishing business. The traditional approach in magazine publishing, for instance, is to get as many advertisers as possible.

Instead, Whittle developed a highly successful group of magazines for college students that had only *one advertiser* for each magazine!

But Whittle doesn't stop here. Challenging basic industry practices, he believes that you have to constantly reinvent your own business. As Whittle boldly puts it, "Being willing to *put your own business out of business* is crucial to preserving an innovative spirit. You have to be willing to make it obsolete. . . ."[10]

UW *says: The only way to move into the future is to let go of the past . . . and the present.*

THE BODY SHOP

In the era of the MBA, where business expertise is considered an absolute necessity for success, Anita Roddick is an anomaly. Contrary to Conventional Wisdom, she says, "We survived because we have no rational business knowledge."[11] The Body Shop, founded by Roddick in 1976, did more than survive. It is now the largest and most profitable cosmetics company in Great Britain, one whose logo is more widely known in England than the McDonald's Golden Arches are known here. Roddick's path to success has broken most of the rules of succeeding in the cosmetics industry.

- In this highly competitive arena, where marketing and sophisticated advertising are critical, the Body Shop does not advertise but relies on word of mouth.

- In an industry where companies spend millions on researching the customer, the Body Shop's only marketing research is a well-used suggestion box in each store.

- In an industry that sells packaging and image more than product and substance, the Body Shop uses refillable bottles originally designed for collecting urine specimens!

- In a manufacturing process that traditionally generates pounds of waste to produce a few ounces of cosmetics, the Body Shop has made some remarkable breakthroughs, both in profitability and in concern for the Earth and its inhabitants. For example, many of their products use banana oil, leaving thousands of tons of banana skins behind. So Roddick and her staff figured out a way to turn these skins into paper. They set up a paper manufacturing plant in Nepal and secured some key contracts. And in an era where bottom-line profit is next to god, *the Body Shop turned the paper plant over to the local community.* Not only that, but each Body Shop store is encouraged to commit 25 percent of its profits to a community project, one that, as Roddick says, captures the hearts of its employees.

Two of Roddick's basic principles for success, in addition to manufacturing terrific products, are that it should be fun to work there and that the work should engage the hearts of the employees. The vision guiding the Body Shop is to help in every way possible to save the planet. Breaking with tradition in just about every way possible, Anita Roddick has created a profitable venture—any way you look at it.

Oh, and by the way, their annual reports are printed on postcards!

PULLING A FEW DIFFERENT STRINGS

Knowing that very few arenas are as competitive as the music business, the Julliard-trained members of the Kronos Quartet broke radically with the traditional image of a string quartet. Most people think of a string quartet as serious and mature musicians dressed in black and performing, in staid surroundings, eighteenth- or nineteenth-century classical music. Well, the Kronos Quartet has a surprise for you.

They wear colorful, "high-punk" costumes, and use electronic devices and elaborate sets. And they play only twentieth-century compositions, bringing together "a passion for exuberant theatricality . . . energy befitting a rock video . . . and a hip sense of humor." Though "Mozart would have been delighted," most of the staid world of chamber music was initially taken aback.

After triumphant tours in the United States and abroad, violinist Michael Harrington expressed ideas common to most Break-It Thinkers: "The purpose of being an artist is to explore bold, new contexts for bold, new ideas with all the abandon I can muster."[12] Harrington's Break-It Thinking applies to all of us.

PLAYING HIS OWN NIGHT GAME

The battle for late-night TV viewers, in which each rating point is worth hundreds of thousands of dollars, is like a war. Because of the high stakes everyone is afraid to take a chance, to try something new and innovative. Accurately assessing the film capital's play-it-safe tendencies, Arsenio Hall says, "Normally, this town [Hollywood] is afraid to do anything new. I understand that. When you fail here, you're gone." But demonstrating the attitude of a Break-It Thinker, Hall adds, "But if I win, I win big."

Demonstrating how he puts that attitude to use, Arsenio gave tradition a spin. Hall looked at all the other shows—Joan Rivers, David Letterman, Pat Sajak, and Johnny Carson—and said, "The mistake the others made was to design a situation just like Johnny's—get a desk, a guy beside you. . . . Carson was the architect of my dreams . . . but you can't knock off a legend. You can't out-Johnny Johnny. Why try to take Johnny's audience? I just want his audience's *kids*. . . ."

Using Break-It Thinking, Arsenio plays with the band, takes cameras on the street, does improv, sings, writes sketches, and asks provocative questions.

In less than nine months, Arsenio's late-night cool helped him climb from last to second place in the competitive TV market. Some industry analysts are convinced it's only a matter of time before he will challenge Carson for top honors.

Demonstrating the Break-It Thinker's attitude toward the extensive firehosing he got from "friends," Arsenio says, "Everyone was telling me, 'It's hard, too hard. Look how Joan [Rivers] failed. Black people told me, 'Yo, baby, you're black.' Let's chill with this color bull. No one told Johnny not to be too white for the brothers in Detroit. I'm gonna be me."[13] And that describes how he plays his own game to the hilt.

COACHING A DIFFERENT GAME

Roland "Ort" Ortmayer, who has coached football the past 40 plus years at La Verne College in Southern California, coaches a different game than most. La Verne's president thinks of him as "a type of Socrates." *Sports Illustrated* calls Ort "the most unusual coach in the United States."[14] "No, more than that," says a former student. "All Ort will do is change your life entirely." Consider a few examples of Ort's Break-It Thinking:

- Ortmayer on winning: "Sometimes I have the feeling that justice will not prevail if we win." So each season he schedules three games he expects to win, three he figures he'll lose, and three toss-ups.

- On the authority of the coach: "If players would rather run something out of the I formation than out of splitbacks, that's okay with me. I teach that it's all right to use your brains. All I insist on is that they come up with something I can understand so I can stay with the program."

- On plays and playbooks: "I call a few plays during the game. It's just that the players don't choose to use them. That's okay. I feel like I should try to make some sort of contribution."

- On winning (Part 2): "I'm having a miserable football season but a great archery class."

Not everyone is as much of a maverick as Roland Ortmayer, but—take heart—you can apply the same rigorous unconventional thinking to anything you do, and on any scale. You don't have to out-Ort Ort any more than Arsenio tried to out-Johnny Johnny. Take a lesson from these people, though, and don't compete head-on—change your game.

BREAK IT . . . AGAIN AND AGAIN

Break-It Thinking is the strategy suited to today's action-packed world. You have to constantly challenge the present in order to make it into the future. You have to *invert* problems and *invent* solutions, day in and day out, to thrive in today's uncertain times.

Break-It Thinking is a process, not a product, a means, not an end. It's a state of mind that fosters continual learning, incessant creativity, and perpetual growth. Success is not its *endpoint*, it's just a step along the way. There is no time limit, no last out, no final curtain in this game.

Levi-Strauss's Dockers® . . . Patagonia . . . Jean-Claude Killy's jet turn . . . Michael Chang's novel serves and returns . . . Dick Fosbury's inventive "flop" . . . Gary Friedman's breaking with the law . . . Sol Price's out-of-the-way stores . . . Chris Whittle's "re-invented business" . . . the high-punk Kronos string quartet—all are instances of Break-It Thinking that is at the heart of the *Un*conventional Wisdom we need as we enter the twenty-first century. To accomplish what they did required daring and creativity. It also meant they were willing to break with tradition, try new ways, and apply Break-It Thinking to every level of their organization.

UW *says:*
Competition encourages conformity,
so break the rules and change the game.

9

Sacred Cows Make the Best Burgers

THE WAY IT'S ALWAYS BEEN DONE

The Break-It Thinkers described in the last chapter achieved dramatic results by having the courage to challenge old ways and break with convention. Old habits—doing things the way they have always been done—are a major inhibitor to innovation, growth, and progress.

"In corporate culture they often have a set way of doing things, some sacred cows," says G. Robert "Bull" Durham, former CEO of Phelps Dodge. "They prevent you from recognizing what you . . . could do."[1]

Sacred cows are those systems, strategies, policies, procedures, and routines that have become "standard operating procedure" in many areas of business. They are sacred because we take it for granted that "that's the way it's always been done." The result is that we spend a great deal of time, energy, and money feeding our sacred cows, supporting the system rather than having the system support us. As MIT's Commission on Industrial Productivity stated, corporate

America is suffering from "a deep reservoir of outmoded attitudes and policies."

Sacred cows are often created by powerful forces that work against change. For example, people trained to behave in one mode attract new employees who believe in that way of doing things. New information that might challenge old habits is eliminated or dismissed by such status quo thinking. Adding insult to injury, individuals who step forward to challenge the prevailing wisdom are quickly spotted and put on the fast track . . . to some other company.

Durham's advice about sacred cows is to "flush them out . . . be mercilessly objective. Nothing is sacred."[2] "Sacred cows . . . stifle our creativity and weaken our competitive strength," comments SPX chairman Robert D. Tuttle.[3]

ROUTINES AND RUTS

It is naive and simplistic to think that we have to eliminate all routines and controls. That would obviously create chaos. Some policies and procedures do prevent us from wasting time and continually reinventing the wheel. But today anything that goes untouched for very long will soon become outmoded, inefficient, and counterproductive.

These habits dull senses, inhibit creativity, and hinder free thought. If we don't rid ourselves of outmoded routines, they will quickly turn into ruts.

SACRED COWS ARE TOUGH TO ROUND UP

Many controls and systems quickly turn into sacred cows because we don't take the time or expend the energy to keep them new and fresh. As a result, they become invisible, part of the environment, fading into the woodwork of our unconscious.

Sacred cows are well camouflaged because many of us are distracted by the pursuit of bigger game—the new contract, the merger, increasing productivity, the new product. Caught up in the chase, it's easy to miss sacred cows, and they go untouched and unchecked.

Others are often thought to be untouchable because they are "the boss's baby" or relate to someone else's "turf" and we think we don't have the requisite power to make changes. So we leave them alone and watch with annoyance as they continue to take valuable time and effort.

It sometimes seems easier to stay with the familiar, even though we know it's not working very well. Changing anything could make it worse, so better the devil you know . . . Trying to eliminate a sacred cow or any other habit takes time and energy, both of which are in short supply these days.

The result of "going along with the program" and not rounding up our sacred cows is that we unwittingly contribute to their perpetuation, even when they have far outlived their usefulness. And when you let them roam, they keep growing and gnawing on your patience as well as on profits and productivity.

Sacred cows come in all shapes and sizes. Among the most common varieties are:

- Corporate cows—obsolete corporate culture

- Company cows—archaic, complex company policies

- Departmental cows—divisive turf wars

- Industry cows—unquestioned industrywide standard operating procedures

- Personal cows—unproductive routines, ruts, and habits

Throughout the remainder of this chapter are examples that will help you recognize some of these generic sacred cows.

Corporate cows

Corporate culture. Often the most pervasive and most subtle sacred cows are those that are inherent in the corporate culture itself—the shared beliefs, assumptions, and values of the corporations. The culture is the *modus operandi*, the guiding principles of the organization, the way it operates.

To keep ahead of change these days it is imperative to have a corporate culture that is entrepreneurial in nature: fast-moving, innovative, and risk-taking. Developing that type of culture often means challenging the basic thinking and structure of the organization from the top down. The MIT productivity study concluded that American executives have to *fundamentally rethink* their assumptions and habits.

Some organizations *are* changing archaic corporate cultures and have made significant changes in their ways of operating, as well as in their beliefs and guiding principles. Many organizations, however, are still carrying over the heavy burden of their past and as a result are having a tough time reacting with the speed, flexibility, and innovation demanded by the marketplace.

Good old Ma Bell. AT&T was a perfect example of this slow-moving, bovine type of culture and as a result went through incredibly tough times after divestiture. People had usually chosen to work for good old Ma Bell because it was safe and sure. After all, what could be more secure than the phone company? As a result, AT&T hadn't attracted the risk takers and innovative thinkers who were needed when the rules changed and competition got fierce in the communications industry. Risk avoidance worked fine while AT&T was indeed *the* phone company. But after divestiture, the telecommunications game changed completely. "Good old Ma Bell is dead," said AT&T chairman Charles Brown. But lots of people hung on to her apron strings well beyond her so-called demise.

After an initially tough time, AT&T is beginning to develop a culture that is more entrepreneurial. They have eliminated layers of managers, given more authority to their people, and are attempting to become more action-oriented; "they can do things without layers of supervisors telling them how," said Jeffrey McCollum, education director at the consumer products unit.

This autonomy is now filtering to all levels. Cathy Ann Gallo, manager of AT&T's Phone Center at Summit, New Jersey, used to need approval before doing something as simple as replacing a broken phone. Now, she says, with the departure of many middle managers, "I've been empowered to do whatever makes my customers happy."

One final example. It used to take over 200 people working 12-hour days and weekends to produce AT&T training courses. By eliminating some of their sacred cows, such as progress reports and compartmentalized efforts, they now have less than 100 people "producing many more courses in a normal workweek," says McCollum.[4]

Back to the past. Often the culture of the corporation reflects the beliefs, values, and even the style of the founder. Though the culture may have been at the cutting edge when the company was established, it's often now outdated and obsolete. The world changes, but the old ways have become law, etched in bronze and followed to a T.

"It's no wonder we manage our way to economic decline," Stanley Davis said. "Our managerial models don't suit today's business. We are still using the model GM founder Alfred Sloan developed for organizing corporate America back in the twenties. As a result we have industrially modeled organizations running post industrial businesses."[5]

The followers syndrome. Although in his day Alfred Sloan was an innovator and a risk taker, many of the people who followed him were not. It is not surprising that when systems, controls, and procedures were developed, GM's innovative, entrepreneurial spirit was deadened.

"The GM system is like a blanket of fog that keeps people from doing what they know needs to be done," said Ross Perot from his perspective as a GM board member. "We've got to throw away Sloan's book [*My Years with General Motors*]. We still believe that we can find the right page and paragraph to give us the answer to any question we have today. . . . We've got to nuke the GM system. . . .

"At GM, if you see a snake, the first thing you do is go hire a consultant on snakes. Then you get a committee on snakes, and then you discuss it for a couple of years. The most likely course of action is—nothing. You figure, the snake hasn't bitten anybody yet, so you just let him crawl around on the factory floor. . . . I come from an environment where, the first guy who sees the snake kills it," Perot says.[6]

No wonder Roger Smith, head of GM, paid hundreds of millions to buy Perot out of GM! Perot was clearly breaking with GM tradition, and Smith reverted to one of the worst conventional responses: kill the messenger.

Breaking locks. William R. Hewlett, cofounder of Hewlett-Packard, is a great example of a leader who worked to keep the entrepreneurial culture alive in H-P. Stopping off at the storeroom to pick up a microscope one day, he found the equipment cage locked. Legend has it that he broke open the latch, gathered up his microscope, and left a scathing note telling the clerk never to lock the room again. Word of the incident spread quickly throughout the company, delivering the message that stifling innovation was worse than risking theft. Decades later H-P is still imbued with that sense of freedom, and fosters a culture of creativity, openness, and "intelligent failure."[7]

Company cows

"It's company policy." In many companies, sacred cows are perpetuated by a classic catch-22: "If it's still around, it must work; and it must work because it's still around." Much of what is offered as company policy and procedure perpetuates this type of thinking.

Most corporate policies and procedures are inherited from predecessors. "It's the policy that was in place when I took the job," one manager told me. Often no one seems to know when the procedure was "born." Fewer still question its utility. It is presumed that if it's "in the bloodlines" of the organization, it must be worth keeping.

Contributing to the reluctance to change is the belief that rules, policies, and systems are sacrosanct. To challenge company policy, even though it is outmoded, is perceived as disloyalty, as if you were "taking on" the company. The sacred cows, therefore, are left free to graze on profits and gnaw at your patience.

Loyalty aside, an increasing number of companies are examining their founding principles as well as the basic assumptions of their company polices. One of the most dramatic examples is that of Harry Quadracci, founder of Quad/Graphics.

The Quad Squad. Harry Quadracci is CEO of the $500 million Quad/Graphics Inc., whose clients include *Time,* L. L. Bean, *Playboy, The Atlantic Monthly,* and *Newsweek.* Quadracci has challenged a dozen or so of the most common sacred cows of American business. His actions offer ideas about what is possible when Break-It Thinking is applied to company policies and conventional business assumptions. As he tells it:

- "Eliminate *budgets.* . . . Use your computer. At any moment I can call up an analysis of any employee, account, or piece of equipment in my company—that's a more timely, accurate control than any budget. . . .

- Using *plans* . . . is like firing a cannonball. It's fine if you are shooting at a castle. But markets today are moving targets.

- *Push staff functions down the pyramid.* Who knows better how to run a department than the guy who's paid to run it? . . .

- *Sell off the purchasing department.* . . . Those who use supplies should be responsible for buying them.

- *Personnel departments can be let go.* Let every manager hire his [*sic*] own people. . . . He'll be more active and ambitious to make it work. . . .

- *Let everybody touch the customer.* Let customers into your plant.

- *Reject your quality control department.* You can't inspect quality into something; QC can be just another bureaucratic process to slow you down. Make everyone responsible for quality.

- *Junk your time clock.* If you don't trust people to work until the job is done, don't hire them. . . .

- *Eliminate as many levels of organization as you can*: you can't build a team among unequals."[8]

Profitable changes. An amazingly diverse number of other companies are busy rounding up their sacred cows. For example:

- Dallas-based oil and gas producer Oryx saved $70 million on net earnings of $139 million in one year—a staggering figure. How, you ask? By eliminating rules, procedures, reviews, reports, and approvals that "insufficiently focused on [their main business] discovering oil."[9] Using a team approach, they were able to cut capital expenditure approvals *from 20 to only 4* and reduce the time it took to produce the annual budget *from seven months to six weeks.*

- When Jerre Stead became CEO at Square D, a leading electrical equipment manufacturer, he was presented with four thick manuals of official policies and procedures. The 760 rules covered such things as who could talk to whom, about what, and under what circumstances. Trimming more than a little fat, Stead pitched the manuals in favor of 11 simple policy statements.[10]

- U.S. West Communications discovered that its employees were spending too much on too little and taking too much time to do so. For example, they had 350 people involved in the preparation of the annual budget! They were able to reduce the number to 100 within one year.

Commenting on what he had learned in the process of ridding his company of many sacred cows, Gary Ames, CEO of U.S. West Communications astutely observed that "at some point in your dieting [i.e., cost cutting] process you come to the realization that if you really want to keep the weight off you have to change your habits."[11]

UW *says: Break-It Thinkers, constantly on the look-out for sacred cows and outmoded procedures, are those who get into the habit of breaking their habits.*

Departmental cows

Turf wars. Many systems appear to be "sacred" and "untouchable" because they are generated by another department. The finance department needs cost analysis; therefore, far be it for anyone in another department to change or challenge it. Grudgingly, others acquiesce, even though the procedures are outdated. Another sacred cow is that other people's turf is sacrosanct. Consequently, turf wars are often fueled by fear on one side, and the desire to retain control and power on the other.

Every organization has its turf wars in which blind allegiance to one part of the business may well work to the detriment of the company as a whole. Manufacturing resists retooling or wants long production runs on unproven products. Marketing wants new goodies, the sooner the better, and could care less what it may cost in R&D or production. Or finance says to cut inventory: the hot items sell, the rest stay on the shelf. In fact, many managers spend more time arguing who pays what than in serving the customer. These turf wars aren't just about money, but about power and control.

Allan Loren, former president of Apple USA, was a president of information systems at Cigna Insurance. Loren's role at Cigna was to get independent agents computerized, thus "moving the locus of underwriting and customer service from a centralized field office to the independent agent, which greatly enhanced service to the customer and improved underwriting." But the behind-the-scenes story was not the distribution of the terminals but the cultural change that was fought for *over a five-year period* with the field officers and key underwriters at corporate headquarters who felt threatened by the "perceived" loss of control and resisted the change.[12]

At Bank of America, as in most banks, one of the turf wars was between the marketing department and the credit department. Realizing the negative effect of these wars, says K. Shelly Porges, marketing senior vice president, "We made a friendly crossing of the fences and began working together more often, . . . and with no marketing dollars expended, we doubled our share of the auto loan business in a year and reached a five percent market share over Wells Fargo and Security Pacific combined."[13]

The walls come tumbling down. A perfect example of how turf wars prevent innovation and hinder productivity comes from Ingersoll-Rand. "It was taking three years to make a tool, then three and a half and it was heading toward four," observed James Stryker, head of business development. This delay was attributed to a succession of walls: marketing would think of a product and throw it over the wall to engineering, engineering would do a design and pitch it to manufacturing, manufacturing to sales . . . who would then try to sell it to customers, who by then didn't want it all that much. To add insult to injury, however, things would get tossed back and forth over the same wall two or three times, and "the point at which a product appeared was often fixed by when people's arms got too tired to throw anything more over the wall."

"We finally said, 'Enough,'" Stryker observed. A half dozen tool designers fastened onto the dream of streamlining the toolmaking process. They formed a cross-functional design unit with representatives from every "walled-in" enclave. As one team member put it, "Everyone would play in the same sandbox. We were going to share our pails and shovels."[14] By sharing their pails and shovels, they cut development time by two thirds.

Toppling walls with superteams. Innovation is not just the engineer's or R&D's job. An increasing number of companies are forming cross-functional "superteams" to solve problems and develop new products. These superteams can include people from sales, manufacturing, marketing, finance, engineering, information systems, and human resources working together and with clients.

One of the beauties of these superteams is that each member looks at the same thing from a different perspective, which results in a much more creative, efficient, and effective output. As seen from the Ingersoll-Rand example, speed is greatly increased when previously competing groups work together.

A few years ago superteams were found at just a handful of companies. Today, according to a survey of 476 of the *Fortune* 1,000 companies, half the companies say they rely on them. To keep innovative and rid our organizations of sacred cows and turf wars, the walls must come tumbling down. The Levi's "Dockers®" breakthrough was created by a team consisting of people from every area of the organization. Some organizations have superteams in every part of their operation. Corning, for example, under the leadership of CEO Jamie Houghton, has *3,000 teams!* Says Texas Instruments CEO Jerry Junkins, "No matter what your business, these teams are the wave of the future."[15]

Industry cows

Following the herd. "Blindly following organizational concepts that have worked elsewhere," says B. Charles Ames, Uniroyal Goodyear CEO, "is a sure way to waste talent and get poor results."[16]

As with any other sacred cows, industrywide practices—"the way it's always been done"—need to be challenged in order to gain the edge on competition. In the last chapter we discussed how people such as Chris Whittle, Gary Friedman, and Sol Price broke with traditional industrywide practices and became leaders in their respective fields. Whittle said, "Pioneering is the best business strategy. I always want people to find my warm campfire because by then I'm already over the next ridge."

UW *says: You can't move fast if you're following a herd of sacred cows.*

Here are some examples of people and organizations challenging the assumptions and habits of their industries and accomplishing some dramatic advances.

Make it overseas? Bettis Rainsford, chairman of Delta Woodside, challenged the textile industry's belief that America couldn't compete with cheap foreign labor, low prices, and government subsidies. Buying old textile mills about to close down; switching product lines; retooling factories with cheap, used machines; and stressing marketing over manufacturing; he "single-handedly revived the U.S. textile industry when everyone else was surrendering to foreign competitors who had both cheap labor and government subsidies."[17]

Hewlett-Packard's Roseville, California, plant recently challenged the high-tech industry belief that you had to manufacture overseas to be price-competitive. By challenging every aspect of their operation, they made dramatic breakthroughs.

In the process, nothing was considered sacred, no detail of the manufacturing process remained unscathed. For example, H-P worked out a special arrangement whereby the supplier of its parts and terminals shipped them in a container that would be reused by H-P for shipping the finished product. This seemingly small innovation saved the cost of paying for additional boxes and packaging materials, and eliminated the necessity of disposing of thousands of tons of cardboard and plastic waste. And this is just one small example. The result was that H-P concluded, "American ingenuity can beat low-cost foreign labor when it comes to high-tech manufacturing."[18]

Turning an outsider in. A normal accounting firm visits clients at certain times in the year to audit the books. But Arthur Andersen & Co., one of the biggest, is hardly normal and has been not so quietly challenging some of the most basic accounting industry traditions. In addition to developing a successful management consulting practice, they now offer an Andersen manager as the CFO for the client organization for a contracted period of time. Thus, the roles are reversed: the outsider becomes the insider, the consultant, boss!

"It's a different world," says Gary Peterson, head of Andersen's contract financial management business. "If you're going to continue to grow you have to do things like this."[19] By challenging some of the industry's sacred cows, Andersen is on the path to reinventing the accountant.

Sacred cards. On a much different level, the president of a small speaker's bureau in Southern California had a paper trail in her office that was longer than the Lewis and Clark expedition. "All my client data is written on three-by-five cards, including upcoming programs, callback calendars, everything. They're the lifeblood of this business, in fact this industry," she told me. "This is the way I learned the business, and this is the way this industry has run for years."

When she realized she was "spending more time making cards than making money," she introduced personal computers to her office. Nothing radical or spectacular. But that small simple step was actually a major break from her own (and the industry's) standard practice.

"I didn't think it was that big a deal," she told me. "I figured, it's the nineties; everybody is cardless and I'm just catching up. Then I went to one of the largest bureaus for a meeting—they are ten times the size of mine—and the first thing I see on a friend's desk . . . is a stack of three-by-five cards. Boy, did I have a good laugh. And I knew I had an advantage too!"

Little things mean a lot. As we have seen, simple changes can mean a great deal to an organization. There are infinite numbers of these in every industry, every company, every job. Take the business letter for example. Few activities are more replete with old habits, assumptions, and sacred cows than the components of a "proper" business letter. "Proper" letters do not necessarily get properly read.

"Formal salutations are a tragedy," says Jay Jones, author of *Write Business Letters Right.* Use a "creative substitution" to "get the readers attention, create goodwill, and put others first."[20] Instead of beginning a letter to a realtor with "Dear Ms. Thompson," how about "Good grief, Carol . . . what's happening to real estate?"

Personal cows

Heading for your first round-up. In my workshops I have people answer the questions at the end of this chapter as a first step to rounding up their sacred cows and putting them out to pasture.

After doing this "sacred cow" exercise with over 10,000 people, more than 90 percent reached two conclusions:

1. They were spending much more time doing things they disliked rather than things they liked.

2. The things they liked usually had to do with people, creativity, and new challenges. The things they disliked usually had to do with paperwork.

I then asked them: Which contributes more to the productivity and profits of an organization, the people or the paper? You can answer that one yourself.

In almost every instance, doing the things you like—the challenging tasks, the creative work, the people work—is much more directly related to the bottom line of the organization than the paperwork.

Many systems that generate paperwork look good on paper but they don't really work that well operationally. They require more people and more time, and they end up costing more money. They also burn people out and prevent them from doing the things that are in fact important.

Very often the paperwork that bogs us down has more to do with mistrust, control, and monitoring than with motivating, innovating, and producing. The paper trail represents people trying to keep tabs on other people.

Contrary to this, Break-It Thinkers know that the purpose of any system is to liberate people to do their most creative work—to free them up, not tie them down; to empower, not control.

Here are several illustrations of people who have successfully rounded up sacred cows that were hindering their productivity, creativity, and motivation. They will stimulate your thinking and give you some useful ideas that will enhance your productivity, profits, and patience.

Cutting reports down to size. One of the sacred cows identified by a division head I know at a *Fortune* 50 manufacturing company was the monthly 10-column financial report sent to all corporate officers. "It takes a lot of time and effort and frankly I question how important it is to get the information that often," he told me. "I mean how much can you use? It's been there longer than I have. . . ." He threw up his hands in frustration.

At a monthly follow-up meeting, one of his managers suggested eliminating two columns because "nobody needs that information anymore. It's outdated." The group agreed and sent out the abbreviated report. Much to their relief there was no criticism. In fact there was no response at all.

Feeling a little more cocky, at the next meeting one of the members suggested combining two sets of numbers, since "they aren't all that different." The group agreed, and that month's statement went out with six columns. Once again, no response.

At the subsequent meeting someone jokingly said, "Hey, maybe there's no one out there! Let's skip a month and see what happens." The division manager, who was responsible for the report, blanched but finally agreed. No report was sent out. And still no response.

Two months later they sent out the *Third Quarter Report*, all *four columns* of it. This time the feedback was swift. A message, handwritten on the report, arrived from the CFO saying, "Great report! Clear. To the point. Keep up the good work." From 10 columns monthly to four columns quarterly . . . and a message was sent out to this man's division. All sacred cows are fair game.

Cutting meetings down to size. These days people are spending more time in meetings than behind their desks. The problem, one woman told me, is meetings that go well beyond their point of productivity. "We have staff meetings every week," a newspaper editor said. "They last an hour and a half, but after three quarters of an hour they are a waste. People are tired, restless, and antsy. The productivity and creativity after forty-five minutes is almost nonexistent."

I then suggested the obvious—set the meeting's duration for 45 minutes. It worked fabulously. "People only brought up topics that were important," she told. "We stopped wasting time. I'll tell you, we got more done in those forty-five minutes and did better work than we did in meetings that were twice as long. An added bonus was that the number of meetings dropped as well."

UW *says: We fill up the time available, so cut the available time.*

The baker's dozen. At another major high-tech organization, the bane of the sales manager's day was the 13 approvals he had to get in order to bid for a government contract. Yes, 13! "A maniacal baker's dozen," he rightly called it. "Everyone has to sign off on it—manufacturing, finance, engineering, legal. . . . Everyone's got their finger in the pie. It takes so long to get them all on board that it dampens the enthusiasm of my people and puts us behind the eight-ball in terms of making government deadlines."

Challenging the system and substituting trust for mistrust and responsibility for supervision, this manager was instrumental in getting the approval process as lean and mean as it comes, going from 13 approvals to . . . *one!*

Vertical meetings. Frequent, unproductive meetings are one of the most common sacred cows, regardless of the industry you are in.

Jack Daly, executive vice president of Glendale Federal Savings & Loan, shared this concern and decided to take it a step further. Daly noticed that meetings held in the lush confines of the corporate conference room were interminable. People would mill around, sit back in the soft chairs (the sacred cow of the meeting room), be slow to start on the agenda, and even slower to leave when the meeting adjourned.

Applying Break-It Thinking, Daly did the only honorable thing: he removed all the chairs! That's it. Everything else was exactly the same, sans soft seats! For the next three months, meetings took half as long, and there were half as many of them. After three months of "conditioning," the chairs were returned, but the meetings retained their newfound efficiency.

Corning Glass, Equitable Life Assurance, and Johnson & Johnson have also joined the vertical meeting brigade. "It does work," says Corning VP Frank Anthony, "no question about it. People don't b.s. They get right to the point because they hate to stand."[21]

The half-open door policy. A senior manager at a major management consulting firm has a sacred "open door" policy that was a double-edged sword. Although it did improve accessibility, accessibility didn't improve performance. She felt increasingly at the mercy of people stopping by and popping in. A minute or two here, two or three there, added up. These seemingly minor interruptions also broke her concentration. Her motto, she quipped, was "Now, where was I . . . ."

So, using Break-It Thinking, she did a seemingly insignificant thing: she turned her desk around and moved a bookcase to block people's direct view.

The payoffs from this simple act were many: "To get my attention now, people had to make an effort. It wasn't just 'stick your head in and start talking.'" The small interruptions, the gossip, and the questions people could answer themselves virtually stopped. "One unexpected result was that my people began making more decisions on their own and as a result felt more involved. Best of all, I also found that I was getting home thirty to sixty minutes earlier every day, in better spirits, and feeling as though I was finally 'catching up'!"

Paper cows. The number-one sacred cow for a West Coast sales organization that sold to sports and running shops was "reading and writing reports." Not only did the salespeople continually face the pressures of ever-rising goals and new competition, they had to write reports on everything: calls made, call results, expenses, credit status of small shops, inventory check, and so on. Then, at the end of the day they still had to read memos, reports, and their mail.

Initiating their own "round-up," five of the reps from the Northwest hired their own secretary. They would then dictate all of these reports while riding from one account to another and send them in to the secretary for typing and distribution. They figured that they saved about 45 minutes a day, which translated into at least one and often two extra calls. And no "drudge" paperwork! Soon this idea was taken up by all of the reps.

But this is not where the story ends. Taking a lesson from his people, the sales manager rounded up another cow. He began putting all of his correspondence to his sales staff on audio tape. In addition to the usual information about sales, objectives, competitive activity, and promotions, he included a "hero of the month" segment, awarded for an action beyond the call of duty. Everyone wanted to be the next month's "hero," so they began trying to outdo each other by creating unusual promotions.

Within six months these two changes had increased sales by 35 percent!

ROUNDING UP YOUR OWN SACRED COWS

These examples of rounding up personal sacred cows weren't dramatic or earth-shattering. The people weren't wild and frenzied mavericks or raving lunatics. These were ordinary people dealing with ordinary, simple things.

At a seminar I conducted for one of Hewlett-Packard's most successful sales divisions, I asked them if they could identify one or two of their own sacred cows that were preventing them from doing their job better. The results surprised everyone. In less than 10 minutes H-P's fastest-growing sales force was able to list 25 sacred cows that needed to be booted out in order for the salespeople to be even more productive.

Sacred cows don't have to be big and burly. Sacred cows are everywhere and come in all sizes and shapes. My advice is to begin by rounding up the most visible ones. The key is committing to the round-up, taking some action now. This helps build confidence and momentum and opens you to new opportunities not foreseen at the outset.

The following questions are designed to help you identify your own sacred cows. Start by identifying the cows, but don't try to do something about them immediately. Going through junk mail after being away on a business trip was one woman's sacred cow. "The pile is that high," she said, holding her hands about a foot apart. "But I have to go through it because some of it may be valuable." Maybe, maybe not. There may be a myriad of other solutions that aren't obvious at first. So don't decide too quickly whether the cow can be rounded up or not. Just write it down. We'll talk about ways of putting them out to pasture later on. Answer the questions with as much openness and honesty as possible.

1. List any systems, procedures, policies, or habits that are outdated and that you would like to change.

2. What are the aspects of your job that you like the least, that are a "drag" and wear you down or seem like "busy work"?

3. Which of the above that you inherited from your predecessor or learned in a course at school are more trouble than they are worth?

4. Which come to you courtesy of another department that you never have challenged because it is a "turf issue"?

5. Visualize yourself going through a typical day (or week). Make a list of your routine habits—when you get up, how you get to work, when you have lunch, what you do when you get to the office, what you do when you leave, how you handle the mail. Which of these habits or routines would you like to break? Why? What would be the benefit?

6. If a comedy group were to do a satire of your day, what specific activities would provide them with the most laughs?

7. Look around your office. Identify something that has bothered you for a while. Imagine that you have done something about it. How would you feel? Would you expect to see a difference in your attitude and/or effectiveness?

By now you should have a clearer sense of your own sacred cows. Keep them in mind as we move on and you'll learn numerous ways of putting them out to pasture safely, easily, and effectively.

Keep in mind the importance of not letting your sacred cows make mincemeat out of you because nothing is sacred.

At this point you should have a clearer sense of your own outdated habits as well as the necessity of changing them. Taking this one step further, the Break-It Thinker is constantly on the lookout for ways to stay fresh and creative. It's important, as **UW** says, to get in the habit of breaking your habits.

UW *says:*
Get in the habit of breaking your habits.

10

Think Like a Beginner

LIFE'S LITTLE LIGHT BULBS

We've all had that "aha!" experience, when the light bulb goes on in our mind. In a moment the blinders come off, tunnel vision vanishes, and a solution to a problem appears when and where we least expect it—in the shower, while jogging, in the car. These are the moments when we roll back our eyes, slap ourselves on the forehead, and wonder why we hadn't seen it before. It was so obvious, so simple.

Obvious? . . . Yes. Simple? . . . Yes. Easy? . . . No!

One difficulty we have in seeing an obvious solution or spotting a new idea is that we have been blinded by our own expertise. We value complexity. We choose the obscure rather than the obvious. So knowing "too much" makes it difficult to see simple answers. Firehosing ourselves, we are sure that anything so simple and so obvious can't be any good—surely someone must have already thought of it before.

Yet Conventional Wisdom is not much help because it assures us that if we want the best advice, we should call in the experts with detailed knowledge of the subject, who boast specialized training. "Got a question?" "Got a tough problem?" Call in the specialists. "Need a detailed evaluation?" Get an expert in, pronto.

That may have been a good strategy at one time, but in today's world, a new idea, technological breakthrough, political shift, or research finding can quickly render obsolete what had been considered state-of-the-art knowledge.

IF YOU USE EXPERTS, USE 'EM WELL

"When I was with the *American Trend Report*," says Louis Patler, "we hired experts, but we were very careful about how we used their thinking skills." Experts have some great qualities—discipline, and a willingness to immerse themselves in a subject, for example, but they can get trapped by their past success.

Patler cautions that "the biggest risk in using experts is that they may be compulsive about being right—they may screen out novelty trying to make everything fit what they already know. That can make them too conservative to be accurate forecasters. And they waste far too much time defending old positions.

"We trained our experts to cross fields and take a fresh perspective. The challenge is similar when we help managers apply trends effectively. You have to be able to think like a beginner—leave dignity to the historians, the future belongs to the bold."

PIGEONHOLING

Thinking like an expert, or bringing one in, to solve your problems, can hinder more than help. Richard Tamm, a Bay Area computer consultant, told me he often sees this happen with software programmers. "Rather than rethinking a program when a new idea or development is introduced," Tamm said, "their tendency is to try to fit the new idea into an existing model or framework, and *poof*, the new idea is no longer new."[1] Experts invariably put new problems into the same old context in order to understand them. They tend to define what is *new* in terms of what is *old*, what is *unknown* in terms of what is *known*, and to pigeonhole new situations into existing and well-established frameworks.

Whether in sales, service, engineering, or manufacturing, experts will literally not see current problems or situations anew, but rather through a filter of preconceived ideas or biases that screen the way they see the world. Additionally, once such people have gained the moniker "expert," their need to be "right" and to retain the title will often bias their opinions and close their minds. As a result they become entrenched in their perspectives as well as their positions and will defend the tried and true ways of doing things in the most articulate and jargon-filled ways. This "expert" attitude reminds me of a Buddhist story.

The man who knew too much

There once was a student who was very knowledgeable. One day he went to his master's house. When they were seated opposite each other, the master began to pour the tea while the student began to tell him what he knew. The more the student talked, the more the master poured. Soon the student's cup was running over, the saucer overflowing and tea spilling on his clothes.

The student asked the master why he had kept pouring the tea. The master replied, "When the mind is filled to overflowing, like the teacup, there is no room for anything new in it." Eventually the student realized what the master knew immediately—that he was all wet!

EXPERT BEGINNERS

"When I became Minister of Labour there were all kinds of experts on labour relations who were willing to share their views about the past 50 years, and especially about the problems," said the Honorable Elaine McCoy, Alberta's (Canada) Labour Minister.

"Experts are often too full of facts about what didn't work in the past to make the leap to the future. But what these experts can never tell us is where to go from here. We needed a fresh perspective. So I spent a year talking with people from all walks of life to develop a vision of where we want to go in the next century. Most important political choices have to do with human values, not just 'expert' information, and have to be made with heart."[2]

THE BEGINNER'S MIND-SET

"It used to be, the bigger the nerd you were, the better the researcher," says François P. van Remoortere, president of W. R. Grace & Co.'s research division. "That's changed now," he says. "Some of the best advice comes from people who know the least about a specific operation."

This isn't to belittle experience, information, or expertise. But the key to keeping ahead of change is to learn to *think like a beginner*. With a beginner's mind you will be more open to what is emerging and better equipped to anticipate change.

The beginner isn't as attached to old ways of doing and seeing things and won't spend a great deal of time "beating a dead horse" or accumulating sacred cows. Looking at the world with a fresh eye and an open mind, the beginner will see things that the expert will miss.

Thinking like a beginner is a state of curiosity where you see situations anew, not letting old information and the "benefits" of experience cloud your judgment. Experience, after all, took place in the past, and the thinking, strategies, and information that worked in the past are often outdated and obsolete.

As a renowned maverick, the French architect and designer Phillipe Starck, has demonstrated, new eyes accompany the perpetual beginner. He says simply, "I am an amnesiac. This is why I always arrive fresh at a problem."[3]

ELINA'S PUZZLE

Children have a way of arriving fresh at a problem. They are filled with curiosity, crave new discoveries, and are open to new experiences. As with Starck's amnesia, they see the world for the first time. This is why a child can ask a question or make an observation that goes to the heart of a matter.

To make this point, I have asked people to solve a puzzle that Louis Patler's five-year-old-daughter, Elina, brought home from kindergarten.

Q: Which of the following letters is the most out of place?

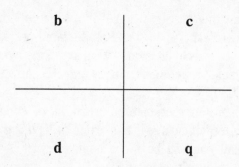

Do the puzzle yourself or with some friends to see who comes up with the right answer.

Answer _____ Why? _____

Some answer that the *c* doesn't fit because it has no straight line attached. Others say it is the *q* because it is out of order. Some, sensing there must be a trick, say something about the *b* or *d*.

Seeing the puzzle with the eyes of a beginner, Elina answered immediately. To her the letter that was most out of place was "the *t*"!

I have shown this puzzle to thousands of people and have had up to 25-minute discussion groups on which letter was the proper choice and why. Only a few noticed the *t*.

Most of us go about solving problems by working through the *b*'s, *c*'s, *d*'s and *q*'s because we have experiences that tell us that is the way to do it. We look for the conventional, rather than the obvious, the complex, not the simple.

NOVICE CONSULTANTS

Recently I consulted at Keystone, a major Colorado ski resort known for its family orientation and fabulous service. John Rutter, vice president of ski operations, was concerned that his people were getting too set in their ways. "They are beginning to think they know it all. I want to shake things up a little and get them to start thinking in a different way about how Keystone can provide even better service for its customers."

Introducing "novice consulting," we divided 25 managers drawn from every sector of the operation into six teams. Once a week, each team would spend half a day in an area of the resort operation in which team members had no expertise. They were told not to try to be an expert and come up with solutions but to be like a beginner and see what they could see, and to ask as many "dumb questions" as possible about things they didn't understand—obvious bottlenecks, sacred cows, missed opportunities.

The results far exceeded expectations! At our follow-up meeting six weeks later, hundreds of the "naive" questions resulted in dozens of new ideas. Many a sacred cow was spotted and rounded up. The resort's entire internal marketing campaign was changed as a result of this effort. Rutter estimated that one of the ideas, involving ticket sales procedures, would save them tens of thousands of dollars a year, and that many of the other innovations would lead to substantial improvements in service and the quality of the product they were offering the public. And all of this was accomplished by beginners doing the experts' work.

SUPE DE JOUR

Novice consulting worked so well that Gordon Briner, director of Keystone's ski school, decided to use "beginners as experts" in his instructor-training programs.

It is conventional to have supervisors give occasional lessons and even to work in staff jobs for a day. That's important, but old news.

The new wrinkle from Briner was to use Break-It Thinking to flip the Conventional Wisdom around. Once a week every senior ski instructor spent a morning as a *supervisor*, a program they called the Supe de Jour.

The novice supervisors spotted many things the experts were missing. They came up with new ideas that improved the teaching climate for the student and instructor, as well as the relationship and communications between the instructors and supervisors. They also changed some industrywide sacred cows, like the slow and impersonal student "line up" for classes.

Both Briner and Rutter reported that managers and instructors felt more involved in the whole resort as well as more empowered. They were listened to, and could see that their opinions and suggestions counted, which in itself greatly improved morale, motivation, and service at Keystone.

THE PERKIN-ELMER FAN CLUB

The Perkin-Elmer Corporation, manufacturer of analytical instruments and semiconductor processing equipment, used the novice approach in a highly specialized area. They brought in people from different departments who had no expertise in engineering to consult on an engineering problem. These nonspecialists helped cut the number of changes required to produce a product by 50 percent, and manufacturing costs as much as 55 percent!

How did they do this? By keeping things simple and questioning everything. On the basis of these "nonexperts'" suggestions, plans for a new bolt-in metal fan were scrapped in favor of a plastic one that snapped into place more quickly, easily, and cheaply, thus making the company—and the customer—much happier.[4]

CLEANING THE SLATE

"We started out by wiping the slate clean," says Max Davis, manufacturing manager of Hewlett-Packard's Roseville plan. Davis was referring to the approach they took in designing the new Roseville assembly line, in which managers questioned *everything*, asking themselves if they really needed a computer system . . . a cafeteria . . . or even design engineers! Over a 2½-year period, H-P totally revamped the way it built everything, from plant to product.

As a result of approaching everything with fresh eyes and an open mind, H-P's five newest computer-terminal models cost from *5 percent to 45 percent less than those made in foreign plants!*[5] Consider these other remarkable results of cleaning the slate at H-P:

- Raw material costs have been cut by 50 percent.

- They went from a 50-screw to a 4-screw design for the terminals, and they are looking for a supplier of a snap-in part that will reduce the number of screws to just one.

- Paperwork has been reduced by 90 percent.

- Labor time needed to build the terminals has been cut 75 percent.

- The number of design and engineering support people went from 50 to 5, a 90 percent reduction! They accomplished this by designing their terminals around available parts instead of requiring custom or proprietary parts.

- Product reliability is so high that only 4 percent of the work force is needed for repair work, compared to 20 percent on older products. That's an 80 percent reduction!

The list goes on. The Roseville plant is making quality products for less than foreign competitors because they were willing to wipe the slate clean of all preconceptions and take a fresh look at *every* aspect of their design and manufacturing process, holding nothing sacred.

No wonder John Young, H-P's CEO, proudly and accurately states that "this is the lowest-cost manufactured product of its type made anywhere in the world."[6] That's the expertise that a beginner's mind-set makes possible.

OUT OF THE MOUTHS OF BABES CAME . . .

Specialists overthink, looking for sophisticated solutions to what are often simple problems.

At a lunch break with several top executives of a major new resort, the general manager told me that everything was working great, with one exception: their new "state-of-the-art" outdoor cafeteria wasn't making money. "People are spending considerably less on food than we projected, and for the life of me I don't understand it. Our research shows that customers think the food is great, the service terrific, and the scenery sensational." He had hired several restaurant consultants and had "covered all the bases. We've tried everything—changed managers, suppliers, themes, interior colors, menus, seating arrangements—everything. And we still can't turn a profit."

At this point I got in line for lunch. I grabbed a salad, a sandwich, and a juice and was trying to make some room on my tray for a dessert. At that same moment I watched the little boy in front of me try to squeeze a dish of ice cream onto his tray, knocking his sandwich to the floor. "I told you not to take so much," his dad yelled.

And the light bulb flashed! I went back to our lunch group and told them what I had just witnessed. "Look, I'm no expert, but have you ever considered buying bigger trays! I think that kid wouldn't have dropped his food, his dad would have had a better day, I'd have dessert, and we all would have spent more money . . . if we had bigger trays!"

Out came the Firehoses. "That tray is the industry standard." "We're getting them at a great price." "They're just the right size for our dishwashing machines." All very rational. Exactly what you'd expect them to say.

However, the general manager took me literally. "Let's try it," he said, "we've tried everything else." Within three months the bigger trays (and the bigger dishwashing machine), produced a $1.50 increase per person, per meal. That represented almost a half million dollars in increased revenue annually—approximately 50 times the cost of the change—and the restaurant went into the black for the first time. Seeing the situation as a beginner, I was able to come up with an *obvious* solution to what had been considered a complex, even mysterious, problem.

"WHY DO PEOPLE BUY OUR DRILLS?"

At a major power-tool company, drill sales weren't up to projections, and the marketing director had brought in consultants and managers from marketing, engineering, manufacturing, and sales to see if they could figure out why. Frustrated that the session wasn't getting anywhere, asked: "Why do you think people buy our drills?"

One consultant said it was the price. Others mentioned the company's reputation for quality and service, the packaging and advertising, the easy availability and good warranty. All good answers.

"Hold on! Wait a minute!" the marketing director interrupted. "I'm beginning to see the cause of our problem. We have forgotten what business we are in. The *real* reason people buy our drills is because—they—want—to—make—a—hole! I think we've gotten too fancy. We've got to stick to the basics and sell them a tool that makes holes."

When marketing started emphasizing how well the product drilled holes, sales increased 15 percent over a six-month period!

WELCOME VISITORS

There are many ways to encourage the fresh and open approach of a beginner.

Here are two easy, practical techniques for invoking a beginner's mind-set:

1. Pretend that you are a visitor from outer space. Take an "alien's" look at your situation. Ask basic, even naive questions like "What's that?" "What does it do?" "Why do you do it that way?"

2. Bring your mother or your eight-year-old along for the day and encourage them to snoop, eavesdrop, observe, and ask questions.

You'll be amazed how much these "visitors" can change your perception of the taken-for-granted world, because what is obvious to them has long since become hidden from you.

UW *says:*
Think like a beginner.

11

Strange Bedfellows Make Great Partners

The most useful attribute of the beginner's mind-set is the wondrous ability to cut through preconceived notions and taken-for-granted assumptions to find the simple, obvious, and creative. Approaching things fresh, like a child, the beginner sees things in new ways and avoids "trained incapacities," the blinders that come from doing the same thing in the same way you were trained to do them.

The Break-It Thinker has fewer biases and assumptions than those who play it by the old rules. Conventional habits often force us to look for the complex rather than the simple, the familiar rather than the new. But the Break-It Thinker turns this around and intuitively looks for the "anomalies," notices the exceptions to the rules, and is drawn towards the unique and innovative.

Conventional Wisdom has taught us to follow rules, making it tougher to discover the exceptions, which is where we find the breakthroughs. There are ways, however, that we can learn to see the world like a beginner. In this chapter we will discuss some Break-It Thinking strategies that will bring out the beginner in you, and free you to be more creative in solving problems and generating new ideas.

I've selected five *un*likely ways that you can look for likely solutions. Each will require that you break one or more "rules." And each has innumerable practical applications that will help you to see more clearly and be more creative, innovative, and successful.

THE CUSTOMER IS ALWAYS RIGHT . . . ESPECIALLY WHEN HE'S WRONG

The Conventional Wisdom for product design and marketing says pay attention to the customers. Learn as much as you can about their needs and wants and then design the product on the basis of information. The customer is then part of your R&D department . . . a step in the right direction.

But the customer can be crucial to your R&D in a totally different and often overlooked way. You can learn a great deal by watching how your customers "misuse and abuse" your product *after* they buy it. Major breakthroughs in new products and innovative product redesigns have come from watching the customer "trash" the original intent and use a product in a totally different way.

Where would millions of American households be, for example, had not someone noticed a neighborhood cat "visiting" an open bag of gravel manufactured to clean up oil and grease? That is how Kitty Litter was born. Other enterprising entrepreneurs noticed that people were using orange crates for storage containers, and copied them in sizes suitable for everything from audio tapes to record albums. Someone turned three-hole binders sideways, miniaturized them, and produced the Rolodex. The list is long and includes many of our most taken-for-granted objects around the house and the office.

The common denominator in all of these examples is that by paying attention to how consumers—and one cat—*actually use, misuse, and abuse* products, you'll have the world's largest R&D team—and an endless supply of ideas with which to work.

Hell's Angels R&D Team

You can make some terrific discoveries by paying attention to unlikely people and looking in unlikely places. When there was a dropoff in Harley-Davidson sales a few years ago, Vaughn Beals, Harley-Davidson CEO, took an unconventional step: He required all senior management staff to make cross-country trips on Harleys, go to biker rallies, and rub shoulders with typical—and atypical—Harley customers, including the Hell's Angels.

Willie G. Davidson, a grandson of the Harley-Davidson founder and vice president of styling, noticed that virtually every Harley at these rallies had been modified and customized. Being a true Break-It Thinker he saw the Angels and other bikers as his R&D team, adapted their best ideas, and incorporated them into later designs. Chopping the chassis, adding chrome here and painting flames there, sculpting gas tanks—all were ideas incorporated into later Harley designs![1]

Harley's wheelin' and stealin' paid off. They now account for 60 percent of the domestic motorcycle market and have had six consecutive profitable years.

Creative abuse

A tactic somewhat similar to Harley-Davidson's involves Candid Camera–like observations of how your product is *actually* used by the customer. You may have a wonderful product, created for one thing, but (like Kitty Litter) it may end up being used for an entirely different purpose.

Robert Milch, who founded Igene Biotechnology, for example, didn't find his "real" product until he understood—with a little unexpected help—that he was selling the right product to the right customers *for the wrong purpose*! He was fairly successful marketing converted whey to bakers as a substitute for nonfat dry milk. But his product, MacroMin, didn't really take off until *bakers told him* that they *also* "misused" it as a partial substitute for egg whites—at a fifth the cost. Bingo!

You can see creative customer "abuse" all the time in the world of fashion: women wearing "men's" shirts, and men sporting "women's" earrings, sport coats made out of heavily starched wallpaper, evening gowns patterned after lingerie. *House & Garden* recently noted that "in certain circles in the United States it is considered chic to use vintage Louis Vuitton steamer trunks as coffee tables, end tables, and television stands."[2]

Levi-Strauss listens and watches

Levi-Strauss has understood the importance of keeping their eye on the customer for some time:

- They noticed that customers were shrinking their jeans to get a tighter fit and just the right length. Levi made preshrunk sizes.

- Customers were taking their new jeans and driving cars over them, then dropping them into the washer and adding bleach . . . Levi-Strauss released stone-washed, prefaded jeans.

- Women were adding darts and pleats to men's jeans to get a better fit. Levi-Strauss introduced a line of women's sizes.

- Baby boomers well into their forties continued to demand jeans. Levi-Strauss produced a line with "a skosh more room" in the fanny and thighs.

- Levi-Strauss recently noticed that kids were wearing ripped jeans. Bingo! New product! . . . preripped jeans!

Watching customer "misuse" and "abuse," Levi-Strauss rolled with them and treated the users as their best R&D people.

Reebok 'robics

A while back, Reebok cofounder Paul Fireman noticed how people were modifying their running shoes and tennis shoes to use in aerobics class. He introduced a line of aerobic sneakers based on the best of his customers' innovations: ankle support, extra cushioning, and bright colors.

He also took note that many women were wearing running shoes to and from work and then changing into dress shoes. Seeking both comfort and style, "they were modifying, painting, and padding hi-top *men's* basketball shoes."[3] Fireman "stole" many of these modifications, and released a complete line of comfortable and colorful walkers. Taking the "misuses and abuses" of their product seriously, Reebok went from *$13 million in sales in 1983 to $1.4 billion in 1987.*

When wrong . . . is right!

The moral of the Harley-Davidson, Levi-Strauss, and Reebok stories is to pay attention to how the customer uses, abuses, or misuses your product. Below are some "abuses" I have been seeing lately:

Junior high school kids are wearing two socks of bright, contrasting color on each foot, the opposite color out. Sock manufacturers take note: what an opportunity to sell twice as many socks!

I'll bet that nearly as many hollow-core doors are used as desktops as they are for closets. I'm waiting for an office furniture supplier to take notice.

And Vuitton's descendants might as well start designing leather coffee tables and TV stands before some enterprising soul beats them to it.

Paying attention to customer abuses and misuses can keep millions of R&D and marketing researchers, as well as a never-ending parade of ideas, at your disposal.

STRANGE BEDFELLOWS MAKE GREAT PARTNERS

Conventional Wisdom preaches, "Keep your eye on the competition" and "Know thy enemy." This mind-set breeds the conformist "me-too-ism" discussed in chapter 8 and blinds us to many new possibilities.

"Incestuous" is how New York marketing consultant Carol Farmer refers to retailing. Everyone wants to know what the competition is up to. "Whatever is working for Benetton is being studied"—and copied. But "as long as its competitors keep playing catch-up, Benetton should have little to worry about."[4]

When watching and copying the competition, the best you can do is follow *their* lead, a strategy that automatically puts you in second place trying to catch up, at best gaining a small, short-term advantage.

Take a look around

UW *says: New ideas most often come from "outside" your field.*

Using a sports analogy, instead of watching how your competition is playing the game, observe a different sport and look for things that might be applicable to your team.

Smart businesses do the same thing. Try looking outside your field or industry. You may be pleasantly surprised at what good ideas (and friendships) come from the strangest bedfellows. You'll find that seemingly disparate ideas and strategies from other fields are applicable in your own. Break-It Thinkers are drawn to contrast and novelty, they practice juxtaposition, placing things side by side that would not usually be found together.

How does this work? Let's look at some recent examples.

The "Alice's Restaurant" bank

"Banks today face perhaps the biggest challenge because they were regulated for so long, they have no entrepreneurial legacy," Jack Wilborn, consultant to many banks and partner at Arthur Andersen & Co. recently told me.[5] Consequently, banking's ranks are filled with conservative, Type B personalities, people who wait for the customers to come to them. This was acceptable in the old days, but in this era of deregulation, when the competition is fierce, it is a strategy that no longer works. Banks need to be more innovative and creative than ever, while avoiding the irresponsible practices of many S&Ls. But that's easier said than done.

"The problem with banks is people who think we have to do things the way we always have," says Casey Mackenzie, executive vice president of First Nationwide Bank. Seeking to attract the volume and traffic found at discount stores, she got the mountain to come to Mohammed. McKenzie was instrumental in opening First Nationwide branches in 164 K Mart stores.[6]

Bank One's branch near Columbus, Ohio, is a financial center that, as *Fortune* magazine reported, "resembles Alice's Restaurant: you can get anything you want." Laid out like a shopping mall, complete with the inevitable rock music and neon signs, it has been designed by the company that does K Mart, WalMart, and Sears stores. To reach the teller's window located along the back wall, customers walk past minishops selling everything from real estate and travel services to discount stock brokering. The bank is a roaring success. After just two years of operation, it has more than 9,000 accounts and a whopping 35 percent share of local deposits.[7]

BANKS LEARN HOW TO USE THE "S" WORD

To most of the managers who had come up through the ranks of a major midwestern bank—part of the old generation in banking—selling was anathema. It was referred to as the "s" word, ranking it right up there with flashy fingernails and cheap perfume. With deregulation, all of that changed. The importance of creative selling and servicing has now hit the banking business with a capital *S*, and managers are scrambling to change their tactics. The old "s" word, *sales*, has moved out of the back alley, and into the hiring room.

But while the idea of selling seemed clear to these midwestern bankers, they were having a difficult time turning their understanding into action. Reading only the *Wall Street Journal* and the financial industry press, they only compared themselves to other banks.

Then they would try to beat the other banks, but shortly thereafter their competitors copied them. Consequently, most of their new products were only variations on the old themes and they never made the major breakthroughs that would put them—let alone *keep* them—ahead.

Noting the need for more aggressive selling and for changing old patterns, habits, and assumptions, we used some creative Break-It

Thinking and sent these managers right into the lion's den. I had them spend a week at the top local car dealerships to observe sales professionals in action—a kind of wisdom-by-exaggeration, an "odd coupling" if you ever did see one.

After their stint on the showroom floors they came away with a much better understanding of what selling was all about: how to find and attract customers, how to get them in the door, how to listen to what customers really want and meet their needs. For those who made it through the week—and some didn't—the experience was vital to gaining a full picture of what they could do to succeed in today's fierce world of modern banking. As a result, many changes were initiated. They even sold the car dealers on a program to get special rates for bank customers, proof to me that they had come full circle.

By taking their eye *off* the competition and looking at another industry, they were able to improve business, raise morale, and make their customers happy simultaneously.

Used-car lots meet the circus

Fred Ricart took his father's failing car business in Columbus, Ohio, from near doom in 1981 to being a $220-million-a-year company in less than seven years. The dealership sells nearly 25 times more cars than the average lot. His formula? Pure Break-It Thinking. He combined elements of amusement parks and the circus with used-car sales and fashioned his own unique car-buying experience.

- The showroom is called the "welcome center" and has *no* cars in it, just lounges and snacks and live music and greeters to direct you to the right area of his 66-acre lot where *you* can find the car *you* have in mind.

- His servicemen make house calls, often fixing problems *not* covered by the factory warranty, *free!*

- He runs goofy ads that include him singing, and his salespeople are infused with the motto, "Entertain people, and they spend money. . . . Most people come here because they trust me, and they want to have fun."[8]

What can a hospital learn from *The Love Boat*?

With increased competition from new types of health-care facilities, insurance reimbursement problems, and incredible changes in levels of care, hospitals are in a fierce struggle for survival. To keep their heads above water, many are adding new services and programs to bring in added revenue. Courses on aging, chemical dependency, sports medicine, nutrition, parenting, and fitness are making some hospitals into health universities.

But hospitals have a "public relations" problem. Ever know anyone who *liked* to go to a hospital? The "vibes" and atmosphere of most hospitals put people off.

To help a group of administrators from a large hospital chain understand the image problem, I made an unconventional suggestion: Experience a business totally dependent on "intensive care." I had each administrator spend a few days on a cruise ship, to learn about catering to people's every need.

I suggested they pay attention to everything—how they were welcomed, the way the cabin steward showed them to their room, how the tables were set and the food displayed. I told them to focus on the attitude and demeanor of the staff and on how they felt on the receiving end of another kind of "intensive care."

Eight managers went on separate, week-long cruises and returned with a combined list of over 100 improvements they wanted to make. "We've got to make people who come to us feel special," one manager said, "let them know we really care about them. We've been treating people as though they were lucky to be in our facilities. We've got to treat them as though we are happy to have them and it is a privilege to serve them."

Changes were made in the hospital decor, in the training of nurses and administrators, and in the printed information given to patients. The administrators adjusted hours, added incentives to the nursing staff (based on their experiences with their cabin stewards), and modified clothing codes for employees. They repainted the walls with more pleasing colors and had soft music in the waiting rooms. They even had a greeter to give information, began offering special gourmet meals, and put flowers in the halls. Within eighteen months, the environment had become totally different. As one manager said, they had "put 'hospitality' back in 'hospital.'" The changes worked out better than anyone expected as profitability increased by 15 percent.

2 + 1 = WATER

If you combined two spoonfuls of hydrogen and one of oxygen and mixed them up, you'd get something in the bowl that bears no resemblance to either: water. Combining the two seemingly disparate elements creates a totally new one. You can use a similar strategy to create a product or start a business.

Many of the success stories of the last decade are attributable to this type of synthesis: combining disparate trends, tastes, and tendencies to create new products or offer new services:

• Roy Speer and Lowell Paxson realized that (1) people like to shop, (2) people like to watch TV, and (3) people like to shop or watch TV when they damn well please. The answer: Home Shopping Network, Inc., a 24-hour-a-day TV shopping channel that grossed over $700 million in 1987.[9]

• Noticing the huge office products market ($67 billion in 1988), the skyrocketing growth of super discount stores like the Price Club (a membership program of The Price Co.), and the increase in the number of small businesses and entrepreneurial activity, Thomas Stemberg put them all together and opened "Staples," a super discount office supply store. *The New York Times* likened Staples to a Toys 'R' Us for small business people, adding that Staples, like all amalgams, "is a classic 'category killer.'"[10]

• As the "baby boomers" age, more and more are wearing glasses. And they want them to be chic and fashionable. And they don't want to wait to get them. So, who ya gonna call? Lens Crafters, the McDonald's of eyecare, a Jiffy Lube for lenses. By combining fashion with health-care needs, the desire for quick service, and a wide selection of styles, Lens Crafters has grown enormously in a short period of time.

• Noting the rising interest in gourmet food, the continuing demand for health food, the consumers' love of discount prices, and the travel boom, Joseph Coulombe "grafted" a store with a name and decor reminiscent of a South Seas odyssey, Trader Joe's. At Trader Joe's customers find a wide array of gourmet and health food staples—from Wolfgang Puck pizzas to no-cholesterol mayo to raw macadamia nuts—all at discount prices. Trader Joe's is now trading about $200 million a year at 30 stores.

• Jacqueline Clark, a 30-year-old business school student doing market research for a class assignment, noticed a phenomenon: the birthrate was sky high, and the number of working mothers of preschool children was skyrocketing, too. Against her adviser's cautions, she quit school to start a nanny referral service that connected well-screened and well-trained nannies with working parents. The response was incredible and the synergy led to other services. Soon she was offering Red Cross training to the nannies, compiling lists of college students willing to babysit, and offering "tutor-sitters" to help children with schoolwork in the late afternoon before their parents got home from work. She now has franchises in 30 locations.

• Perhaps most ingenious of all was Will Parish's hot combination of ideas. A former lawyer whose specialty was conservation and the environment, he was well aware of rising energy costs and diminishing fossil fuel resources, as well as the enormous problems associated with waste disposal. Parish was in India when he "ate a meal heated by flaming cow dung" and the light bulb flashed. Thus was formed National Energy Associates, which collects and burns 900 tons of "cow chips" a day and produces enough megawatts to light 20,000 American homes. Now, he say, "I combine doing well with doing good,"[11] and *Fortune* magazine has labeled him the prototypical "entre-manure."

There are hundreds of other examples of the power of making one and one equal one squared, such as Duds 'n' Suds, part rumpus room, part laundromat. The list of such enterprises goes on and on, but all are based on the same premise.

UW *says: Look for the "odd coupling," the strange bedfellows and the synergistic products and services. This will give you a decided edge.*

LOOKING IN UNLIKELY PLACES

UW *says, The Break-It Thinker is one who learns to expect the unexpected, savor those light bulbs when they appear, and act on them.*

The Break-It Thinker knows that this can happen anywhere at any time, in likely and unlikely places, at likely and unlikely times.

• One day, while on a business trip to college campuses promoting vacation trips, "nature called" Richard L. Weisman. "I remember staring at the back of a stall door and thinking, 'What a tremendous waste of space.'" Bathroom walls were spotless at best and filled with dull graffiti at worst. But "*Aha!*" thought the attentive Weisman, "I decided to fill up the walls by sticking my vacation fliers there." That was the seed of his $12 million-a-year company, Stallwords, Inc., which sells advertising space that turns bathrooms into billboards.

• If it's true that "one man's ceiling is another man's floor," as Paul Simon sang, then how come there are a zillion companies that will clean one man's floor and nobody cleaning the other man's ceiling? "*Aha!*" said Kaadah Schatten, who recognized this obvious need. Thus began Ceiling Doctor, Inc., whose proprietary cleaning techniques can save a customer up to 85 percent on ceiling tile replacement, the traditional method of "cleaning." Her franchises are in dozens of locations throughout the United States and Canada, and total revenues now exceed $5 million annually.[12]

• Jim Jenks liked surfing. Jim Jenks liked pizza. But what he didn't like was the flimsy trunks for surfing and the "blah" shorts that were available for going out to eat. One day, at a pizza joint in Encinitas, California, he looked down and said, "Look at this tablecloth. This tablecloth print would make a neat pair of trunks."[13] That was the day multi-million-dollar Ocean Pacific Sunwear was formed. Using wild colors and patterns, combined with rugged construction to handle surf conditions, Jenks devised "jams" and "baggies" suitable for his two great pleasures, surfing and pizza eating.

The new greening of America

As concern for the environment increases, a variety of innovative products are hitting the market. For example, Steve Sommers, the president of Alexander Fruit & Trading, was under pressure from his five children to be more "environmentally correct." Sommers has now developed a new way to cushion his shipments of ginger honey sauce and cabernet sauvignon: substituting popcorn for plastic foam pellets.

"It's naturally biodegradable . . . nothing goes to waste . . . and using this will make me feel a whole lot less guilty about how I send my goods."[14] It also makes good business sense too, as each bag of popcorn costs about $4 less than plastic.

Golfers have left millions of plastic tees strewn all over the world's golf courses for decades. To tackle this problem in an environmentally correct way, biodegradable, compressed, organic materials have been made into tees. In 1989, one company sold 300 million of them![15]

"HAPPY ACCIDENTS": WHEN THE BEST-LAID PLANS GO ASTRAY

Question: Cornflakes. The microwave. Post-it's. Walkman. Teflon. ScotchGard. Aspartame. Volcanized rubber. Rogaine. Kitty Litter. Ivory soap. Velcro. Rayon. Frozen food. Skateboards. What do they all have in common?

Answer: None of these common, now seemingly indispensable, products, was planned. All were "accidents," unexpected treasures found by observant individuals paying attention to what was right in front of their noses. While trying to get one thing right . . . the thing turned left! Undaunted, they followed the path to the port side.

"You have to be alert to serendipity," says S. Allen Heininger, corporate vice president at Monsanto.[16] Plans rarely work out as expected. Inevitably, while you are looking for one thing, something else turns up.

UW *says: Expect the unexpected.*

In science, serendipity has been crucial to many significant discoveries. The "invention" of the microwave (from finding melted chocolate in a scientist's pocket), of ScotchGuard (from spilling an industrial compound on shoes), and Aspartame artificial sweetener (from licking a finger after cleaning up some experimental fluid) are but a few of the widely known instances of looking for one thing and finding another.

In these examples, the "inventions" really discovered their inventors. They were there all the time, like a cosmic gift quietly waiting to be noticed.

Unexpected successes

"No other area offers richer opportunities for successful innovation," writes management guru Peter Drucker, "than unexpected successes. [They] are likely to open up the most rewarding and least risky of all innovative opportunities."[17] A perfect example occurred back in the fifties, when, for unexplained reasons, sales of appliances at fashion-conscious Bloomingdale's were going through the roof. Most major department stores at the time felt it was beneath their dignity to have appliance departments. So the Break-It Thinkers at Bloomie's exploited the trend and vaulted into the number two position in their market.

"The unexpected success is almost totally neglected," continues Drucker. "Worse, management tends to actively reject it," because it calls their planning, forecasting, and judgment into question and challenges their assumptions about the rules of the game."[18]

"Sometimes they stick to you." One crucial ingredient in capitalizing on unexpected success is having the curiosity to look for an open door, even when there is no door in the architectural blueprint. For example, for centuries hikers have had burrs in their socks. But it wasn't until 1948 that Swiss mountaineer and chemist George de Mestral got an idea; while peeling burrs from his socks he realized that nature had provided us with a natural fastener. He turned that observation into a marvelous product with a million uses, *Velcro* ("velvet hooks" in French), the world's first man-made burrs.[19]

Sometimes they hit you smack in the face. Sometimes an idea has to slap you in the face; it's the only way providence can get your undivided attention. "It was a beautiful Lake Michigan day—puffy white clouds, light breeze, not too hot," recalls 23-year-old Joanne Marlowe. "I was pretty depressed about my business, and decided to walk across the street to the beach, something I had never had time for. I laid out my towel. To pamper myself, I spent a lot of time putting suntan oil on. Just as I stretched out, a gust of wind picked up the towel and covered me in sand. I hit the roof.

"A friend said, 'Joanne, instead of getting angry, why don't you figure out a fix?' . . . So instead of relaxing on the beach, I spent the day coming up with prototypes in my mind."[20] Eight weeks later she introduced a line of *weighted beach towels* and sold 4.5 million dollars' worth of them, out of her house, within the first year!

BREAK-IT THINKER'S YELLOW PAGES

You can train your beginner's mind by playing a Break-It Thinker's game with your Yellow Pages. Turn to three different sections at random. Write down the first service or product from each page that hits you. Then spend some time trying to combine them.

On our first turn we got "pest control," "kitchen design," and "discount furniture." How about a pest-proof kitchen design at discount prices?

Our second turn was a little tougher. We got "copying," "carpets," and "concrete sawing." Louis Patler came up with carpet-like patterns imprinted onto concrete. How about a Persian driveway or a Navajo-style patio?

It's more than a great party game; it helps you exercise your Break-It Thinking muscles. You won't "hit" all the time and sometimes two out of three will work. But remember, you only need one good idea and a few small steps to begin turning them into action.

BASIC TOOLS FOR BREAK-IT THINKERS

Most people learn to do what is expected of them, but the truly successful have learned to do the unexpected, to follow the exceptions, to break the rules. To develop and enhance this ability here are some tools from the Break-It Thinker's toolbox:

- Watch how people use, misuse, and abuse your products and services. When the customers are doing it "wrong," they may be right.

- Look for strange bedfellows and odd couples, then use the idea.

- Follow the exceptions, break the rules!

But the most important tool is your attitude. How you approach everything you do will make the crucial difference. Your most important tool is your willingness to change.

UW *says:*
Make exceptions to the rule.

12

Take Risks . . . Not Chances

**If the earth had waited
for a precedent, it never would have
turned on its axis!**

—Maria Mitchell, astronomer (1818–89)

THE BIGGEST RISK IS NOT TO RISK

It should be clear by now that we must continually change our thinking and behavior. Taking risks is a necessity, there is no other choice. Playing it safe is dangerous and futile, and the notion of a comfort zone illusory. There is no safe harbor from this storm.

To survive, much less succeed, you must learn to be out in front of the wave. Wait too long and the wave will pass you by, leaving you struggling in the backwash, treading water. Break-It Thinkers know that riding a wave of change requires bold and daring action. They know that modern life guarantees nothing but change and that if we aren't taking risks and in constant motion, we will neither adapt, nor prosper. It is not surprising to find this advice coming consistently from top performers in many fields. The biggest risk is not to risk.

"Most people," says Lee Iacocca, "are looking for security, a nice safe prosperous future. And there's nothing wrong with that. It's called the American Dream." Yet their biggest nightmare is "the fear of screwing up—the fear of failure, of not achieving that American Dream. And fear of failure," he continues, "brings fear of taking risks . . . and you're never going to get what you want out of life without taking some risks. Remember, everything worthwhile carries the risk of failure."[1]

Tom Truax, hang-gliding champion, swears, "If you are supercautious all the time it's almost more dangerous because you're never pushing yourself and becoming proficient enough to handle the tougher situation when it comes up."[2]

Chuck House became a legend at Hewlett-Packard in part because he "defied" H-P chairman [David Packard] to "bootleg a product" in which he believed. "It's said that I took great risks," House said, "but I never saw it that way. To me, the risk was in NOT doing it."[3]

Ross Johnson, the CEO of RJR Nabisco, tells us that "the decisions we're making on new products right now are very gut-feel decisions with limited market research. You've got to take risks, and you've got to know that you can't bat a thousand."[4]

THE ONLY WAY TO PLAY

Peak performers know you can't succeed without taking risks. To make it to the top level at whatever you are doing demands boldness and daring. This is often obvious in sports.

"Trying to steal [the ball] at that point, I knew was a risk," said NBA Hall-of-Famer Walt Frazier, describing playing against another future Hall-of-Famer, Earl "the Pearl" Monroe, in an NBA championship game. "If I went for the ball and missed, Earl would go right by me for an easy basket. I may have known it but I didn't consider it. *If you're going to be the best, you have to take risks.* They didn't even seem like risks; they were the only way to play."[5]

Great artists are also committed to taking risks. Starting out on stage as a Shakespearean actor, Sir Laurence Olivier later became a major film star. Discussing the wide variety of roles he played (from Hamlet to spies and maniacal dentists), Olivier said he had to keep taking new roles and trying new material in order to continue learning and growing as an artist and an actor, and to prevent himself from growing stale.

Similarly, Timothy Hutton, making the reverse shift from Hollywood movies to the Broadway stage, likened this risk to "working without a safety net," but added, "You'll only be as good as you dare to be bad."[6]

The element of risk is one of the things that opera star Kiri Te Kanawa most enjoys about performing, and on some occasions she purposely goes out of her way to raise the emotional and artistic stakes. During a performance at Carnegie Hall, she sang a program half of which she'd never sung in front of an audience before. "The Conventional Wisdom would hold that was crazy," she said. "Supposedly you polish your material on the road and only do the tried and tested in the major halls. But I wanted the material to be fresh, with an edge of discovery in it. If a piece fails to go over, well, it's not the end of the world."[7]

"If you don't expose yourself to risk, you can't possibly learn anything," says Gifford Pinchot, author of the best-seller *Intrapreneuring*. "If you are 100 percent certain of the outcome of an action, what do you learn from taking that action? Not a thing. If you don't expose yourself to risk, you can't possibly learn anything. . . . If you risk nothing, you learn nothing."[8]

IF YOU DON'T MAKE WAVES, YOU'LL DROWN

Several years ago I was doing a program on risk taking for a major telecommunications organization. The news on the business page reported merger talks were under way and this was generating "downsizing" rumors among the employees.

Prior to the meeting, the CEO and general manager, aware of this, had discussed with me the importance of changing his organization's culture from one of "maintenance thinking" to one of risk taking and innovation. "With the industry changing as fast as it is and becoming more competitive every day, we won't survive unless we think more like entrepreneurs," the CEO said. "It's essential that everyone understands and acts on that. We want, heck, we *need*, risk takers in this organization. Even if the risks don't work out, at least we'll know these are the kinds of people that we need if this organization is to succeed. Those who are just putting in time and going through the motions are holding us back. We've got to weed them out."

Like many other large companies experiencing radical changes, this one had many employees still clinging to the "don't make waves" philosophy. They viewed risk taking as a threat. One middle manager said to me, "Take risks? Are you crazy? *I'm* not taking any chances. They'll be cutting like crazy after this merger. You do one thing wrong and you lose your head. I'm keeping my head down so no one notices me."

But those who kept a low profile became invisible—unknown and easy to cut. Indeed, nobody did notice the guy who kept his head down. That was his problem, and hiding with his chin on his chest, he was laid off. He didn't understand that taking risks is not only a success strategy, but a survival strategy as well.

UW *says: If you don't make waves, you'll drown.*

THE "TOP GUN" PRINCIPAL

"Good principals are like Tom Cruise in *Top Gun*—they are on the edge of what can be allowed out there. They're flying their jets upside-down," said Leonard Pellicer, director of a nationwide study of secondary schools and their principals. Pellicer's research indicated "a relationship between an individual school's success, as measured by students' eagerness to learn and staff satisfaction, and the *willingness of its principals to gamble on new ideas.*"

They also found that risk-taking principals were much less frustrated than peers who would "go through channels." The more successful principals "often bypassed red tape or acted pending approval. They simply refused to let bureaucracy strangle innovation." Break-It Thinking principals became red-tape busters who consistently acted first and got approval later. The study concludes with a finding that offers good advice for anyone in any field: "The more risks taken, the better the outcome."[9]

FRIGHTENED ENTERPRISE

There is an enormous amount of negative "loading" around the term *risk.* I often ask people for synonyms and they suggest: "dangerous," "scary," "failure," "foolish." It's no wonder that C. J. Silas, chairman and CEO of Phillips Petroleum, recently gave a speech to the Forum Club of Houston asking, "Where have all the risk takers gone?"

"We've exchanged free enterprise for frightened enterprise," Silas said. "In America the threshold of tolerable risk has now been set so low . . . that 'the morbid aversion to risk calls into question how Americans envision the destiny of their country.'. . . I believe unless American business leaders are more fully convinced that risk is a necessary—and beneficial—element of doing business, we'll continue to wander outside the gates of the global village. To think that we can create a business environment in a riskless vacuum is more than naive—it's bad business."[10]

NO "WILD AND CRAAAZY" GUYS

Why be surprised that there is an aversion to risk taking in our culture? The conventional stereotype of risk takers is captured by Steve Martin when he says he is a "wild and craaazy guy." Risk takers have a daredevil image. We commonly associate taking risks with leaping off buildings attached to bungie cords or scaling the World Trade Center using bathroom plungers as suction cups. When we think of risk takers we think of people like Julie Ridge swimming the 28.5 miles around Manhattan Island for five consecutive days, or Evel Knievel jumping over cars and canyons on speeding motorcycles. Conventional Wisdom conjures up images of putting your life on the line every time you take a risk.

The truth is light-years away from that disastrous image. The greatest risk takers, including the professionals, are *neither* wild *nor* crazy *nor* only guys. Quite the contrary. Great risk takers are actually quite sane and of both sexes.

"What seems clear," wrote *Time* magazine in a special feature on risk takers, "is that no adventurer, in his own mind, is a daredevil. Even the most extreme risk taker talks like an astronaut of safety gear, of weather carefully calculated, of redundant strengths to cushion failure."[11]

This doesn't mean they are boring bean counters; rather, they are very precise, particular, and prepared when they are going into a difficult situation. "What really protects them," *Time* goes on to say, "seems to be their abnormal awareness of how very much alive they are."

UW *says: Although risk takers thrive on risks, they don't take chances.*

RISKS, NOT CHANCES

Pioneering sports psychologist Dr. Bruce Ogilvie completed a research project a few years ago that sheds light on the important distinction between risks and chances. Ogilvie studied several career risk takers, including sky divers, Grand Prix drivers, and aerobatic pilots, and came to the conclusion that risk takers "are extremely cautious people."

What he discovered was that "an extraordinary amount of intelligence goes into preparing for their activities. They have analyzed every factor that can operate against them."[12] Such assiduous planning increases confidence, commitment, and self-control and helps conquer what would otherwise be debilitating fears.

IF I THOUGHT "IT WAS DANGEROUS . . ."

Research on stuntmen and -women shows that they take every imaginable precaution, carefully choreograph each stunt, and practice and train accordingly.

Terry Leonard, for example, has appeared in over 175 films and has been a stuntman more than half his life. Among the most durable and successful in the business, he says his formula is simple: to minimize the risks, "You've got to keep sharp, keep in tune, and practice, practice, practice. . . . You pyramid your knowledge, rig it this way, and figure out how it's going to work. . . ."[13]

Reinhold Messner, the first man to climb Everest solo and without oxygen, said that if he had thought it was dangerous to make that climb he wouldn't have done it. Messner wasn't some ordinary climber who took crazy risks just to prove something. Rather, he was one of the most skilled climbers in the world. Tracking his incredible career, one could see that his amazing feat on Everest was a natural next step based on where he had been and what he had done before.

FROM MOUNTAIN PEAKS TO BUSINESS PEAKS

Former world-class climber Yvon Chouinard has reached great peaks in the business world as well. Patagonia, the company he founded, is one of the hottest outdoor clothing companies around.

Because of his reputation as a mountain climber and his incredible success innovating new styles, materials, and equipment for the active person, many people consider him a daring risk taker. But pay attention to how Chouinard approached a recent risk: having his successful Baggie shorts manufactured in Panama where the production standards were of unknown quality. He approached this risk just as he approached any peak he scaled—by doing his homework. Prior to the agreement his managers examined the machinery to see if it was adequate and well maintained. They watched the local operators in action. Patagonia even had their own quality-control people in the factory during the initial run. This accomplished, Patagonia lowered costs—and prices—on their whole line of Baggie shorts.

KNOW YOUR LIMITS

Ken Casey is a successful entrepreneur who runs three Northern California companies: a real estate investment business, a property management group, and a CPA firm that specializes in taxation. Casey attributes his way of doing business to lessons he learned from risk-oriented sports.

Ken is a white-water rafter supreme, having made first descents on two of the most treacherous rivers in the world, the Franklin River in Tasmania, and the Bashkaus River in the Altai Mountains in south-central Siberia, as a member of a Russian-American team.

Before taking any new river, Casey told me, "We get the team together, we scout each part of it, we practice together." But there are other factors, too. The people he rafts with are also very experienced and most have been with him on previous expeditions. They make sure they have good backup, so that if something does happen there is a way out. They never go without support. "If some section is too tough, we do what the water does, we find a way around the obstacle."

Casey credits his success in and out of the white water to great preparation, and knowing himself and his limits. I asked him if he would ever take a river without scouting it first. "I may take risks, but I'm not crazy," he said. "Based on my experience, I have a real good idea of what I can and can't do, and what can and can't be done. And," he cautions, "I don't go beyond that. If I do, my confidence breaks down and I don't think clearly. That's when guys drown."

Whether he is investing in a new building or running a new river, "My philosophy is the same in business as in rafting: Take risks, but be prepared."

CAUTIOUS RISK TAKERS

Most of the successful risk takers I have met in business share philosophies similar to Chouinard's and Casey's. They take risks and make unconventional moves, but they don't do stupid things. They do their homework before acting. In fact, the most successful risk takers are usually precise, sober, realistic people.

UW *says: Risk takers live—or die—by three cardinal rules: Rule 1: Prepare. Rule 2: Prepare. Rule 3: Prepare!*

You may be surprised at the picture I am painting of the *cautious risk taker.* Yet I don't believe this term is an oxymoron. We view the feats of risk takers with awe and amazement because usually we see only the breakthrough, the final event, the actual stunt, the outcome. We have images of the little flag atop the big mountain, the begoggled swimmer crawling to shore, or the venture capitalist who turned $5,000 into $5 zillion in five weeks. We see the outcome first, not the preparation. We see the final destination, not the journey. We don't see the months or years of preparation that led up to that moment. Therefore we don't understand that the breakthrough was a carefully anticipated, natural next step.

BORN RISK TAKERS

Another common misconception is that risk takers are a special breed, a rarity. Wrong! The truth is, we are all born risk takers. How else do we learn to walk, talk, ride a bike, ski? You can't learn without taking risks. It's the way we have mastered everything. Growth and creativity come from trial *and* error.

Research shows that we learn more, and faster, in the first five years of our lives than we ever will subsequently. That's no accident. That's the period when we are taking the most risks, when we are exploring the unknown, the untried, and untested all day long. That's the prime time for making mistakes, then picking ourselves up, dusting ourselves off, and trying again, undaunted.

Risk taking is natural. In fact, it is unnatural *not* to take risks. Can you imagine a baby thinking, "I don't know if I should try to stand. I know I'll fall. I know it will hurt. Maybe I'll wait a few years until I'm bigger and stronger"? If that were the case we'd all end up on our hands and knees. Yet this is exactly what I see in the business world: scared people crawling from one quarter to the next.

Nobel laureate Albert Szent-Györgyi said the basic human instinct is to evolve, to keep growing and learning and progressing to the next level. The only way we can do that is continually to take on new challenges. To do otherwise is unnatural. To stop ourselves from taking risks goes against human nature, and the larger laws of Mother Nature. Life is a process of constant change and evolution. Complacency brings entropy and extinction. Worse yet, standing still stops us from experiencing the joy and excitement of exploring the unknown.

UW *says: Stand still and you'll never soar.*

THE NATURAL STEP IS THE NEXT STEP

The key to successful risk taking is to understand that the action you are taking should be the natural next step. One of the mistakes we make when confronting a risk, whether it is learning a new skill or starting a new project, is to focus on the end result.

I saw this frequently when taking skiers to a difficult slope. Going to the edge of the run they would look *all* the way down to the bottom. From where they were the hill looked too steep and too difficult and they backed away.

My instruction to them was to see if they could make just one turn. If they couldn't I assured them we would go to another run. This changed their focus. They were now seeking a natural first step, one they *could* do, (rather than looking at all they couldn't). Then I asked them to take that one turn and stop. I repeated the same instruction several times. After a few turns they were more confident and without any prodding would take off down the run.

The same approach can help you. When starting something new, always seek out the first step and make it one you are reasonably sure of accomplishing. This small-natural-next steps approach will build your confidence, increase your commitment, and, most importantly, get you moving.

Lots of little steps will enable you to reach your goals much faster and easier than you thought possible. Toyota uses this thinking in developing innovations. "While many other companies strive for dramatic breakthroughs, Toyota keeps doing lots of little things better and better. . . . One consultant calls Toyota's strategy 'rapid inch up': take enough tiny steps and pretty soon you outdistance the competition."

UW *says: Dream Big but take lots of small steps.*

"STICK OUT, DO IT DIFFERENTLY"

I can sing the praises of taking risks. I can tell you that risks are good for your health. I can remind you that they are exhilarating, that they are fun. But Break-It Thinkers are in the minority. In fact, most people begrudge taking risks, venturing out only when they "gotta." They have to force themselves to take even the smallest risk, and fight it all the way. If we feel forced to take risks, and look at them as a threat to our well-being, we will do so reluctantly, or as a last resort. Then we'll only give a halfhearted effort, which will practically ensure failure and reinforce our initially negative attitude about risk taking. It's no wonder that, as Phillips chairman Silas said, most people have "a morbid aversion to risk taking."

When we approach a risky situation with trepidation, expecting it to be painful, exhausting, and unpleasant, we overlook the incredible excitement of facing a challenge head-on. Whether kayaking a rapid or presenting to a client, for the Break-It Thinker there's a feeling of increased energy, the adrenaline flows, and awareness is heightened. You have a greater sense of aliveness. Life assumes a richer hue. IBM chairman John Akers says, "The people who are playing it totally safe are never going to have either the fun or the reward of the people who decide to take some risk, stick out, do it differently."[15]

Professional risk takers, those who earn money taking physical risks, talk repeatedly about the sense of heightened awareness, and the intense concentration and application of skills when they are taking risks. They know that at these times they experience more of themselves and draw on more of their innate abilities than at other times. Everything seems to dovetail during these moments.

Willy Unsoeld, part of the first American team to climb Everest, said that taking risks and challenging yourself throws you into a state of "total concentration," where every ounce of your attention is in the present moment. "There is no past, no future, only the present," he said. "You're not thinking about where you were or where you are going. You are totally focused on what you are doing now . . . The present seems to expand, things slow down, you seem to have more time, you see more, feel more, and know more. You are more connected to yourself, to others, to the environment. It's an exhilarating experience. You also tap into skills and strengths that enable you to go far beyond what you thought you were capable of doing."[18]

Americans today are increasingly seeking this experience through action-packed, adventure vacations—white-water rafting, mountain-biking, safaris, wilderness challenges, trekking in exotic places, skiing virgin slopes in deep powder. These adventures are invigorating and exciting. They renew us, they refresh us, and make us feel more fully alive. There is romance in exploring uncharted territory . . . but for many, it seems, only *on vacation, not* on the job.

Our lives have become bifurcated. We separate business and pleasure. The same people will return to work after spending two weeks confronting raging rapids and huge boulders and shrink before their boss or turn their backs on a new and challenging project. But to Break-It Thinkers work too is an adventure, one that is exhilarating, rejuvenating, and stimulating.

KING OF THE RISK TAKERS

You can get the same sense of exhilaration and adventure when you take a mental risk as you can by taking a physical one. Breaking a bad habit, giving a speech in public, trying a new way of marketing your product, replacing an old rule, starting a new business, or calling someone for a first date—all can be accomplished in a spirit of challenge and adventure.

"There is an exhilaration, a heightened feeling in crisis situations that is like nothing else," says my friend, David Miln Smith, who was on the cover of *Sports Illustrated* and was called "King of the Risk Takers" by the *Today Show*. In his book *The Healing Journey*, David chronicles some of the risks he has taken: kayaking 2,000 miles down the Nile; being the first person to swim the Straits of Gibraltar from Africa to Europe (against the current!); running a marathon in the Sahara; fighting bulls without a cape; and much more.

"We can learn a lot about taking risks at work and in our 'regular' life from taking physical risks," says Smith, who now finds himself using what he learned in physical challenges in pursuing "mental" feats which include his current work as a speaker and expert on risk.

Recently, Smith has embarked upon a new career. He is the producer and promoter of le Tour de San Francisco, a 50-kilometer bike tour that draws upward of 10,000 cyclists. David put up a substantial sum of his own money to get the project off the ground. To make this event a reality, he then had to get major sponsorships from such organizations as Peugeot, Vuarnet, American Airlines, Yoplait, and Sara Lee.

In the process he also had to take a lot of risks and challenge himself in ways he had never done before. Like a salesman he had to make cold calls to big corporations to get them to underwrite the event. He then had to find an insurance company, do his own p.r. and lobbying, and work with the local police and mayor's office to get permission to hold the event. To develop public interest in the event he had to organize and implement a marketing campaign.

"The type of risks I am taking now are different," Smith told me. "But the feeling is the same. Whether putting myself on the line physically or mentally there's that same feeling of excitement. There's a purity of purpose which enables me to focus totally on what I'm doing to the exclusion of everything else. At these times I find more of myself and am able to pull off things that I never thought I could. The physical risks were great training for producing the Tour. The same qualities that helped me to be successful in the wilderness helped me to be successful in business."

ENJOYING THE OCCUPATIONAL HAZARDS

The feeling of heightened awareness and the balance of anxiety and excitement is endemic to risk taking of all kinds. Erik Brown, a "million-dollar roundtable" insurance salesman, once told me he loves cold calling, prospecting for new clients, something most salespeople hate. He relishes the intensity of sitting across from someone he has never met and having to react quickly to who they are and what they are saying. "That first call is incredibly exciting. You don't know what will happen. It's like being at the starting line or going on a first date. You can feel the adrenaline pumping and you are totally focused. It's a great feeling. Lots of people don't like cold calling, but I wouldn't do without it."

When I give speeches, I try something new each time—a new story, a new exercise, a new joke or anecdote. For example, in a talk to 2,000 people, I had them get up and play a game. I knew there was a danger that the group was too large and I would lose their attention, but I also felt excited at the prospect that it could be sensational. I was scared, but I tried it and it worked. I learned how to adapt an exercise for 200 to an audience 10 times the size and won a standing ovation for my effort!

Doing something new at each talk prevents me from becoming complacent. I'm much more present when I'm trying something new. And these little risks keep me improving and on my creative edge.

DEATH WISH VERSUS LIFE WISH

For many people the stakes in taking risks are treated like a life or death situation. And they are right—risk taking is a matter of life or death—but for a different reason than you might think. Let me explain.

At a program I gave for psychiatrists, physicians, and surgeons, one session was devoted to risk taking. I asked these health professionals if there were any mental or physical effects associated with taking risks. Unanimously they described why risk taking is good for your physical *and* mental health.

"*Not* taking risks is what takes a toll on people," one physician said. His comments were corroborated by the 300 or so in the audience. "I see it especially in people over forty. I can tell just by looking at them when I walk into the examination room. They droop. In an instant I know their story. They are burned out, not liking what they are doing, but feeling trapped. No choices, no way out. They are afraid it's too late to start over or try something else. Consequently," he said, "they show signs of aging much sooner and much faster. You can see it in the way they walk. They slump, move more slowly, have less color in their cheeks—there's just less energy left in them."

Although quick to qualify their opinions by saying their comments were based on observation, not research, the psychiatrists agreed that people who didn't take risks seemed more depressed, more likely to overeat or overdrink, and had more stress- and/or depression-related maladies than other patients. In contrast, those who were more adventurous were generally healthier and had more energy, more vitality, spring in their step, and had a more positive outlook. Risk taking is good medicine for your mind and body. Playing it safe can be hazardous to your health. I don't know if risk taking will lengthen your years, but taking risks will enable you to live a more vital, rewarding, and fulfilling life.

EATING SOME SAND EVERY DAY

Break-It Thinkers keep their eyes and minds open for new opportunities to grow, learn, and challenge themselves. It's like what the surfers do: They keep watching the "outside" horizon for the next big set of waves, because great waves make for great rides. Then, *before* the wave is upon them, they start paddling out to meet it. Sure they *might* wipe out. Sure, they *might* eat some sand. But there's also the chance that they'll catch an incredible wave and ride it all the way to the beach. Break-It Thinkers are continually on the lookout for a big wave. They *want* it, and rather than waiting for it to come to them, they head out to meet it. As we saw in chapter 1, we can learn a great deal from the avid surfer.

Taking risks and continually challenging yourself will keep you ahead of the waves of change in your own life. You will experience more learning, more growth, and more joy. To the Break-It Thinker, the fact that there's no guarantee makes it all the more exciting. To the Break-It Thinker, risk is the breakfast of champions.

So take risks, not rests. Risk taking is fun, it will rejuvenate you and keep you more healthy and vital, physically and mentally. And remember where there's no dare, there's no flair. Living is risking.

UW *says:*
The biggest risk is not to risk,
we are all born risk takers.

13

Fear Tells Lies . . . Break the Cycle

One of the biggest inhibitors preventing us from taking risks and confronting the many challenges facing us is fear. Fear keeps us from turning our innovative ideas into action, from following our dreams, from performing well under pressure. We're afraid we won't accomplish our goals or "make it to the top." We worry about missing a deadline, a flight, or a dinner date. We fear what might happen at an important meeting and we worry about arriving late to meetings that never start on time.

LEARN TO THINK BEYOND THE FEAR

Fear prevents us from thinking clearly and creatively and causes most of the stress we experience. It is the greatest hindrance to successful risk taking and to performing our best under pressure. To keep ahead of change and to successfully confront the many challenges facing us, we need to learn how to overcome this insidious obstacle.

The good news about fear is that we have plenty of company. We all fear failing. Before taking a risk or tackling a challenging situation, *everyone* is afraid. Nobody lives without fear. In fact, if you tell me you have no fears, I will assume one of two things: Either you are playing it much too safe and not taking any risks, or you are totally out of touch with your feelings.

FEAR FRIGHTENS EVEN THE BEST OF US

Even the greatest performers are afraid before going out onto the stage, the court, or to the conference table. Helen Hayes says she used to go "stone-deaf" on opening nights. Ann Miller would get dizzy and nauseated. Dame Margot Fonteyn has said she felt so much fear before dancing *Swan Lake* in Moscow that she felt clumsy, awkward, and nearly immobilized. Gloria Steinem recounted that the idea of speaking to a group, much less a big audience, was enough to make her heart pound and her mouth go dry. Even Winston Churchill used to say he felt as though there was a block of ice in his stomach every time he was to address Parliament.

In our culture, the tendency—especially for men—is not to acknowledge fear. Being afraid is not "macho." Yet many peak performers have readily admitted to "stage fright." Bill Russell, one of the greatest basketball players ever, used to throw up before most games. Edwin Moses, Olympic gold medalist and former world-record holder in the 400-meter hurdles, who went *years* without a defeat, says that each time he races, "It feels like I'm being led to my execution."

Fear is a common experience even with the "swashbuckler" types who always look cool. Dennis Eckersley, the Oakland A's All-Star relief pitcher, generally considered one of the best "closers" in baseball, says that every time he goes out to the mound in the late innings, when the ball game is in the balance, he is scared. "At the All-Star game, I sat down with Jeff Reardon [of the Twins]. He's been a great closer for years, and he always looks so cool out there. The first thing Reardon said was that he's a basket case, too. God, was I glad to hear that. I'm scared . . . every time I go out there."[1]

FEAR IS NATURAL

Fear is normal. It's the *appropriate* response in challenging situations, when you are doing something new and unprecedented. It's important to understand that, before taking any kind of risk—prospecting for new clients, talking to an angry customer or employee, presenting a new idea at a conference, speaking up at a meeting, or asking for an order, a raise . . . or a date—*you should expect to be afraid.*

In fact, fear is like a weathervane that indicates that you *are* doing something new, that you *are* changing, that you *are* not being too cautious or complacent. Break-It Thinkers know that fear will be a constant companion throughout their lives. They not only learn to live with it but to thrive on it.

"I've always felt that if you're not afraid, then you're not doing anything very interesting," says Bruce Engel, CEO of WTD Industries Inc., fifth-largest lumber producer in the country. With $3,000 of his own money and assets of less than $300,000, Engel bought a dilapidated lumber mill in the middle of a recession. Five years later he had 24 mills and a personal worth in excess of $80 million. "If you're really trying and aspiring," he says, "fear is right there with you all the time."[2]

GOING OVER THE WALL

"Heroes and cowards feel exactly the same fear," said Cus D'Amato, the legendary trainer of many boxing champions, including Floyd Patterson and Mike Tyson. But like all champions, D'Amato says, "Heroes just react to fear differently."

Fear is like a wall that limits your view and creates boundaries to your growth and creativity. Heroes, peak performers, and Break-It Thinkers know that the breakthroughs in their own creativity, learning, and growth lie beyond the wall. Top performers get to the top by taking on the things they are afraid of. The rest of us either deny our fears or try to avoid the things we are afraid of, which doesn't work. Sooner or later you will bump into it again on another project, in another job, another relationship, another place.

To get over the wall of fear, first you have to be willing to acknowledge it. Experience will show that when you look at fear directly, a way over the wall will become obvious. You may find a "ladder" or see a "door" or "window" that was hidden to you when you were too scared to look. By confronting your fears, the wall will never be quite as big or intimidating again.

Break-It Thinkers understand that there is no choice but to confront fear and turn anxiety into excitement and action. "You gain strength, courage, and confidence by every experience in which you really stop to look fear in the face," Eleanor Roosevelt once said.[3] Conversely, if you run from fear, if you deny its existence, it will chase you, track you down, and grow in size with each step.

LOOKING THE MONSTER IN THE EYE

A Southwest American Indian tribe relates the following story to teach its children the importance of facing their fears and looking them in the eye.

Fear is like a 60-foot two-headed snake as big around as a ponderosa pine. Avoid it and the snake grows larger and comes closer, rearing its huge ugly head, ready to strike. But if you look the snake in the eye, it sees its own reflection, gets scared, and shrinks away.

In the balance of this chapter (and in the next chapter as well) I will discuss ways to look the monster in the eye and turn anxiety into anticipation, excitement, and positive action. Having fear as an *ally* will enable you to take risks more successfully and perform at peak levels under pressure. To start, let's look at the fear cycle.

THE FEAR CYCLE

One of the reasons fear is so insidious is that it feeds on itself. Fear creates a vicious cycle which is self-fulfilling, self-perpetuating, and self-reinforcing. Once under way, it gathers its own head of steam, like a snowball rolling down hill.

Understanding the Fear Cycle is the first step in breaking it. In the following pages, we'll examine each link in the chain of fear in order to understand it better.

Link 1—The Doomsday Syndrome:
Fear exaggerates "imagined consequences"

The Fear Cycle begins with the imagination running wild, making everything seem worse than it is and magnifying the possible consequences of failing until they expand to horrible and catastrophic dimensions.

When you are caught in the Fear Cycle, doomsday seems to lurk just beyond every meeting for which you are late, every sale you might not make, every deadline you might miss. Worse still, it is not only those specific things (the meeting, the sale, the deadline) that are on the line, it is *you, your* pride and *your* self-esteem. Fear eats confidence and self-esteem for breakfast.

One of the most common fears people have is the fear of speaking in public. In fact, one fellow quipped that he fears speaking in public more than death! The Fear Cycle starts when speakers begin worrying: They fear not having enough time or not being able to fill the time allotted. They're afraid they'll bore the audience, or forget an important point. They are afraid people will walk out or, worse yet, fall asleep. When you are caught in the Fear Cycle, the imagined consequences become horrific: I'll be fired; I'll never work again; I'll be the laughing stock of the industry; my life will fall apart. The Doomsday Syndrome has taken over.

Athletes can scare themselves into paralysis by imagining the worst. As part of my Inner Skiing programs I used to take intermediate skiers to an expert slope, but one I knew they could handle. En route to the hill they would see the black diamond sign that designates an "expert" slope. The result was instantaneous. Some people panicked just *seeing* the sign. "Black diamond equals broken bones!" or, as one person put it, "Black diamond! Black means death and that's what's going to happen to me if I go down there. Forget it!" By changing their focus to small turns and fundamentals I could coach them down the mountain.

The same strategy applies in business too. Recently I talked to a salesman who was in a panic at the thought of not making his monthly quota. I watched him begin the Fear Cycle right in front of my eyes. "If I don't set up some appointments today and open up some new accounts, I won't make my target," he said desperately. "If I don't make quota I won't make my monthly draw, and if that happened I could get fired and it's a tough market right now, it might be a while before I could get another good job. In the meantime I got payments to make, my car, my house, my kids in school . . ." By the time he was done reciting his doomsday scenario he had himself on Skid Row drinking cheap wine out of a paper bag!

When I had him look at each "leap" he had made he could see how his fears had exaggerated everything out of proportion.

Link 2—The Uh-oh's:
Fear distorts perception (and you see what you believe)

Having exaggerated the imagined consequences, it is a small step to also exaggerate the perceived difficulty of a situation. Suddenly everything is more difficult and urgent than it really is. Time seems to shrink to nothing and you "know" that your task will take an eternity to finish.

To scared speakers, the audience appears hostile and unfriendly, like opening-night critics waiting to pounce. Looking out at the group, they "see" Darth Vader, Jack the Ripper, and the Wicked Witch of the West glowering in the front row.

To the golfer who is afraid of missing a putt, the hole looks the size of a quarter; to the tennis player the server's box shrinks in direct proportion to the amount of pressure the server feels. The frightened skier sees the rocks, not the deep powder, the scared surfer sees the coral, not the waves, the scared speaker only sees the person with the frown or someone looking at her watch, never noticing that the rest of the audience is interested.

The same is true at work. Molehills appear mountainous. You walk into your office worried about meeting a deadline, and the pile of papers on your desk resembles the Matterhorn. Four phone messages to return seem like 40. Writing a simple sales report or a recommendation to your boss seems like writing the Great American Novel. Making the deadline for the new brochure appears about as likely as walking on water. The anxious salesperson sees the client as Godzilla in a three-piece suit.

Fear also distorts perceptions by drawing your attention to what you fear the most. Everywhere you look you see imagined obstacles that will make your job harder.

Link 3—Thump, thump thump: The physical response

Fear is sneaky. Often you are not even aware of it; consequently, you may not "see" how your mind is exaggerating, making everything seem more difficult and catastrophic than it is. And you may not notice how your perceptions have changed. Yet if you *listen to your body,* your physical responses will often give you the first evidence that fear is affecting you. Your heart may pound so loudly you're sure your old college roommate vacationing in Guam can hear it. Your mind leaps from one thought to another like a ball in a championship Ping-Pong match. Your palms feel like the Okefenokee Swamp, while your mouth is as dry as the Sahara. The intensity of these symptoms indicates how caught up in the Fear Cycle you are.

Fear also plays dirty tricks. A scared speaker's larynx tightens, making their voice come out about three octaves higher than normal. A frightened salesperson will be all thumbs and drop a case of samples on the client's toes. A friend told me, when describing her first professional golfing match, at the onset of fear she had to pry her fingers off the club.

Link 4—The fear response: Freeze or frenzy

The two most typical responses to fear are to freeze or panic, to slow down or speed up, overreact or underreact, jam on the brakes or floor it. Fear stops us dead in our tracks or gets us running like hell. Each of those exaggerated responses sabotages innovative thinking and effective action.

In the "freeze" mode you procrastinate and avoid what seems too frightening or uncertain, reverting to "busy work" instead. I see it everywhere: the scared surfer waxing his board all day, watching the big waves roll in but never getting into the water, the petrified teenager pacing by the phone unable to call for the first date, the executive who puts off making a return call to an irate customer by cleaning his desk.

The "panic" mode is the opposite: You get the Gotta's and speed up. With the Gotta's (see chapter 5), you don't communicate well and can't concentrate or think clearly. Your mind darts like a hyperactive hummingbird, and you act without thinking. Actions taken at these times are not well thought out and often result in your falling on your face or running at top speed . . . in the wrong direction.

Link 5—Thumbs down: Your (worst) expectations are fulfilled

The result of freezing or panicking is a performance that is below your ability. Not surprisingly, in fear's grip your performance matches your distorted expectations.

Desperate to meet a deadline you either write in a hurry and don't take time to think clearly or creatively, or you stare at the blank page, sure that you'll never get it right. Of course, when you are in a hurry you make more mistakes and have to do it over again.

The fear has become self-fulfilling. The skier who is afraid of falling holds back, leans up the hill, and falls. The speaker worried about not convincing the audience . . . doesn't. As a result, you think you really must be a lousy skier or a poor speaker . . . *and now you have concrete evidence to prove it.* The cycle is complete.

And next time

Since humans learn from every situation, what we learn from such experiences is that indeed our fear was well founded. Once our fear has been "confirmed," it becomes "proof" and self-incrimination begins.

The next time you are in a similar position the most recent experience is the freshest. The skier vividly remembers the fall and tightens up on the next run. The speaker remembers the poor speech and worries even more about the one coming up. The cycle continues.

The tragic part is that when you are afraid your performance is not reflective of your ability or skills. Poor performance isn't due to a lack of knowledge or skill; it's because fear took control.

Here is a visual representation of the Fear Cycle using the example of the frightened public speaker.

The Fear Cycle
LINK I:
Imagined Consequences

"I'll look stupid, be boring, never get another job."

"I'll lose my credibility."

LINK V   **LINK II**
Worse Expectations Fulfilled   **Fear Distorts Perception**

"I was right. I am a lousy   "Audience looks like opening
speaker."   night critics."

LINK IV   **LINK III**
Freeze or Frenzy   **The Physical Response**

Talk too fast   Heart Pounding

Forget key points   Sweating

Stumble, mumble, bumble   Eyes darting

                                  Looking at floor

BREAKING THE FEAR CYCLE

The Fear Cycle can be broken at any point. But to do so, to *re*cycle the energy in a positive way requires using Break-It Thinking at each link in the chain.

Apply the diagram to your own life. Take a look at the following diagram and imagine a challenging situation in which the Fear Cycle applies: taking a risk you have been avoiding, starting a new project, telling someone you love them, starting a new job or business, quitting your job—you name it. Then fill in each part of the cycle. What are your imagined consequences? What are your physical symptoms?

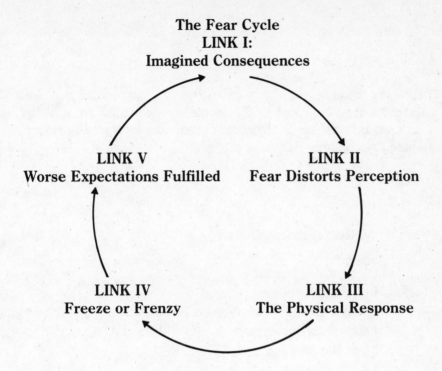

The Fear Cycle
LINK I:
Imagined Consequences

LINK V
Worse Expectations Fulfilled

LINK II
Fear Distorts Perception

LINK IV
Freeze or Frenzy

LINK III
The Physical Response

The worst-case scenario test

The first step in breaking a Fear Cycle is to do a worst-case scenario test of your imagined consequences. Look at the challenge you are confronting, or the risk you are contemplating, and ask yourself, "What is the worst thing that could possibly happen?"

I have worked with some of the world's biggest risk takers in sports and business, and almost without exception they start each new project or venture by rehearsing a worst-case scenario. They all scrupulously investigate the worst imaginable outcome to determine the best possible strategy to use.

Make a worry list

To prepare for any eventually, you must worry about *everything*. Make a *worry list* of all the "what if's," even the ones you think are unlikely to happen. Be creative; the more far-ranging your worry list the more prepared you will be. Here's an example:

What if . . .

   . . . the flight is canceled?
   . . . the boss (or client) says no?
   . . . the new idea bombs?
   . . . I give a lousy presentation?
   . . . he says, "Not tonight, I have a headache"?
   . . . I don't make my quota?
   . . . I lose this job?
   . . . I don't make this deadline?
   . . . (fill in a few of your own)

Change worry to anticipation

The second step is to *change the worries on your list to anticipation*. This is the step that takes you from inertia to action. It changes the "what if" to an "if, then." It looks like this:

Change "What if the worst happens?" to "If the worst does happen, then I will. . . ."

Change "What if the flight is canceled?" to "If it is canceled I will. . . ." Change "What if the boss says no to my recommendation" to "If she says no, then I will. . . ." Change "What if I lose this job?" to "If I do, then I will . . ."

Changing worry into anticipation makes you better prepared for anything that might occur. Going from "What if?" to "If . . . then . . ."

is empowering, putting you into a *can do* state of mind. It moves you from anxiety, negativity, and high stress to a state of positive anticipation, readiness, and confidence. Below are two techniques for turning anxiety into anticipation that enable you to feel more positive in even the most difficult situations:

Speculating. John F. Kennedy was great at this. He was the first President to have press conferences routinely televised, which was pretty gutsy, since many members of the press were less than friendly, and there were some very hot issues like the Vietnam War, civil rights, Krushchev, and Cuba. "Before every presidential news conference, Kennedy and a half dozen of us would sit down and go over every possible question that he might be asked," reported Dean Rusk, Kennedy's secretary of state. "When he went to a news conference, he had been briefed to the gills. So he almost never got surprise questions."[4]

Walking a mile in their shoes. Another way to turn worry into anticipation is by role-playing: Put yourself in another person's place and imagine what he or she would do. One CEO told me that before a stockholders meeting he goes down to the auditorium and sits in several different seats. "I imagine myself as a person who will be sitting there, and what I would be feeling, thinking and wanting if I were them. What questions would I have? What would be my concerns? I then figure out how best to respond. I prepare for all important meetings by trying to fully understand the concerns of everyone there."

On AMEX Life Assurance's Pioneer Team, staff often hold meetings with a chair in the middle of the room to remind them to keep the customer at the center of their thinking. They take turns sitting in the special place and role-play customers' responses, needs, and concerns.

Anticipation to action—Find the "can-do"

After anticipating all possible scenarios, it's important to get into action. Positive action often defuses fear. There is always *something* you can do to improve a situation and prevent the worst case from happening.

For instance, I was in a car racing to a meeting recently when the parkway turned into a parking lot. Rather than be frantic, pound the horn, and end up in the panic zone, I used some Break-It Thinking. Realizing that I couldn't do anything about the traffic, I focused on what I could do. I reviewed my notes, visualized all the people in the meeting, thought about their agendas, and anticipated any and all questions they may have.

I did arrive at the meeting late (by about ten minutes), but I was calm and composed. Another speaker who was also caught in the same jam arrived at the meeting hassled and out of breath.

When things seem out of control, Break-It Thinkers always find something they *can do* to turn it around. You can't control a situation but you can control how you respond to it.

". . . there'd be a lot more dead people around"

One of the most positive things about confronting your fear and doing a worst-case check is that *the reality of the situation is almost never as bad as fear makes it seem.* The perceived risk is always greater than the actual one. The chances of the worst case coming to fruition are usually much less than you think. Dean Smith, the great basketball coach at the University of North Carolina, once said that "if all the things that we act as if [they] were life and death were really life and death, there'd be a lot more dead people around."

Quite unexpectedly, I had experienced this in 1989. I was going to be the keynote speaker at three national conventions, all taking place October 18–20. The dates had been planned at least six months in advance. Then on the seventeenth the earthquake hit San Francisco. So much for planning! All the airports were closed, making it impossible to travel. The phones were also out, so I couldn't even call anyone.

My first speech was due to begin a nine the next morning in Phoenix. Fear started creating "doomsday" scenarios in my mind: "My agents will think I'm unreliable and won't trust me"; "The word will get out"; "My career will go down the tubes. . . ."

When I finally reached my agent, at about 1:00 A.M., not only was he very understanding, but he also had already begun planning for the eventuality that I would be unable to get there. When I called the client the next day, he was actually more worried about my welfare than about their meeting and assured me not to worry. They even hired me for the following year, adding "Earthquake permitting!"

I have seen the same thing happen over and over again. The reality of the situation is almost always less catastrophic than a fear-driven mind makes it seem.

NOT DOING VERSUS DOING

Sometimes fear immobilizes us, seducing us into "not doing" what we know we should be *doing*. At a training program for district sales managers for a major computer company, a manager volunteered to talk about the biggest challenge she was facing, one she was dreading. Like many managers she admitted that it was difficult for her to handle "problem" people and to confront negative situations. She was currently anxious about telling one of her salespeople that he wasn't cutting it. "I keep putting it off, hoping the situation will somehow get better," she said. "But it's not. In fact, the more I put it off, the worse things are getting and the harder it is to confront him."

A worst-case scenario check helped her realize that what *was* happening was far worse than the worst case that *could* happen if she confronted him. She immediately felt more comfortable about facing the situation head-on.

A few days later she called me. "I did it! I talked to him. And, you know what? He was actually relieved! Can you imagine that? He knew he wasn't performing well and had wanted to talk to me, too, but was feeling guilty, so he kept putting it off," she said. "All my anguish wasn't necessary." As they talked it through, he told her that he was burned out on selling, but still loved the company. As a result she was able to get him out of sales and into human resources, which, it turns out, was where he always wanted to be.

At our next meeting she was bubbling. "I tell you, it was so much easier than I thought it would be. I've got three or four other things I've been avoiding. I can't wait to tackle them. I'm on a roll." As a result her management style changed and for the next six months her district led the region in sales.

AND WHAT IF THE WORST *DOES* HAPPEN?

No matter how well you prepare, no matter how many reality checks you do, sometimes the worst *does* happen and your fears *do* materialize. What happens then?

My wife, Marilyn, is very courageous about taking risks mentally and socially. But like many women who were discouraged from playing sports when they were young, she is cautious about taking physical risks.

A number of years ago she decided to face her fears and signed the family up on a white-water rafting trip down the Salmon River. I don't think she loosened her jaw the entire trip. We kidded her that she singled-handedly had changed white water rafting to white-knuckle rafting. But she did it, was proud she had faced it, and loved it. She has since done several more increasingly challenging river trips.

Last year I kayaked a river while Marilyn rafted nearby. Going through huge rapids in my flimsy little craft was one of the most exciting things I have ever done. Marilyn was interested but was also petrified of capsizing.

Well, to make a long story short, she decided to run a rapid with me in a double kayak. Within minutes we got too close to a rock and pitched over. Her worst fear was realized as we went sailing (sans boat) down the rapidly moving water.

Later, after getting back into the raft, she bragged that she hadn't lost her paddle and said, "That wasn't as bad as I thought it would be"—and started laughing with sheer joy.

That experience, in which her fears *were* realized, was a break-through and her Fear Cycle changed to a Success Cycle. She has since become quite an adventurer, regularly riding on difficult mountain bike trails and ocean kayaking. What Marilyn found out was that even when your fears *do* come true, they are usually not as bad as you had imagined, and can lead to new levels of confidence.

HAVING THE MONSTER IN YOUR CORNER

When you are afraid you either put off taking risks and new challenges that are essential, or if you do take them you don't perform up to your ability. Great teachers, coaches, and leaders know that a performer who does not confront fear won't be a peak performer. Left unchallenged, fear will inhibit creativity, clarity of mind and purpose, and self-control.

Having the courage to confront your fears, to look the monster in the eye and break the vicious Fear Cycle, is critical. With the release of fear working for you, you'll have more energy, think more clearly, and be more in control. You'll then have turned fear's vicious cycle into a high-energy vital cycle.

Remember:

- Fear is natural. If you have no fear you're playing too safe.

- Fear tells lies. It distorts, exaggerates, and magnifies, making everything seem worse than it is.

- Focus on what you can do—not what you can't.

- The worst is never as bad as fear makes it seem.

- Turn anxiety into anticipation. Change "What if?" to "If . . . then."

A word of caution. No one beats fear all the time. But practicing the techniques in this chapter and the next will decrease the likelihood that you will get trapped in a Fear Cycle. You'll be able to think more clearly and creatively under pressure and feel more confident and committed.

UW *says:*
Fear tells lies . . . look beyond it.

14

Mistakes Are
a Good Investment

> If you want to succeed,
> double your failure rate.
>
> —Tom Watson, Jr., IBM

"TO ERR IS HUMAN"

No matter how much you anticipate, do your homework, and prepare, prepare, prepare, prepare, one thing is certain: When you are taking risks, learning a new skill, trying something new, entering a new situation, developing a new idea, testing creative solutions, or challenging yourself in any situation . . . *you will make mistakes!*

Nobody learns to walk without falling. Nobody learns to ski without eating some snow. No one learns to surf without a few wipeouts. No writer, salesperson, or senator escapes rejection. No one bats a thousand if they are continually challenging themselves to learn and grow, and be more creative and innovative.

Charles Lynch, chairman of DHL Corp. (a former nationally ranked college tennis player and a top salesman) told me that when he interviewed prospective salespeople he would begin by asking them about the accounts they had *lost.* "When a salesman tells me he's never lost an account I think either he's lying, or he's never played in the big leagues. When you are working against top competition you will lose accounts, just as when you are playing tennis against the best you will lose matches. Losing is part of winning."

TRIAL *AND* ERROR

Lynch is employing good Break-It Thinking. Every Break-It Thinker knows that learning is a combination of trial *and* error, not trial without error. Mathematicians understand that there are "probabilities" and margins of error. And certainly scientists know, as Chaparral Steel's president, Gordon Forward, has said, that scientific experiments are "designed for mistakes."

"A decision is a judgment, it is a choice between alternatives," writes Peter Drucker. "It is rarely a choice between right or wrong. It is at best a choice between "almost right" and "probably wrong."[1] In either scenario a margin for error exists. All risks entail the possibility that mistakes will be made."

"I believe the overall quality of work improves when you give people a chance to fail," says Mike Markkula, vice chairperson of Apple Computers.[2] In organizations where failure is encouraged and not considered a "crime," people are more willing to experiment and more open to learning. It's common knowledge, for instance, that at 3M, one of America's most innovative corporations, risk taking is encouraged. Failure to meet expectations, which happens about 60 percent of the time, is viewed as an opportunity to learn and try again.[3] In a world where Monday's ideas, ideologies, and institutions are obsolete by Tuesday night, if you are not constantly learning you will be pounding the pavement by Wednesday. And mistakes are a natural part of the learning process.

"We teach people that mistakes are like skinned knees for little children," says the inimitable Ross Perot. "They're painful, but they heal quickly, and they're learning experiences. My people are covered with the scars of their mistakes. They've lived out in the field; they've been shot at; they've been hit in every part of their bodies; and they're real. By the time they get to the top, their noses are pretty well broken. The chances of their getting there with a clean nose are zero.

They get there by producing, and the by-product is to make mistakes."[4]

MISTAKES OF INACTION

Often mistakes result from inaction as much as action, with the real mistake being procrastination—simply doing nothing: plodding along in a career you despise. Not buying the starter home when you had the opportunity. Failing to stand up to your supervisor when you knew you should have. Tolerating unethical business practices in hopes of "keeping the peace." Standing there waiting for the right time. Waiting and waiting until finally the waves of opportunity and change have passed you by. Not taking the risk to ——— (you fill in the blank). Break-It Thinkers know that the right decision made too late is as wrong as the wrong decision made too early.

Passive, play-it-safe mistakes can be just as devastating as mistakes resulting from action. What makes them worse is that you can't even say, "Well at least I gave it my best shot."

LEARN MORE FROM MISTAKES THAN FROM FAILURES

"Crisis can often have value," John Sculley says, "because it generates transformation. . . . I have found that I always learn more from my mistakes than from my successes. If you aren't making some mistakes, you aren't taking enough chances."[5]

All of us have had occasion to learn more from our mistakes than our successes. This can be seen quite clearly in sports. In tennis, when a good player tries a new shot, say a backhand slice, and hits it into the net, s/he will go over the fundamentals to determine why s/he made the error. Then s/he'll incorporate the necessary adjustments and take practice swings to cement the new learning. The next time s/he'll hit it better. The correction has helped the player perfect the shot, upping the level of his or her game. Contrast this with players who don't take any risks. Satisfied to get the ball over the net, they play it safe, try nothing new, and their game doesn't improve.

This phenomenon is true in many areas. If you aren't making

mistakes you aren't growing or learning. Or, as one chief executive says, "If you're not making mistakes, you're not doing anything worthwhile."

FAILURE BREEDS SUCCESS

Conventional Wisdom tells us, "Success breeds success." Apple's Mike Markkula says just the opposite. Research on innovation demonstrates that "success does not breed success. It is failure which breeds success."[6] Mistakes help you to rethink, reconceptualize, and restrategize. The result of "going back to the drawing board" is usually substantially better than the original idea. Every Break-It Thinker understands that anything worth doing . . . is worth doing wrong.

SUCCESSFUL FAILURES

We all know, for instance, that famous people like Lincoln, Edison, and the Wright Brothers had a number of major failures and made innumerable mistakes before finally achieving the successes for which they are remembered.

In any walk of life, in any era, those who have succeeded are usually those who have learned from their mistakes and failures, persevered, and gone on to new levels of excellence because of what they learned along the way. In fact, many of the most successful breakthrough ideas came after people had first failed. Remember that the average millionaire entrepreneur has gone bankrupt *3.75 times*.[7]

Here are some examples of little-known "failures" that led to major successes.

A scrapbook of "successful failures"

- When UCLA's legendary basketball coach John Wooden introduced the fast break to college basketball, his team committed the highest number of turnovers and fouls in memory. But Wooden knew "mistakes were part of learning." He expected them, and "knew that every opportunity for failure was equally an opportunity for success."[8] Wooden's teams went on to perfect the fast-break offense used today by nearly every team in the nation. His teams also won 10 national collegiate championships in 12 years, one of the most remarkable team achievements in all of sports history.

- *Sports Illustrated*'s success was a long time in the making, having lost money for the first 11 years! But as the *New York Times* once said, "No one could, or would, tell [publisher] Henry Luce to quit."[9]

  Just out of college, Phillip Moffitt, along with four other partners, started *Campus Voice*, a magazine that served as a campus guide for a college's activities. Realizing a small profit on the first edition, they decided to branch out and published 20 editions. They lost $100,000. Thinking they had the right formula but needing to increase volume, they then published editions for 60 colleges. They lost $300,000. Still not deterred, they continued expanding and published 100 editions and *lost half a million dollars!* And Moffitt was still only in his midtwenties!

  "Failure is always a part of success," says Moffitt. Learning from these failures, he and his group went on to several very successful ventures in publishing. Eventually Moffitt, with partner Chris Whittle, bought *Esquire* magazine when it was in a tailspin, turned it around, and sold it to Hearst.[10]

- Fidelity Select Leisure Fund, one of the highest-performing investment portfolios of the late 1980s, faced an uphill battle from the start. In May and June of 1983, the first two months after founder Morris Smith hung out his Fidelity shingle, his investments took a big drop. "I wanted to jump out the window," said Smith. Instead, he looked at the market, learned from his mistakes, and has offered investors sizable yields (e.g., 56.5 percent in 1987) ever since.[11]

- **Q:** Tom Landry, Chuck Noll, and Bill Walsh accounted for 9 of the 15 Super Bowl victories from 1974 to 1989. What else do they have in common?
  A: They also had the *worst* records of first-season head coaches in NFL history.

Even 1989 San Francisco '49er coach George Seifert (who was only the second rookie coach ever to win a Super Bowl) was fired from his first head coaching job at Cornell after going 1–8 and 2–7 his first two years—in the Ivy League!

- The name L. L. Bean and mail-order catalog sales are nearly synonymous. Their product line and money-back guarantee have set the standards for an entire industry. However, few people realize that their first and most famous product, the patented Maine Hunting Shoe, was a huge flop when first introduced. Ninety of the first 100 pairs were returned by irate customers because the stitching that held the leather tops pulled out of the soft rubber bottoms. But since Mr. Bean had guaranteed each pair, he scraped together enough money to correct the mistake and replace the shoes. Impressed with his honesty, those 90 people became L. L. Bean's satisfied customers.[12]

- In 1988, Dennis Conner received about $5 million in return for product endorsements, second only to Michael Jordan. What we forget is that those endorsements came, on large part, because Conner had *lost* the America's Cup in 1983, made adjustments, and won it back in 1987. Though Conner had won the cup previously (in 1980), only an elite group of sailors was interested in him then. His coming back from defeat aroused the country's attention. Rebounding from adversity made him both rich and famous.

- Ted Turner, himself a victorious America's Cup skipper, recounts, "Nothing ever came easy. My first eight years of sailing I didn't even win my club championship. But I just kept working and working and working."[13]

DOUBLE RECORD HOLDERS

Max Shapiro, founder and president of Sportsworld, which runs sports clinics and camps for promising young athletes and Sports Fantasy Camps for adults, said that great athletes frequently hold double records for both accomplishments and *failures*. Consider these:

- The Boston Celtics' Bob Cousy, arguably one of the great passers and ball handlers in basketball history, consistently led his team in assists, *and* in "turnovers" (passes gone awry).

- Rickey Henderson, in the year in which he set the major league record for stolen bases, also set the record for the most times thrown out while attempting to steal, Max said, "Many players don't get thrown out forty-two times in an entire career!"

- Babe Ruth for many years held the major league record for strikeouts as well as home runs.

"In my business, I try to remember those things about Cousy and other great athletes," said Shapiro, no stranger to taking risks and learning from mistakes. "A few years after I started Sportsworld, I sold it. I regretted the decision and I learned my lesson. Four years later I bought it back and within a year doubled the enrollment."

MAKING TOO MANY VERSUS TOO *FEW* MISTAKES

Increasingly, leaders in industry are becoming aware that mistakes are a natural and necessary part of learning and innovation. Rather than the conventional attitude of fearing mistakes and risks, they encourage—and in some cases demand—them. "The trouble in America today," said the president of Nike footwear, Philip Knight, "is not that we are making too many mistakes, but that we are making too few."[14]

In a changing, unpredictable world, the irony is that not making enough mistakes means you are not taking enough risks and leaves you at a disadvantage. Break-It Thinkers realize that in their companies the real mistake is taking too few, rather than too many, risks. Consequently, a growing number of companies have come to understand that taking risks, and making mistakes in the process, is good business. For example:

- Scandinavian Airlines: "I want (employees) to make mistakes," says SAS president Jan Carlzon. "I heard once about a company president who told his people, 'I want you to make at least two mistakes a week.' What was he really saying? 'I know you're so good that to make two wrong decisions a week, you must be able to make twenty to thirty right ones. I want you to make decisions.' The same goes for me. The dangerous thing is to not make decisions.[15]

- IBM: There is a famous story about IBM's founder Tom Watson and *big* mistakes. One of Watson's vice presidents took the initiative on the development of a new product. The product was a colossal flop and cost the company an estimated $10 million. Watson summoned the man to his office, saying there was something he wanted to discuss with him. When he arrived in Watson's office he was holding a letter of resignation in his hand. Watson turned and said, "Let you go? We just spent ten million dollars giving you one hell of an education! I can't wait to see what you're going to do next." Learning from his father, Tom Watson, Jr., who was responsible for major IBM progress, said, "If you want to succeed, double your failure rate."[16]

- Johnson & Johnson: One of Johnson & Johnson directors, Jim Burke's, first stabs at innovation, upon becoming head of the new products division, was a children's chest rub. It failed miserably, and Burke worried that he might not get a second chance. "Are you the one who just cost us all that money?" asked J&J chairman General Robert Wood Johnson. "Well I just want to congratulate you. If you are making mistakes, that means you are making decisions and taking risks and we won't grow unless you take risks." Some 30 years later Burke is still spreading that word. "Any successful growth company is riddled with failure and there's just not any other way to do it," he says. "We love to win, but we also have to lose in order to grow."[17]

Tom Peters rightly put it, "The essence of innovation is the pursuit of failure . . . to be able to try things and make mistakes . . . without getting shot."[18] The assumption that all of these leaders share is that we all need to keep experimenting, innovating, and being more—not less—bold and daring in our thinking and actions. Break-It Thinkers understand that you can't be innovative and not make mistakes.

TAKE AN INVENTORY

Take a moment to do an inventory of your experience. Reflect for a moment on one of your mistakes or a failure you have had. Describe that failure and what you have learned from it.

Then ask yourself, Is there currently a risk I am not taking, a challenge I have been avoiding because I am afraid I might fail or make a mistake?

Risk is no longer an option. It is an imperative. And, as we shall see in the next chapter, making mistakes is not against the law; but to the Break-It Thinker, failing to learn from mistakes ought to be.

UW *says:*
The biggest mistake is not making any.

15
Failure Is a Good Place to Start

Walter Wriston, former chairman of Citicorp, said, "Failure is not a crime, failure to learn from failure is. . . ."[1] The difference between the "best" of us and the rest of us is not determined by how many or how few mistakes we make, but by how much and how fast we learn. The sign of true champions in any field is not just a great performance but, rather, how quickly they respond to their failures and what they learn from them.

In order to be innovative and creative and to keep ahead of today's challenges, you must take risks and you will inevitably make mistakes. It's not *if* you make mistakes but *what* you do *after* you make them that determines how well you will do.

TO ERR IS TO LEARN

Mistakes are inevitable. The real problem is that we don't automatically learn from them, and so they get repeated. Resolving not to make the same mistake again doesn't work. You have to know what caused the mistake to correct it. But sometimes we fail to look closely enough at our mistakes because we attach a stigma to errors. We believe that we should know how to "do it right the first time." This is a particular problem for bright, well-educated people who are used to being rewarded for being "right."

Early in life most of us find out that mistakes can be painful. When we started in school, parents and teachers rarely praised us for mistakes. Quite the opposite; our mistakes were faulted in front of the class. We felt foolish, humiliated, and embarrassed. These early experiences often affect our behavior for a lifetime.

Since no one wants to appear foolish, or think of themselves as stupid, we often to go great lengths to avoid admitting we made a mistake, even to ourselves. This response blocks the objectivity needed to learn, and bounce back. Here are some of the defensive ways we respond after making a mistake.

DENY IT TO YOURSELF

One of the toughest defenses to dismantle is denial, because it's so hard to catch. Denial is a habit that gets started early when a kid who has been criticized too much learns to duck first and ask questions later . . . or maybe never.

When you deny you made a mistake, you fail to accept responsibility for it. You wind up lying to yourself, distorting the facts about even small errors. This makes it much harder to create a firm basis for quick learning.

"While I design seminars for executives who want to see their managers on a fast learning track, I find that I have to discuss this issue early so they learn the connection between being willing to recognize mistakes and gaining ability to use them effectively," says one consultant.

"It is even a tougher issue for government managers. We are based in the District of Columbia and work daily with people who spend vast amounts of public money but are afraid to acknowledge and learn from their mistakes. And so, more public money gets spent to cover up old problems. What a waste."

COVER IT UP

If mistakes are viewed as bad and failure is frightening, then to fail and be found out is catastrophic. Consequently, people will go to great lengths to avoid being perceived as a failure or to admit a mistake ever happened. Trying to cover up mistakes, they hid the truth and hope no one will notice.

Harvey Mackay wrote in *Swim with the Sharks Without Being Eaten Alive*, "Stubbornness in refusing to recognize a problem has destroyed a lot of bottom lines. . . . You can't solve a problem unless you first admit you have one."[2]

Cover-ups take a lot of energy. Often the defensive, elaborate disguises become so intricate and complex that they end up having a life of their own. To cover up usually requires a labyrinth of supporting lies to shore up the original "big" one. A cover-up uses all the creative juice that could have been used to learn from the original mistake—and fix it.

A classic example was the incredible chain of events that began with the White House–sanctioned break-ins at the Watergate complex. The early denials, and the ensuing cover-ups, became much more of a problem than the initial mistake. Eventually, exposing the elaborate cover-up led to the resignation of former president Richard Nixon.

UW *says: Deny a mistake, and you deny yourself the chance to learn from it.*

"I SCREWED UP"

Monty Python's John Cleese, a successful businessman and film producer in his own right, relates the philosophy of Peter Parker, the head of British Rail. Parker has found, "The most difficult person in management is the mistake concealer. If someone walks into my office saying, 'I screwed up,' I say, 'Come in.' In the healthiest organizations the taboo is not on making mistakes, but on concealing them."

"Having a positive attitude towards mistakes," adds Cleese, "allows them to be corrected rapidly when they occur. . . . The problems come when mistakes are denied." Cleese, one of the great Break-It Thinkers says, "If we don't acknowledge a mistake, we can't very well correct it."[3]

POINTING THE FINGER

Blaming occurs when a mistake is so obvious it can't be denied, so you try the "next-best" thing: pointing a finger at someone else, you say, "It's not *my* fault!" The boss blames the staff, marketing blames research and development, the teacher blames the student. The blamer tries to put everyone else *on* the hook.

Consider the golfer who tensed up and overcompensated and hit a drive into the rough, a natural mistake that could be corrected next time. But instead, he blames the course's narrow fairways, the architect for designing it that way, the wind, other people's loud voices, and his caddy. He is willing to blame anything rather than admit an error.

Sounds familiar, doesn't it? We do it all the time. We blame the client for not buying, the boss for not listening, the audience for not clapping, the baby for not eating.

A partner in an East Coast investment group, talking about a client of his who had fallen on hard times, said it was tough to find the real problem. "They were all too busy pointing the finger. They were blaming the boss, the customers, new laws, unions, or a new competitor. Anything but themselves. And as a result, they never got to the heart of the problem."

Turnaround specialist Timothy Finley said about a company he bought that he found the president "pointed the finger of blame at the sales manager for the lack of profitability, and the sales manager pointed the finger of blame at the president." Looking at the facts objectively, Finley discovered that both had made mistakes. But according to him each was so busy passing the buck that there was "too much blaming and not much learning."[4]

Blaming others is tempting in order to escape the consequences. But when you blame a mistake on others—be it your boss, your customers, or your kids—you simply deprive yourself of an opportunity to learn.

"ARRGGHH!"

Who hasn't seen (or been) the tennis player who smashes her racquet on the ground after a bad shot, the skier who whips the snow with his poles, or the executive who pounds on the desk after a bad phone call or meeting? Fury and anger are very common responses when we make a mistake. They are such intense emotions that they overpower you and those around you. Sometimes the anger is "other-directed," irritably and often irrationally used to attack others. But most often it is directed inside as we assault our own self-esteem with both fists.

Any form of anger leaves its emotional bumps, bruises, and scars which prevent you from thinking clearly and rationally. Anger that is still smoldering prevents you from getting back into the "game." The golfer, still angry at himself for missing a putt, is still tense as he stands at the next tee. Upset, tight, and gritting his teeth, he overswings, turning a bad putt into a bad drive and a bad drive into a triple-digit round!

Similarly, the manager, angry at herself for making a mistake in a meeting or on the phone to a client, doesn't calm down and focus on the next task. The next thing you know, the phone rings and she vents her anger on the *next* caller.

DAMN!!! I DID IT AGAIN!

While avoidance and denial skirt the issue, and blame flings it at others, another mistake we make is to point the finger at ourselves. We've all felt this way. We rehash an error ad infinitum, beating ourselves into the ground. We run the "I did it again!" tape over and over.

Dwelling only on our mistakes is a way of playing a mental failure tape. The more you ruminate on the mistake, the more deeply it becomes etched in your mind, and magnified out of proportion. Blow a putt or shank a drive and our inner voice says, "Damn!!! You did it again. You'll never be any good at this game. You'll never learn anything." The incident is then generalized to other aspects of our lives.

Failing in a *specific* situation gets blown up into treating yourself as a failure in *general*. You move quickly from poor performance to poor self-image to lower self-esteem and reduced confidence. We continue to replay our "failure tape," rehearsing for future repeat performances. The next time you are faced with a similar situation, up pops the past failure tape from your memory bank, and you think, "Uh-oh, here I go again." It's a vicious cycle.

This phenomenon isn't restricted to mortals like you and me. It even happens to star performers like San Francisco 49er quarterback Joe Montana, a two-time Super Bowl MVP and arguably one of the greatest pressure performers in sports. One September in 1987 he had the worst game of his career against the New Orleans Saints. He was 12 of 26 for 120 yards, was sacked 6 times, and threw 2 interceptions. Hardly vintage Joe Montana.

Later that season, when they played the Saints again, Montana had a difficult time getting untracked in the first half. He was worried about what happened the last time San Francisco played the Saints and didn't want to be missing guys again who were wide open. Having dwelt on his poor performance in the *last* game with the Saints, Montana carried it over into the next one.

"SHAKE IT OFF"

At the other end of the spectrum is letting things go too quickly. During a recent softball game, our third baseman made an error on his throw to first. "Shake it off, forget about it," he was told. "Don't think about it. Concentrate on the next batter." He nodded and turned toward the batters box. Next inning he cleanly fielded a hard grounder and threw it over the first baseman's head, *again*. He had repeated the mistake because he hadn't figured out why his throw went awry in the first place.

What "Shake it off" means is don't get down on yourself—don't take the mistake as a personality defect. Shake off feeling stupid or foolish and get on with the game. But all too often we tend to hold on to the frustration, and neglect the error that could now be corrected.

Shaking off our mistakes is good advice, but *only after you have learned* from the situation. After making an error you often see baseball players take a few imaginary practice throws to correct the mistake and get back in the "groove." If you move on without reflecting on what you did, or if you avoid facing the problem, chances are you will repeat it.

NEW YEAR'S RESOLUTIONS

While most of us know we should learn from our past mistakes in order to prepare for the future, this is far from an established routine. It is more like our New Year's resolutions. It is not enough to "resolve" or just "promise" not to make the same mistake twice. The real question is *how* to learn from errors.

"There are no pitchers who do not give up home runs; there are no batters who do not strike out," writes English professor David Huddle in an article in the *New York Times*. "[They have] learned to survive giving up home runs and striking out. That much is obvious. What seems to me less obvious is how these 'failures' are put to use. . . ."[5]

Here are four *active* steps to take to ensure that your mistakes become stepping stones: these Four *R*s—*Admit Re*-sponsibility, *Re*-view, *Re*-place, *Re*-hearse—will not only prevent you from repeating the same mistake, but will enable you to learn, grow and turn past failures into successes.

R 1: Admit *Re*-sponsibility.

Start by acknowledging your role in the situation; this gives you real power to effect change. A study of 191 top executives at *Fortune* 500 companies indicated that virtually all had suffered "hardship experiences" ranging from missed promotions to firings to business failures. The survey conducted by the Center for Creative Leadership, found that the executives who bounced back did so *"because instead of blaming others, they were able to admit their failures, and then move on"* (Emphasis added).[6] They could analyze effectively, and then learn from what happened.

Similarly, good research and development departments have the capacity to stay focused on one key question: "What are we learning from this project?" In every experiment (or experience in life) something goes "well," and something else goes "wrong." An excellent scientist doesn't worry or try to cover up for something that didn't go exactly as planned. Instead, he turns on his curiosity because he wants useful and reliable information. He builds on his mistakes.

Admitting to a mistake extends beyond your own direct concerns. If you are managing a team, for example, and someone else makes a mistake, you need to share in the responsibility. The best leaders are willing to take responsibility for things that occur on their team.

Yet you can't learn from something if you don't know what you did. Accepting responsibility makes it easier to learn from an experience and convert the mistake into a success the next time around. It also gives you more clout in a situation because you look at things accurately.

UW *says: It is not a mistake to fail: failure is the best place to start.*

R 2: *Re*-view your script

If you were taking an automobile trip and got lost you'd probably check your map to determine where you were. Once you see you're in Omaha, instead of Ohio, you can decide how to get back on track. It's the same with any mistake.

After you've made a mistake, go back in your mind and *re-view* the situation as if you had a mental videotape in your head. Rerun the tape from start to finish in order to see the whole process. In the case of a bad decision, start the tape with the information you had and the research you did. Run through your whole decision process and "watch" it, then go to the meeting itself and "watch" it through to the end. As you review, find the point or points where you would change things next time. Was your information complete? Were you in too much of a hurry? Did you wait too long? Were you too worried about the cost? Be as specific as possible.

Actions are preceded by thoughts. Once you isolate what didn't work you can find out what you were thinking at that moment. The golfer's overswing made him shank the drive; but it was the *thought* "I've gotta hit the cover off the ball" that created the overswing.

Or, it could have been an attitude, or an emotion. A "play-it-safe" attitude may have caused you to delay making the decision. Or the Gotta's might have caused you to move too quickly, without looking at all the information.

The key in a *re*-view is to look at both your behavior *and* the thought that led to it. Look at the point where the mistake was made, and then back up to identify your thoughts and the assumptions which contributed.

R 3: *Re*-place the old footage

It's not enough to just flag the error. To ensure that you don't make the same mistake again, develop an alternative response so that the next time a similar situation develops, you are ready. Learn to replace the old picture with a better one. When you "edit" the "mistake" footage out of your mental movie and replace it with something better, you're "splicing" in thoughts and actions that will help you to respond better the next time.

For example, if the Gotta's caused you to act too quickly, and not do all your homework, your new movie would show you doing a "worst case" scenario check while you gather your composure. Or, suppose the mistake came from procrastination because the project seemed too formidable; in the new movie you would see yourself breaking the job into small doable steps.

Next, replace the "error" tape with a "success" tape in your mind, giving you an alternative way of thinking and acting and providing you an alternative way of thinking and acting and providing you with additional options for handling the situation. You can't guarantee that the re-edited version will ensure complete success but it will work better. You won't repeat what you did the last time. And you'll feel more confident, a big step in improving the outcome of any situation.

R 4: *Re*-hearse the new moves

The last step in the cycle is to mentally rehearse the new movie. The more you rehearse the "re-edited" tape, the more it becomes your natural response. Then, when a similar situation occurs, you won't repeat the old mistake. The desired behavior, if well rehearsed, will become automatic. Consequently, rather than repeating a mistake you will have imprinted a more desirable response onto the situation, which can lead to a breakthrough to an entirely new level.

TEACHING THE FOUR Rs TO URBAN HIGH SCHOOL

One of the most rewarding experiences of performance coaching I ever had was with Urban High School's volleyball team, which my son Otis played for. Urban was the lowest-ranked team in the playoffs. Though they lacked experience (this being only the second year the school had a team) and had a height disadvantage, their worst problem was a mental one.

In a session before the playoffs, I went over the Four R's with the team. They correctly admitted that their problem wasn't mistakes but how they reacted to them. Reviewing the team dynamics they confessed that they would yell at a person who missed a spike, a set, or a pass. They would glare at the offending teammate, yell at him to "wake up," blame him for not being positioned right, and in general "get on his case." Some players also described how they'd get down on themselves after an error and lose concentration for the next few points.

We then explored ways to replace these negative responses. I asked, "What could you do differently when someone makes a mistake?" One player said, "We have to respect each other." Another said, "Yeah, we have to make each other feel good, not bad, after a mistake. You feel bad enough already."

I then had them mentally rehearse these positive responses and encouraged the team to visualize them that evening and before the next game.

It was an inspiring session and everyone left feeling better, but the real surprise came the next day at the first playoff game. The opponent served and one player blew an easy set. They all ran over to the player and gave him a "high five" and some encouraging words. The same thing happened when the team's big hitter muffed one. Normally he would get down on himself. This time, though, he cracked a little smile, and quickly practiced a better move and got right back into the game.

Meanwhile the opposition seemed to unravel as my team became more and more upbeat. The entire tournament went that way: They beat teams that were, on paper, far superior to them.

But the real test awaited them in the finals, a rematch with a school that had slaughtered them in an earlier meeting. We won the first game, lost the second, won the third, and lost the fourth. It was so tense you could taste the pressure. In the last game, as the lead went back and forth many times, the Urban team never lost its cool. The kids encouraged each other and kept their spirits up. Their opponents, though, became increasingly more tense. Finally, with the game in overtime, like in a Hollywood movie, undersized and underskilled Urban won. It was the school's first championship in any sport, and the team knew it wasn't luck. They had developed a new set of mental muscles that allowed them the flexibility to make mistakes, and like winners in all fields, had gained the ability to recover.

Learning from mistakes will enable you to keep moving, but as you will see in the next chapter, we don't always win the game we think we are playing.

UW *says:*
Failure is success in the making.

16

Plan on Changing Your Plans

Though we are cautioned to plan our work and work our plan, Break-It Thinkers know that at any moment everything can change. Everything.

The sky can open up, a wall in Berlin can fall down. First there is communism, then there isn't. Poets become presidents, presidents outcasts. Plan as we may, the future has plans of its own.

Break-It Thinkers know that though it's important to have a plan, sometimes it's even more important to abandon it!

I learned about this years ago while teaching people how to mentally prepare for difficult rock climbs. Looking up from the bottom we would mentally plan a route to the top. However, once the climb began, and we had progressed a short way up the mountain, the view was totally different. From the new vantage point we could see other, more promising routes that were impossible to see from below. So we would change the route.

When we take risks or face challenges of any kind, we can plan, prepare, and rehearse until we're blue in the face. But once the journey begins, in this era of intense change, we can count on running into something unexpected very shortly after we're under way. For the Break-It Thinkers that's an exciting prospect. They welcome the unexpected—even thrive on it.

For many, however, the unexpected is a source of anxiety. But for the Break-It Thinker, change—planned or unplanned—is an ally. Peter Drucker has said, "No other area offers richer opportunities for successful innovation, than [the] unexpected."[1]

THE TRIPLE DOUBLE

As unpredictable and uncontrollable as things are today, there are three things you *can* in fact count on. I call these the "triple double." You can assume that anything new will invariably take twice as long, cost twice as much and involve twice as much work as you thought!

I learned about the triple double several years ago. A client had what seemed to be a "perfect" product. It was unique, and had an untapped market that filled a major market need. It had everything going for it. He had developed a marketing plan, gotten financing, hired a project manager and off he went.

But at every step of the way the unexpected appeared. Everything—the research, the package design, the sales, promotion, and distribution—had taken him twice as long as he had planned.

Additionally, other possibilities as well as problems emerged as he went along. He decided to get a national sponsor rather than try to market the product himself. He also found a different and more economical way of distributing the product, which he hadn't known about at the start of the project.

At the point I stepped in, his original time line and budget projection had as many lines in it as a 2,500-year-old man's face and he was discouraged and disheartened.

Because of the triple double, one of the most difficult phases of any new project or venture is in the middle. This is where the unexpected has wreaked havoc on carefully developed plans. Seeing that the goal which has seemed within reach and doable is now way down the road and tougher to attain causes many, like my client, to lose heart and feel as though they have run out of gas.

Here are three steps that will defuse the triple double and refuel any project: Step one: Readjust your goal. Given everything you *now* know, you may want to shift your goal, direction, or strategies. Don't stick with the plan if the plan hasn't stuck with you.

Step two: Reaffirm your original commitment and vision. Remember the dream that inspired the project. This will help to "refuel" your fire and get your original excitement and passion back.

Step three: Begin with a victory. Small wins will help you regain momentum, reinforce your dream, and get you back on track again.

LESSONS OF AIKIDO

You can't control the unexpected, but you can control your *response* to it. Practitioners of Aikido, a form of martial arts, know that they may get thrown if they resist an attacking force. So they learn to blend *with* the force and use an attacker's energy for their own advantage.

By analogy, if you resist the unexpected by sticking to the original plan, you will be "thrown," and your progress impeded. Being flexible enough to shift your direction so that you move *with* this change, rather than against it, will give you more energy and power. When you go with the flow of change, the unexpected becomes your ally, not your adversary.

SIGN POSTS

Many people feel that changing is an admission of defeat, incompetence, or inadequacy. But this rigid attitude often causes you to miss many opportunities along the way.

For example, going on a journey, if you are not paying attention to anything but the map, you will miss signs indicating more scenic or faster routes. Then, upon arriving at your destination, you will discover that all the accommodations have been taken by those who had their eyes open and saw the signs along the road.

No one can plan for everything. There will always be changes and signposts that will present new opportunities or directions. Unlike most, Break-It Thinkers anticipate that contingency plans are usually the best plans of all.

KEEP YOUR EYE ON (AND OFF) THE PATH

Break-It Thinkers understand change and serendipity so they have little trouble getting started. They assume they'll learn new information, meet new people, hear of new developments, and see new possibilities that they could not have known at the outset.

This happened to me shortly before the release of my book *The C Zone: Peak Performance Under Pressure*. Prior to the book's publication, I mounted a huge promotional campaign. As a result of my persistent early-morning calls, *U.S. News & World Report* did an interview. Then something unexpected happened. Contrary to what I had assumed, the article didn't sell appreciably more books. But I did get one phone call a month later—from someone who had come across the article—which significantly changed my work, because he invited me to give a speech.

Business history is full of such stories. Clarence Birdseye revolutionized the retail food industry and built a giant company because he seized upon an unexpected opportunity. While on a fishing trip to Canada he noticed an Eskimo's fish frozen in ice. That observation gave him the idea for "frozen food." Similarly, the Upjohn pharmaceutical company was testing Minoxidil, a crystalline solid developed for reducing high blood pressure. Volunteers reported moderate success with their blood pressure, but an unexpected side effect was that they began growing hair. With modification, enter "Rogaine" hair enhancer.[2]

BACKING INTO A CLEARING

The Break-It Thinker understands—and assumes—that the unexpected can happen at any moment. If you want to avail yourself of the opportunities inherent in an unpredictable future you have to keep your eyes and ears open, and your intuitive antennae up.

In these fast-forward, unpredictable times, in serendipity we trust.

We must assume from the outset that for every new problem, solutions will present themselves, and for each obstacle new paths will open.

UW *says: We can learn to* back *into a clearing.*

THE BIOBOTTOMS STORY

Anita Diamonstein had a Physician Assistant degree and a new baby. But her medical training was of little use when facing a choice between cloth and disposable diapers. "I hated the idea of disposable diapers," she told me. "Plastics were unappealing and wasteful and with cloth you had all those pins."

Then, while at a friend's house a strange looking woolen cover with no pins arrived from Japan. She had another friend translate the Japanese label, ordered 50 pairs, and spread them around her neighborhood.

The product, Biobottoms, was the talk of the neighborhood. All her friends wanted some. Friends of friends were calling her. Taken by the potential of Biobottoms as a natural, healthy alternative, she wrote to Japan, inquring about the possibility of selling them in the United States. The response was immediate. They offered her sole distributorship for the United States! She had backed into a clearing.

Taking advantage of serendipity, she is no longer practicing medicine. She is now president of Biobottoms, Inc., selected as one of Inc. 500's fastest growing private companies in 1990. Biobottoms offers not only the original product, but an entire mail-order line of all-cotton infant and children's clothes.

EXPECT SERENDIPITY

Nowadays, uncertainty and surprise are normal. You can assume that is reality. You can also assume that the unexpected can't be controlled. What you *can* control, however, is your attitude toward the unexpected. You can look forward to it, and be ready to act on it, or you can be intimidated by it and procrastinate indefinitely.

Break-It Thinkers trust the future. Their attitude is they have a firm belief that once you get going, providence steps in. "Start down the road, and you'll find all sorts of interesting alternate routes." They find change an exciting rather than ominous prospect. Like the Sioux Indians, they assume that everything in the environment—every change, every surprise, every unexpected event—is a potential ally that can assist rather then hinder progress. In an unpredictable world, trusting in serendipity is a more viable attitude than living in constant fear of impending doom. Expecting and welcoming the unexpected is a good first step.

Genius and Magic

I leave the summing up of this chapter to a quote by Goethe, which arrived in my office one day, unexpectedly, on a postcard.

There is one elementary truth the ignorance of which kills countless . . . splendid plans: that the moment one definitely commits oneself, then providence moves too. All sorts of things occur to help one that would never otherwise have occurred. A whole stream of events issue from the decision, raising in one's favor all manner of unforeseen incidents and meetings and material assistance which no man could have dreamed would come his way. Whatever you can do or dream you can, begin it. Boldness has genius and magic in it. Begin it now.[3]

UW *says:*
Trust the unexpected.

17

Play Your Own Best Game

POLISH THE STONE, DON'T RESHAPE IT

Everyone has been on the receiving end of the conventional wisdom that warns us to shore up our game and improve our weaknesses. But plugging up holes in your game can be a very frustrating and time-consuming activity. It also, as every Break-It Thinker knows, distracts you from honing and perfecting your strengths, from polishing the stone.

DON'T FOCUS ON YOUR WEAK POINTS

Plugging the holes in your game causes you to spend too much time on what doesn't work. Though you may go from poor to fair, you rarely excel at that which is not your strong suit. Then, because you are spending so much time focusing on your weak points, you don't have time to hone the skills you are good at. The result is that you never excel at anything.

My desk usually looks like Hurricane Hugo has just hit. Following the Conventional Wisdom, I decided to shore up this weakness and clean up my desk. To help me get organized and make better use of my time, I hired a consultant. After a week of following me around, he gave me a "daily planner" and told me how to use it. He also taught me how to set priorities, to handle papers just once, and he encouraged me to clean my desk up at the end of the day so I would be ready to start in the morning. All of his advice was good common sense, practical, and not difficult to implement.

I followed his regime faithfully for a month and found three things: (1) I *was* a little more organized. (2) I had a roaring headache all day long. (3) My speech dates dropped 30 percent, and I hadn't written any new material all month.

It was at that point that I realized I was never going to be well organized and that was okay. Organization wasn't my game. My game was selling, coaching, motivating people, and writing. If I kept doing these things well, I concluded, my business would do just fine. The bottom line is that my desk is still a mess and my business is doing quite well.

WELL-ROUNDED IS FLAT

"If you try to become proficient at what you are weak at, it will take an inordinate amount of time. That means you don't have time to keep improving at what you are already good at, so that skill gets rusty, and you end up mediocre at everything," said Sandy Mobley, a manager of training at McKinsey & Co., the giant management consulting firm. "The so-called well-rounded personality," she explained, "is really, in my experience, very very rare."

UW *says: Well-rounded often means flat.*

COP VERSUS COACH:
EMPLOYEE PERFORMANCE REVIEWS

In most performance reviews, managers gloss over strong points and focus—usually in great detail—on "areas for improvement." Sure, "strengths" are mentioned, but rarely are they given the attention of "weaknesses." Performance reviews have become a critique, a mechanism for telling employees what they are *not* doing, what's *not* working.

There's more "cop" than "coach" in these sessions, a subtle but crucial distinction. A cop catches you doing something wrong and a good coach brings out the best in you. Many managers and supervisors act like they're patrolling the neighborhood watching for what might go wrong, not what goes right. When they "cite" what they've noticed, it's no wonder their employees feel more "busted" than trusted.

UW *says: Focusing on weaknesses usually reinforces them.*

"Don't focus on building up your weaknesses," writes management guru Peter Drucker. "Understand your strengths and place yourself in a position where these strengths count. Your strengths are what will carry you through to success. . . ."

Obviously, if something you are doing (or not doing) is severely hindering progress, you should do something about it, but not at the expense of your strong points.

UW *says: You'll* get by *by improving upon weaknesses, but you'll* get great *by building on strengths.*

MAKING THE GRADE

I knew all about focusing on strengths and not emphasizing weaknesses, I had read the research, I had even written about it. Yet it slipped my mind when dealing with something much closer to home. My son's report card in his first year of high school consisted of an A, a B, two Cs, and a D in math. Now here's a tough question for you: What grade do you think the great humanistic coach Kriegel focused on? The D of course! I railed at him, I told him he had better "shape up" or his future was in jeopardy . . . I pulled out every Firehose imaginable.

I was complaining about his D to a friend, who immediately chastised me for not practicing what I preach. Realizing that Otis had unusually strong "people skills" for a person his age, I stopped focusing on the math, his weakness, and emphasized what a gift of leadership and communication he has and how important being a good "people person" was in every area of life. And I kept reemphasizing it every chance I had.

At the end of his sophomore year, Otis told me, "Dad, I've decided to run for president of the student body!" Suppressing my initial instinct to firehose him because of his grades, I said, "Great! With your leadership ability, I know you have a strong chance." He got 70 percent of the votes and became the first junior in the history of the school to become student body president.

But the most interesting part of this proud-papa story was yet to unfold. The next year, while serving as president, his grades improved by almost a full grade point and without any yelling and shouting on my part. He was, as he says, "so jazzed," that it affected everything else he did.

When we focus on strengths, as I did with Otis, and then he did with himself, it reminds us that we *are* good. This enables us, as a friend says, "to step out of life's puddles and onto good, solid earth," and build self-confidence, self-esteem, and positive momentum.

When I talk about strengths, I'm not talking about acquired skills like the ability to do WordPerfect or analyze a financial statement. I'm talking about strengths that are basic to your nature, qualities and traits that are essential to your makeup, like being a great problem solver and detail person, having a curious, inquisitive mind, being adventurous, loving change, or being naturally gregarious and enthusiastic.

The problem is that most people are much more aware of and attend to their weaknesses rather than their strengths. We've all had more than enough of the negative to contend with—so much so that most people tend to shrug off their positive traits and/or take them for granted.

But building on your strengths will not only help you become a peak performer and increase your confidence to take risks. The ripple effect will keep you growing, learning, and challenging yourself in other areas as well. To ride the big waves today we all need as much confidence and encouragement as we can muster.

BUILD ON WHAT WORKS

When taking on a new position or a new project it is not unusual to think you have to change and be different from before. The ace salesperson becomes sales manager and shifts basic styles to meet the challenges of the new position. Great communications and motivation skills that were so effective in the field now play second fiddle to trying to be an administrator and organizational person. Soon the great salesperson becomes the not-so-good manager because he didn't realize that sales skills—the ability to communicate and motivate— were invaluable assets in any position.

When he became the president of Scandinavian Airline Systems, Jan Carlzon tried to shape himself to fit what he thought were the contours of his new position. He was nervous about how he would be perceived by the managers who had formerly been his peers. "How would they look at me now?" he wondered. "I felt I had to show them I was the right man for the job. The company was in a bad situation, with big losses. I thought, 'Now I have to be the boss.' I had to prove I knew everything better than the others did—that I was quicker in analyzing things and making decisions and everything."

Carlzon was lucky to have some real friends around. One of them who saw what was happening said to him, "What the hell are you doing? Do you think we chose you to be our boss because we wanted you to be somebody different from who you were? If you don't get back to being yourself you will be a failure."

Taking his friend's advice and reverting back to his strengths, Carlzon turned SAS around dramatically, from a company that was chalking up huge losses to becoming one of the strongest competitors in its field.[2]

IMPRACTICAL VISIONARY

When a person is taking on a new challenge, there will be external and even self-imposed pressures to be different. I was working on a project with one of the visionaries of the environmental movement, Huey Johnson, who had been the director of the Nature Conservancy, a cofounder of the Trust for Public Land and had served as secretary for resources for the state of California.

Never one to rest on his laurels, Johnson is now working on a project he calls the "Green Century," a revolutionary plan to re-establish U.S. and global environmental quality.

To turn Huey's vision into reality, everyone, myself included, was pressuring him to be more concrete. We were all trying to bring him down to earth (pardon the pun) so that a specific plan and tangible first steps could be developed. But for Huey, small practical steps are like walking in wet cement. After two meetings I realized we were going about this in the wrong way.

Here was this "visionary" whom we were trying to get to be "practical." Huey's strength is in his vision and his ability to inspire people. This insight totally changed the way we worked. We took Huey's vision and developed practical strategies for turning it into action, using him as a sounding board to make sure we stayed on track. By utilizing everyone's collective strengths, our team ended up with a powerful plan.

THE ODD COUPLE

Another way we seek to improve is by copying another person's strengths. We find a role model and emulate this person who has the skills, the "style," or the attitude that we think we need to develop. The futility of this is something I learned awhile ago.

When *Inner Skiing* was published, my coauthor, Tim Gallwey, and I scheduled promotional events around the country. Expecting 50, we found that 500 people showed up at our first program. I had never given a speech before a large audience and was petrified. So Tim went first. He sat down on a chair on the stage and just talked calmly and eloquently. He was great!

Using Tim as my model, I, too, pulled up a chair and tried to emulate his relaxed, thoughtful style. I used the same approach, sat in the same damn chair, in front of the same audience, yet while he was great, I bombed.

If you knew Tim and me you would immediately understand how ludicrous it would be for either of us to try to emulate the other. Tim basically is reserved and intellectual, whereas I am more enthusiastic and speak with lots of expression and body language. We are, truly, the odd couple. On hindsight, trying to copy Tim was ridiculous because in "finding him," I lost myself.

DON'T BE A "WANNABEE"

Kids today have an expression for those who copy others, "wannabees." These are the people who "want to be" like someone else. They mimic the way their hero dresses, talks, and walks, affect the same mannerisms—everything. There are Madonna wannabees, Elvis wannabees, Michael Jackson wannabees.

You've seen it at work, too. There are Iacocca wannabees, Tom Peters wannabees, Mary Kay wannabees. In many businesses there are the "boss" wannabees who mirror those in a position of power. They wear the same kinds of clothes as the boss, effect the boss's mannerisms, walk like the boss, talk like the boss . . . the whole nine yards.

In my speech I was a Tim wannabee. The problem with being a wannabee is no matter how much you may *wanna*bee, you ain't *gonna* be! A good carbon copy is still a copy, and is nowhere near as good as an original. I was a lukewarm version of Tim. Trying to use what worked for him, I didn't use what worked for me. I wasn't making the most of my own strengths, my own uniqueness. If you become a wannabee you will never be more than second best. No one is better than the original. And in a laser-fast world, second best isn't good enough.

POLISH, DON'T RESHAPE THE STONE

Great risk takers and leaders are unique. In fact, that is precisely the key to their prowess: they have built on their own special combination of strengths. They know their pluses *and* their minuses, but they have elected to build on the positive side of the equation. They don't try to copy others or attempt to be what they aren't. They make the most of what they have, what they know, what they do best, and who they are.

Lee Iacocca is a case in point. When he took over Chrysler he had to orchestrate the biggest bailout in U.S. economic history, which included incredibly detailed financing. Yet he didn't try to be what he was not, a financial genius and number cruncher. Through it all Iacocca remained Iacocca. A great communicator, motivator, and marketer, these strengths had been the keys to his success, and utilizing them in this very trying situation enabled him to succeed.

Break-It Thinkers share one trait: they build on their strengths. *They don't try to be what they are not; they remain true to who they are.* They don't imitate, clone, or copy someone else. Knowing their strengths and weaknesses, they choose to polish, not reshape, the stone.

UW *says: You'll be better at being yourself than at being anyone else.*

BE GREAT AT ONE THING

If you have ever watched Chris Evert or Ivan Lendl, it would be immediately obvious that these already great tennis players could have improved their games by coming to the net more often and volleying better. Yet neither of these athletes, who were ranked number one in the world, worked on this part of their game.

Break-It Thinkers know they can't be good at everything and don't try to be. Knowing their strengths and their weaknesses, they defy conventional wisdom by continually building on their strong points. If you look at top performers in any field, they aren't good at everything. They are usually great at one thing. That's what gets them to the top.

Break-It Thinkers build on what they are good at *until they become great at it*. If you try to be well rounded, you won't peak at anything.

But, you may ask, "Doesn't working on our strengths keep us in our comfort zone?" Actually, Break-It Thinkers know the opposite is true. Building on your strengths will give you the confidence to take risks, keep growing, and change much faster.

NOTHING NEW UNDER THE SUN

Most people resist change. One principal reason is a lack of confidence in their ability to adapt to an unpredictable environment. The conventional way we look at change actually skews the picture further and makes change look harder and more intimidating. We tend to focus on what we *don't know*, what we're *not good at*, and what we *still have to learn*.

A good example of this occurred recently in an electronics firm undergoing major restructuring. The customer service representatives were told they had to begin selling service contracts for their equipment in addition to installing and repairing them. This generated a great deal of resistance. To the service representatives, learning to sell was a very different game from what they had been playing. But it turned out they already knew a lot more about sales than they thought.

For example, the first step in servicing or installation was talking with the client to understand how they used the equipment. The same is true in selling. The salesperson first has to learn about the customer's needs. The service reps also had a great deal of product knowledge and hands-on experience, which is obviously important in selling.

Seeing the similarities helped the reps feel more confident, less as though they were in unfamiliar territory. They realized that they already had mastered many of the basics needed to sell. They still had to learn closing techniques, how to handle objections, and other sales skills, but these seemed far less daunting when being built on a base of strength.

Most challenges won't take you into territory that is entirely different from where you are now. No new situation is so different from your current one that you can't utilize your own strengths. If, for instance, your strong suit is communication, or problem solving, or organizational development, you can utilize these to help you adapt more quickly or easily to whatever your next challenge or opportunity is. Your strong points serve as a bridge, making you more likely to succeed.

When Gary Friedman went from being a trial lawyer to a mediator— two very different areas—he found he could utilize many of the strengths he had in his former practice. As a trial lawyer he was skilled at analyzing situations and evidence, finding solutions for complex situations, questioning people to get to the heart of the matter, and understanding the essentials of the law. Each of these strengths helped him excel as a mediator.

In every new situation you will need to learn new skills, new information, new roles or rules of the new game. But nothing will be so dramatically different that you can't utilize your strengths in the new context. Furthermore, realizing that you already have core strengths will help you adapt more quickly and confidently.

THE POTTING LAWYER

One of the most startling changes happened to an old friend of mine, Jim Hayes. An honors graduate in engineering from Notre Dame, Jim went on to Harvard Law School, eventually working for a large New York patent law firm. Jim's ability to simplify complex issues, to understand how things worked, and to solve problems, combined with an inventive, inquiring, and curious nature, made him very successful, very quickly.

After working for this firm for three years, Jim made a radical career change. He moved to the northern California area and became a potter and sculptor. On the surface of it, you couldn't pick a more different path. Yet Jim became a successful potter and sculptor because he utilized the same skills that made him a good patent attorney: curiosity, inventiveness, and problem solving. As a potter he was always inventing new and better tools and trying new materials, shapes, and designs and was constantly searching for new ways to extend his art.

The lesson, of course, is to utilize your existing natural strengths in whatever context presents itself. In any new situation you encounter, look to the strengths you already have. Using strengths as a foundation for change will give you a strong base from which to take any risk or face any challenge that you may encounter.

FINDING WHAT WORKS

Though there are many sophisticated tests and measures to help you identify your best traits and qualities, there are some simpler techniques as well. Because we are good at certain things and they come easily and naturally to us, we tend to overlook them completely.

STRENGTH ASSESSMENT

Below are some ways to identify and acknowledge your areas of strength. Answer the following questions, and watch out for the Firehose!

1. What are some of the strengths you utilize in your current work?

2. Review your accomplishments of the past five years. What do you think are the main qualities, characteristics, and strengths that enabled you to do well?

3. What are the things you like to do the most, the ones you do in your spare time? What qualities do these activities bring out in you? (Often those qualities that seem the least related to work will give you information that you have been overlooking.) Here are some examples:

- White-water rafting, rock climbing: love of adventure, challenge and risk

- Crossword puzzles: problem solving, working with details

- Tinkering: problem solving, inventing

- Gardening: patience, caring, problem solving

- Travel: doing and seeing something new, love of adventure

- Teaching, coaching: motivating people

4. Who are your heroes and heroines? What qualities do they exhibit that you admire? How do you express these qualities in your own life? Where are the opportunities to express more of these qualities?

5. What qualities do people admire in you?

6. Imagine you are a good friend of yours giving frank feedback to you about your strong points. What would she be saying?

DESIGNING YOUR OWN GAME

It is more critical than ever to work in an area in which you are utilizing your strengths and natural skills. You'll not only be more productive and creative, but you will also enjoy what you are doing more, which will further increase your effectiveness.

In spite of this, many people seem to be working in jobs or careers in which they are not utilizing their strengths and therefore don't feel fulfilled. This is a major reason why over 70 percent of white-collar workers are dissatisfied in their work.

Before throwing in the towel and changing everything, there are two steps you can take to utilize your strengths at work and make your job more satisfying, and both are within your power.

Answering the following questions by applying them to your own life will enable you to assess your strengths and the extent to which you are using them on your job.

1. Change your role

- What strengths do you have that you are not using in your work?

- Which of your strong points could you be using more often and how?

- What are some opportunities for you to utilize more of your strengths that you aren't making the most of?

2. Change the rules

- If you were to redesign your job description to better utilize your strong points, how would it look? Write a paragraph that redefines your job to reflect your interests and assets.

- If you were to give yourself another title, what would it be? What would you be doing in this "new job"? What new roles would you have and what attributes would you be using?

- Create the *ideal* job for yourself; one that utilizes your strengths to the max. What would it be? What would you be doing and what strengths would you be utilizing that you aren't now?

- Where are the natural overlaps between your current job and your ideal?

- How can you begin to transform your current job into your ideal one?

UW *says:*

- *In order to excel in a changing world you must build on your strengths.*

- *Don't try to be good at lots of things; be great at one.*

- *If you strive to be well rounded, you will probably end up flat.*

18

Don't Look Where You Don't Want to Go

THE DON'TS

There are times you may think that you are acting in your own best interest when instead you are unwittingly choreographing your own defeat. In these situations, without realizing it we mentally rehearse our own defeat by spending far too much time anticipating the worst. Break-It Thinkers know that subtle shifts in thinking can enable you to perform at your best, and that shift accounts for the margin of victory.

Recently I was talking to a young lawyer about to begin her first jury trial. She was very nervous about it, and in our conversation I asked her what impression she wanted to make on the jury. "I don't want to look too inexperienced, too young or naive. I don't want them to suspect this is my first trial. I don't—"

This young lawyer had fallen victim to "the Don'ts." The Don'ts are negative goal setting. They focus on what you don't want to have happen, instead of what you do. Ironically, thinking about what you don't want will often make it happen. When you have the Don'ts, you are mentally rehearsing what you don't want to happen. It's like the suggestion that you *not* think of a pink elephant. What's the first thing that comes to your mind? A pink elephant.

It's like the golfer who, faced with a water hole, tells herself, "Don't hit it into the water"; or the manager going into a meeting thinking, "Don't lose your temper!"; or any one of us telling ourselves, "Don't worry," "Don't do this," "Don't think that."

JP's nose

George Wheelwright, one of the founders of Polaroid, tells an aprocryphal story that illustrates this point. When he was trying to get investment capital to form the company, J. P. Morgan was interested and invited him and his family to his house for dinner. It was a formal affair and Wheelwright was understandably nervous, because Morgan had the reputation of being one of the most ornery of people.

There was one other aspect of J. P. Morgan: he was also very sensitive about his nose, which was purported to be like that of W. C. Fields—big, bulbous, and red-veined. Prior to the dinner, Wheelwright coached his young daughter by telling her, "Don't say anything about his nose. Don't stare at his nose. Don't even mention the word 'nose.'"

The evening went smoothly, and Morgan was warm and friendly. When the butler served the dessert and coffee, Wheelwright's daughter, looking adorable in her party dress, picked up the sterling-silver sugar and creamer tray, went up to Morgan, and in the cutest little voice you ever heard said, "Mr. Morgan, how many lumps of sugar would you like in your nose!"[1]

The mind works in pictures

Little Ms. Wheelright was so well-versed in the Don'ts that she didn't know what *to do*. The Don'ts are self-fulfilling because the part of your mind that controls your behavior works in pictures. That's why when you tell someone *not* to think of a pink elephant, the picture they see is of a pink elephant. In effect, when you say *don't* do something, you create *that* picture in your mind, minus the caution "Don't." The late Italian psychiatrist Roberto Assagioli wrote in *The Act of Will* that "images and mental pictures . . . tend to produce the physical conditions and external acts that correspond to them."

Stanford neurophysiologist Karl Pribam calls the phenomenon whereby our mental images precede *and* effect all our actions "feedforward."[2] Pribam's research showed that an image in the mind fires the *same* neural connections in the autonomic nervous system as does the actual act of doing something. So "thinking" and "doing," as far as the autonomic nervous system is concerned, are no different!

All of this is another way of saying that having a mental picture will create a corresponding *physical* response. The picture in the golfer's mind when she thinks, "Don't hit it into the water," is a rehearsal of a ball-going-into-water. And guess where it is likely to go? The picture in the manager's mind when he tells himself, "Don't lose your temper," is manager-blows-his-cool. And guess what probably happens?

UW *says: Thinking about what you don't want to happen increases the odds that it will.*

Beating the Don'ts

I learned a wonderful lesson about beating the Don'ts when I played for the New York Lacrosse Club. Several players were Native Americans who were at ease at great heights and worked constructing Manhattan skyscrapers. At the time I had a fear of heights, so I asked one of my teammates for help in overcoming my fear.

He told me to meet him at one of the building sites. He said he would take me to the top and show me how to overcome my fear. I tried to talk him into *telling* me how to do it while we were on the ground, but he just laughed, gave me directions to the building, and encouraged me to come.

Having gathered up my courage, I arrived at the building and we went up. Leading me to the edge of a roof on the thirty-third floor, he told me to look down. I was terrified. My stomach felt woozy, I was dizzy, and my legs felt like shaving cream.

Then he told me to look across to another building. In other words,

I was now looking out rather than down. No problem. No butterflies. *That* I could do just fine. Then he said something that was so simple and so profound that I have never forgotten it and I use it in every area of my life: *"Don't look where you don't want to go."*

Similarly, when faced with a challenging situation, *don't* think about what you *don't* want to happen. Don't think about what you *don't* want to say, what you *don't* want to do, how you *don't* want to look, or the result you *don't* want. Zero in on what you *do* want to do or say or have happen.

THE DO'S

Before going into any pressure-packed situation, give your mind a positive mental picture to shoot for. Focus on what you do want to have happen. Look where you *do want to go*. See yourself accomplishing your goal. Remember, the term that best describes the attitude necessary for peak performance is *can do*.

Having a positive mental picture will help create the corresponding behavior. "How *do* you want to be in the courtroom?" I asked the lawyer before her first trial. "I want to look professional, self-assured, like I know what I am talking about."

I asked her to create a picture of what "self-assured" would look like. To her it meant she would move confidently around the courtroom, would use convincing body language, would make eye contact with the witnesses and jury, and would project her voice so that it could be heard from the bench to the back door. Then I had her imagine a skillful closing argument, quick jury deliberations, and a winning verdict. First she won her trial in her mind; a few weeks later she won it in court.

Visualization is valuable not only for personal performance. You can also use it when developing a new process, product, or program, to run through the process mentally from start to finish and make sure there are no glitches and to check that you have planned for everything, even the unexpected and undesired.

I had a political fund-raiser visually run through a major event he was planning. He played the part of a prospective donor and, in his mind, ran through the time he entered the hall till the time he left. It was amazing the little things that came up that had been overlooked, like the potential traffic jam going from registration to the coat-check area, which would annoy everyone, and the absence of signs for the restrooms. And, as the fund-raiser said, "An annoyed donor is usually not a donor."

Visualize your way to the top

Visualizing success is a technique that many top performers in all fields use: Jack Nicklaus, one of golf's living legends, is a prime example. Nicklaus attributes 10 percent of his success to his setup, 40 percent to his stance and swing, and 50 percent to the mental imagery he uses before he takes each stroke. "I never hit a shot, not even in practice, without having a sharp, in-focus picture of it in my mind. It's like a color movie." He imagines his swing, the ball in flight, and where it will land.

Baseball great Joe Morgan said he would visualize himself swinging a bat "even when I'm in the bathtub."[3]

Phil and Steve Mahre, the gold and silver medalists in the slalom at the 1984 Olympics, were seen on television visualizing their runs as they waited in the starting line. The list goes on and on. Just about every top athlete today uses one or another form of creative visualization.

Bobbi Bensman, one of the hottest rock climbers in the world, talks about the importance of visualization before making each climb. "I use [visualization] on extreme climbs," she says. "In my mind, I put my shoes on, I go to the climb and try [visualizing it] over and over. . . . I tie into the rope, chalk up and start. I imagine myself doing every move, precisely as I memorized it, seeing every foot and hand hold . . . right to the top. It's so real," she adds, "that I feel like calling my friends and telling them, 'Hey, I did the route.' The next day I usually walk up and do the climb."[4]

It's well known that visualization works in sports, but it is extremely effective in any situation, mental or physical, at work or at play. Top performers in medicine, politics, law, and the arts all use mental imagery.

Increasingly, top business executives utilize mental imagery as they prepare to undertake challenges. For example, Dick Munro, former co-chairman, co-CEO, and director of Time Warner, told me that as part of his preparation for an important speech he imagines the whole environment. "I will see in my mind what the room looks like, who will be there, how they will be seated and how I want to come across."

"Windmilling" is what Bettina Parker calls her process of mental rehearsal. When Parker, president of a large international marketing and consulting firm, is working on an important project, she visualizes it over and over in her head, rehearsing it until it plays out perfectly.[5]

Charles Lynch, chairman of DHL, who was a top salesman and a championship collegian tennis player, told me that "before a big match or a big presentation I mentally prepare for anything that might occur. I imagine the worst and how I would handle it. But right before the event, be it a match or a meeting, I visualize myself winning."

Prepare, prepare, prepare . . . UGH!

Most of us know that that preparation, rehearsal, and doing your homework is a key to peak performance in any area of life. Yet we'll do anything to avoid it. Even the most minor distraction is a welcome interruption.

Roger Craig, the All-Pro fullback for the San Francisco 49ers, has a surefire method for keeping himself motivated through his rigorous off-season training schedule. Craig, who feels his conditioning program sets him apart from other backs in the game, starts his workouts just two weeks after the Pro Bowl, a full six to eight months before the season starts.

Asked how he does it, Craig says, "I see what the first game will be like. Man, that will be a physical game. Ricky Jackson, Vaughan Johnson . . . those guys will be looking for me and I better be ready . . . Every time I might have thoughts of easing up on my program or every time I get a little tired in training camp, I just think of games like that and I keep going."[6]

You can use Craig's visualization technique to overcome procrastination and be better prepared for any pressure-packed situation. Visualize the upcoming meeting at which you are going to present or the boss reading your report. Imagine the toughest questions and responses coming your way. Visualizing yourself in that pressure situation will help to overcome your lethargy and get you into action now, so you'll be ready and in top form later.

Building the fire

We procrastinate because the picture in our minds of all the possible difficulties and all the potential disasters involved in the upcoming task far outweigh the positive images. As a result we wait until the balance changes—or, worse, until time is running out.

Parenthetically, people often say that they do their *best* work as the deadline nears. That usually is not the case. The truth is, that is the *only* time they *do* the work. At the last minute, necessity finally overcomes procrastination and they attack the project with the Gotta's, working in a frenzy to finish. But as has been discussed, the Gotta's not only create enormous stress, they minimize quality, creativity, and clear thinking.

Break-It Thinkers know that waiting until the last minute or until someone else does the job ensures mediocrity. To overcome the obstacles that prevent them from getting started, Break-It Thinkers begin by changing the pictures in their mind and by utilizing motivation's push or pull power.

Push/pull

The "push" comes by utilizing dissatisfaction with the status quo. Where you are now and what you are doing is so unpleasant and awful that there is lots of energy to change it. Almost anything would be better than continuing.

The sales manager of a management consulting company had become increasingly discouraged. He felt that top management wasn't listening to his suggestions or keeping up in the marketplace. He no longer trusted the company's priorities or principles.

He had tried everything to effect change from within and was frustrated at every turn. Yet when I mentioned looking for another job, he told me, "I'm making a lot of money here and will become vested in three years. I'll live with it. Besides, who knows what's out there?

I could just as easily get into the same fix someplace else or, worse, end up out in the street, and I've got lots of expenses, two kids in college. At least here I know the enemy. Better the devil you know . . ." He shrugged.

I asked him to visualize himself two years from now doing the same job, for the same company. Imagine, I suggested, how that would feel. "Awful!!! I don't think I could look myself in the mirror if I were still here in two years. I really do have to start looking to make a change." Feeling the push of his negative picture, he began looking around. Today he is the president of a smaller firm, a job that he loves and that stimulates him.

To utilize the "pull" side of motivation, work from the opposite direction. When the vision and possibilities inherent in a challenge are so attractive, you feel absolutely drawn to it. When a dream is great, you will devote incredible amounts of energy to achieving it. The potential with a new client is so terrific you will overcome any obstacle to land 'em. The possibilities in a new business, project, product, or system are so fabulous that not starting on it would seem foolish or crazy.

Take a "two-year picture"

To go from procrastination to action, from stalling to starting, you need a change of mental scenery. Visualize yourself in two years in much the same situation you are now: the same job, same income level, "same old, same old." How does it look? What do you "see"? How do you feel?

Or from the opposite direction: visualize that the risk or challenge you are now contemplating has worked out perfectly. See yourself having successfully completed the project. Imagine the positive ramifications—faster access to information, an innovative new product, a larger income, greater acclaim, perhaps a promotion. As you visualize a successful project, how do you feel? What are the benefits you have realized?

Whether it takes a "push" or a "pull," the two-year visualization exercise will get you excited about future possibilities and moving ahead. Being fired up by your visualization will often "jump-start" a stalled motor and get you going again.

I can't tell you how many people have told me about their valuable experience with visualization. Like Jack Nicklaus, Charles Lynch, Dick Munro, and Bettina Parker, people from every walk of life have found visualization a powerful tool.

The power of the mind's images

Several remarkable studies have confirmed the power of visualization. Research on prisoners of war is especially telling. One POW visualized himself playing a round of golf on his favorite golf course every day that he was in prison. Shortly after his release he shot the best round of his life.

Desperately wanting to learn to type, one man pictured a keyboard and visualized himself typing on it every night. When put in front of his first typewriter he could type 45 words a minute! And in another well-documented example of the effectiveness of visualization, a world-class pianist was back performing professionally within three months of his release from seven years in a POW camp!

A simple experiment done in a college physical education class has become a classic tale illustrating the effect of visualization. Three groups were told that they had a month to prepare for a best-of-20 free-throw contest. At a pretest they each took 20 shots and then were split up as follows: Group A was told to practice shooting 100 free throws a day for 30 days. Group B, the "control group," was told to do nothing differently and play when they felt like it, but they weren't to do any more or less free-throw shooting than they would normally. Group C was told not to touch a basketball for a month. Rather, they were to spend 15 minutes every day visualizing themselves shooting free throws.

At the end of the month's time, Group A, (the group that practiced) and Group C (the group that only visualized) had essentially the same scores, while Group B's score decreased. Solely by visualization the people in Group C rehearsed their way to a peak performance.

Mind to body

Visualization can help you achieve some of your health goals as well. In a study done by Canadian physicians, postcoronary patients were divided into two groups.

One group was given a daily program of jogging and exercise. The other group only did mental imagery. "They imagined themselves jogging or pictured themselves in a beautiful meadow filling their lungs with fresh air and feeling the oxygen going through their whole body, reaching the heart."

After a year the results were identical for both groups. Weight and body fat were down. There was an increase in grip strength and EKG tracings. Blood pressure was lowered, as was adrenaline production.

Your personal mental movie

Here are some guidelines that will help you gain the greatest benefit from visualization. Although the term is *visual*ization, not everyone actually see pictures when they practice this technique. Mental imagery can be auditory, kinesthetic, or olfactory, as well as visual. Some people are more inclined or oriented toward one of these senses than the others. Many people who use visualization very effectively never actually *see* their mental movies. Some get a *feel* for the picture or *sense* it. A good friend of mine *listens* to it. Although I use the word *see* in the guidelines below, this word is meant to encompass any of the other ways you may experience your mental movie.[7]

1. Relax. You can't take a good picture if your camera isn't steady. Similarly, visualization is most effective if your mind is steady. The more relaxed and free of distractions you are when visualizing, the clearer your mental pictures will be and the more deeply the images will imprint. Start practicing at home in a quiet spot a few days ahead of a challenging situation. That way the mental picture will already be imprinted and you can bring it up on the mental screen more easily.

2. Make it real. The effectiveness of your imagery is largely dependent upon how specific and detailed it is. Your mental movie should be as close to the real thing as possible. If you are rehearsing for a meeting, for instance, start by seeing something familiar and build upon it until you can see the whole scene fully. Take your time. Keep adding details until you have a sense of being there. Then see yourself going through the same step-by-step sequence that you would in the actual situation.

3. Your own role in the movie. There are two roles you can play in your movie. You can play the *observer* and watch yourself perform. This is helpful when you are reviewing a past experience or using an ideal model, as it allows you a more objective look at your performance. You can also play the *participant*—be the player in your own movie. Being the subject of your own movie is particularly useful when you are rehearsing for an upcoming situation. To get the greatest benefit from your mental movie, play both of these roles. See how it looks from the outside, and feel and practice it from the inside.

4. Experience it fully. A friend told me that when Olympic triple gold medal winner Jean-Claude Killy visualized a ski race, he could hear the crowd, feel the wind and the cold on his face, feel his legs pumping, and feel the edges of his skis carving through the snow. Experiencing your mental movie with all your senses is the most effective way to fully imprint the visualization and affect your subsequent behavior. Mental movies can come to life.

On the advice of a sports psychologist, an NBA team made a tape of a slumping player's personal highlights—slam dunks, great passes, timely steals, perfect assists—and showed it to him 20 times over a 30-game period. During this time his point production increased 41 percent and steals per game improved by 60 percent!

REVIEW TO PREVIEW: BRINGING THE PAST INTO THE FUTURE

Several visualization techniques can be used to prepare for new challenges and worrisome changes. One is to choose a past "win" in a similar type of situation. Play it back in your mind in as much detail as possible. Review how you prepared for the event and the feelings and specific behavior that helped you to be successful. Look for the little things—the gestures you used, the routines you set up, how you moved—anything that helped you then.

Then review the accomplishment of that past goal, shaking hands with the client who signed the contract, seeing the boss give the okay to your proposal, finishing the project. Visualizing yourself achieving that goal and reviewing how you got there will help you to reexperience the same feeling of confidence, exhilaration, and well-being that you had at that time. It will also remind you of things you did that enabled you to accomplish that goal.

The next step is to transfer these attitudes and skills from the past into the future. See yourself performing with the same "winning" qualities in the upcoming situation. Visualize yourself *in action* accomplishing your goal.

BILL AND I: IDEAL MODELING

I was very nervous when I first began to give keynote speeches to large audiences and often came off flat and humorless. Then I happened to watch a tape of Bill Cosby talking about education. I loved the way he combined humor with a more serious message. "That's how I'd like to be," I said. I watched the tape over and over, focusing on the qualities that I wanted to emulate.

Then I began visualizing Cosby giving a speech to my audience. My mental picture focused on his humor as well as his personal power. Gradually I replaced his image with mine until I could visualize myself combining these two qualities in a style that was my own.

To use an ideal model, pick someone who expresses the qualities that you want to develop, as I did with Cosby. Then visualize this person expressing these characteristics. Gradually edit yourself into the tape until you can see yourself performing with them. *Don't try to copy your role model.* See yourself expressing these same qualities in *your own unique way.* You'll find the more you visualize the more you will be expressing those desired qualities, that already exist within you naturally and easily.

PREVIEWING VICTORY

You can also preview an upcoming event without the benefit of a past victory or an ideal model. Prior to a pressured situation take a minute and sit in a quiet spot. See yourself performing the way you want and accomplishing the goal. Make the "movie in your mind" as real as possible. The following is a good example of how to visualize a preview.

A creative director for a large advertising agency was going to be part of a presentation to a new and potentially very large client, one that the agency had been trying to land for years. He was nervous, because not only was his presentation a critical one, but it was also his first at the agency and he was under a lot of scrutiny. After doing the catastrophic-expectations check (discussed in chapter 13), which helped him regain his composure, he prepared by previewing the upcoming event.

He visualized himself walking into the conference room and sitting down. He then made his mental movie as real as possible. He saw all the details in the room: the flip charts, slide projectors, videotape player, where he sat, and where everyone else (including the prospective client) was seated.

Then he visualized himself going up to make the presentation. He saw himself feeling calm and sure of himself, making eye contact with everyone in the room, using appropriate gestures to emphasize his points. He saw himself responding well to tough questions, and running the video to show the agency's commercial reel. Then he visualized himself finishing the presentation successfully and leaving the conference room.

After several mental run-throughs he was much more relaxed and positive about the situation. He later told me that his presentation was a snap. "I felt like I'd been through it before. But I'll tell you, the movie in my head was much harder than the actual one."

Before any challenging situation don't think about what you don't want to do. See yourself accomplishing your goal. Make it real in your mind, feel it, see it, believe it.

Visualization is a powerful tool you can use to mentally prepare yourself to perform at peak levels under pressure. It will help you feel more confident and in control when entering any new and challenging situation. By utilizing this tool to harness the incredible powers of your mind you will continually surprise yourself and perform at levels beyond what you have before, do more than you thought you could, and be more than you thought you were.

UW *says:*
Picture perfect.

19

Like It?
. . . Log It!

No matter what we're doing these days we all face high-pressure, stress-filled, anxiety-provoking situations. We deal with tight deadlines, take difficult tests, face stronger competition, have meetings with dissatisfied clients, or have to digest as much information as in the Congressional Record in ten minutes! Sometimes we rise to the occasion, sometimes not. Break-It Thinkers understand that frequently the best way to keep an advantage is to keep things in proper perspective. There are times when you have to reach around and pat yourself on the shoulder and say out loud: "Well done."

No one bats a thousand. Many of us, however unconsciously, start a negative fear cycle by taking our wins for granted and only remembering the losses. If you have seven pars and two bogies, what do you remember? The bogies of course. If you struck out twice and then got a hit, what haunts you after the game? The strikeouts. The same is true in any area of life. If you respond well to five questions in a big meeting and muff one, what do you remember? The one you missed.

THE UH-OHS

At a division managers' conference for a major high-tech corp, participants had received written feedback forms from both their staff and bosses. After looking at the forms I asked the managers to write down the comments they remembered. The majority remembered *only* the critical comments. One manager said, "I didn't realize I'd received any positive feedback at all. I raced through, only looking for the bad news."

Focusing on criticism, a past loss, a bad swing, or a muffed question only imprints it more clearly in your mind. Then, when a similar situation arises, guess what your mind jumps to? Consider the tennis player. Remembering his last double fault as he prepares to serve, he thinks, "Uh-oh, better be careful," so he tightens up and serves it into the net. Or the secretary who made a typo on a document. Though his work is normally flawless, he dwells on the mistake and is shaken. On the next report he is tense and makes several more errors. Reflecting on past failures triggers the Uh-ohs and ensures poor performance.

FALSE "TRUTHS"

It seems natural for us to focus on the negative, to the exclusion of the positive. But because we have not factored in positive experiences, our assessment isn't accurate. Dwelling on past failures or mistakes offers us a skewed and unrealistically negative account of our abilities. To make matters worse we then take this to the next level, from performance to self-image. We focus on the putt we missed and begin to think of ourselves as a lousy putter. We dwell on the one question we muffed in the meeting and conclude that we are a poor presenter. We then "carry" this attitude the next time we are faced with a similar situation. And the "lousy putter" tries too hard and blows another. . . .

These unrealistically negative views quickly become vicious cycles, reinforcing feelings of inadequacy about ourselves and affecting our self-esteem. Remembering only the errors, we begin to doubt our ability to handle the job.

Balance the losses with the wins and you get an accurate view of your ability and of how well or poorly you *really* did in a situation. If you are like most people you'll find that you are doing much better than you thought and that, in fact, you aren't giving yourself credit for being as good as you are.

REMEMBERING PAST VICTORIES

Another type of "reality check" can help you build your confidence as you face a difficult challenge. Let me offer three examples from sports.

There were a little over two minutes left in the 1988 Super Bowl, which pitted the San Francisco 49ers against the Cincinnati Bengals. The 49ers were five points down and more than 90 yards from the goal line. To win they had to march the length of the field and score a touchdown. In the huddle, 49er quarterback Joe Montana looked at the rest of the players and said, "This is just like '81."

Those of you who are football fans may recall that in the 1981 NFC title game against the Dallas Cowboys, the 49ers were in almost the identical situation, when Montana, then in only his third year as a pro, led the team down the field and in the final seconds threw a high pass to Dwight Clark, who made what is now referred to in the Bay Area as "the Catch" for the winning touchdown.

In that huddle in the 1988 Super Bowl, Montana wisely got his teammates to remember the successful 1981 experience. In other words, the 1988 drive wasn't unique, they had been "there" before, and they had won! Remembering the Dallas victory calmed the players down, increased their confidence, made them much more effective, and they went on to beat Cincinnati and win the Super Bowl.

In the 1989 Wimbledon finals, Boris Becker was ahead, but the tide seemed to be turning against him. His opponent, Stefan Edberg, was coming on strong. But at one point in the match Becker had a burst of energy and went on to win. Asked afterward what he had been thinking about when Edberg appeared to be catching him, Becker replied that he was remembering his last victory at Wimbledon two years before, what it felt like, and what he had done then to win.

Interestingly, the previous year Becker had lost to Edberg in the finals at Wimbledon. But by thinking about his past victory rather than his defeat, Becker handled the new challenge with more confidence and regained his winning form.

When Greg Louganis, one of the finest divers ever, hit his head on the diving board at the 1988 Olympic Games in Seoul, someone asked him whether he wanted to see a video of it. Luganis declined, saying, "No, thanks. The only pictures I want in my head are of perfect dives." He went on to make an amazing final dive and win the gold medal.

Louganis, Montana, and Becker had taken the time to remember a past victory as a way of bringing out their best. Peak performers like Montana and Becker know that you must learn from past mistakes and then move on, not dwell on them.

Success is one of the greatest motivators and confidence builders. There is nothing like winning to create a winning attitude. The more you *re-mind* yourself of past victories the more you will build a positive reality base for handling tough situations. I'm not advocating trying to talk yourself into believing that you can succeed in a specific situation. It's not that you *can* do it, but that you *have already* done it. You have had the experience and you have been successful. Use past experience to bolster your confidence.

UW *says: Remembering past victories is reality thinking, not wishful thinking.*

THE "WHAT HAVE YOU DONE FOR ME LATELY?" SYNDROME

Often we think of the future as if the past had vanished into thin air. As a result, we look up New Quota Mountain and get a stiff neck because it seems so high. We have forgotten how high the mountain we climbed last year seemed when we were starting out.

I used to work with skiers who, after making it halfway down a difficult run, were feeling intimidated about skiing the rest of the slope. Rather than having them focus on what they still had to do to get all the way down the hill, we would have them look back up the hill and see what they had already done.

The change in attitude from doing this simple exercise was enormous. Looking at what they had already accomplished increased the skiers' confidence, and they usually skied the rest of the way with enthusiasm.

I have used this exercise with many different types of individuals and seen the same change in attitude. I would have students facing a tough exam remember a difficult one that they had done well on in the past. I would have project directors having difficulties getting started on a new project remember a previous one when they had succeeded. The change is always dramatic. When people remember past successes in similar situations they feel more confident and motivated to start on a new one.

KEEP A VICTORY LOG

The president of a major clothing manufacturer told me that he used to get nervous and "filled with dread" before every executive committee meeting. He'd start the meeting tentatively, trying to find a rhythm, and somehow or other would "wade through it."

"After one of these meetings several of my vice presidents came up and complimented me on how well I had done," he said. "I was surprised, since I thought I should have done much better. But they were quite enthusiastic and didn't seem to be playing games. They even offered examples of how I had handled tough questions and turned the tone of the meeting around. I must admit I had seen the meeting differently. In my eyes I had done another just adequate job and had really blown one question.

"But they convinced me that I had done much better than I had given myself credit for. On a whim, I wrote down a few of the things they said on a notepad. Prior to the next meeting, I looked at the positive comments and found myself feeling much more confident. I started the meeting with a bang! Now, after every meeting I keep track of the bright spots and refer to them before the next meeting. I'm telling you, it's like a magic potion!"

Thus was born what he refers to as his Victory Log. He writes down all of his accomplishments in challenging situations and reviews these past victories before entering any tough situation. He doesn't rest on his past accomplishments; rather, he uses the past as a springboard to future successes.

A VICTORY LOG "REMINDER"

I have used the Victory Log© with many, many organizations. Writing down past successes helps people break the cycle of fear by reminding them that indeed they *have* "been there before," that they already *do* know how to play this game. Reading your Victory Log can turn the anxiety of fear into the excitement of having an opportunity to be victorious once again.

The Victory Log given out in my workshops starts with the following message as a reminder:

Throughout your life you will have numerous successes. You will accomplish goals, have moments of great clarity and vision, and some of your dreams will come true.

This VICTORY LOG is a special place for you to record these personal victories.

Read your VICTORY LOG from time to time. It will remind you of your accomplishments and help you remember how terrific you really are.

Your VICTORY LOG will give you insights into your strengths and get you back on track when you are in a slump or running on empty.

Read your VICTORY LOG before a big presentation, embarking on a major project, or prior to any pressure situation. You will find it a source of confidence, inspiration, and power.

Reminding yourself of your past victories helps you identify with your potential rather than your problems. It enables you to act from a position of strength rather than weakness, to feel more powerful, confident, and in control of yourself in any situation.

Each limit exceeded, each boundary crossed, verifies that most limits are indeed self-imposed, that your potential and possibilities are far greater than you have ever imagined, that you are capable of far more than you have ever thought.

The internal rewards of victory are joy, vitality, well being, and the knowledge that throughout your life you will continue to exceed your own limits and break your own records.

Before you close this book, remind yourself of a past success. See it in your mind's eye. Feel it. Experience your power. Remind yourself that the potential to perform at this level, to live at this level, is always there waiting to be experienced and expressed in everything you do, wherever you go.

CUSTOMIZING YOUR VICTORY LOG

It is not necessary to keep a Victory Log in a specific way in order to reap its many benefits. For those who like to write, elaborate descriptions of events will flow easily. For others, a few dates, places, and key words will suffice. If you have a hectic schedule, as I do, short entries go a long way.

I have found keeping a Victory Log to be so powerful that I use it before every speech or seminar I give. As I sit waiting to go on, I read it and flip through the pages to remind myself that I have "been here before." My notations merely consist of dates, a client's name, and something that helps me remember that presentation. Just looking at it brings back the memory of the event. I re-experience the good feelings I had then. Remembering my past victories puts a smile on my face and gets me excited about a repeat performance.

John Ernst, a successful marketing consultant in New York City, told me that when he started keeping a Victory Log he was not prepared for what happened. "Before, I used to do a daily review before going to bed. Most of it consisted of what didn't work right that day and what I could do better next time. As a result I would go to sleep feeling a little frustrated and disappointed in myself. The Victory Log changed all that. I make entries in it every night and review my day's successes. I tell you, I feel differently about myself after reading and writing in my Victory Log. I feel much more positive and upbeat. I realize I'm much better than I ever gave myself credit for. My whole self-image has changed, and that has affected everything, my work, my relationships, even my tennis game."

CHANGING YOUR MIND

Whether in school, sports, or business, reminding yourself of past victories will help to keep you calm and confident. The reality-based Victory Log will help break through the cycle of fear as well as change the mental picture you have of yourself.

You are what you think you are, so reminding yourself of your past victories will elevate your self-esteem. Keeping a Victory Log will change the image you have of yourself. It will give you more confidence and poise and eventually replace a vicious cycle of fear with a vital cycle of success. A Victory Log is a simple, tangible tool anyone can use to encourage themselves to take more risks, blaze new trails, and become more of a Break-It Thinker. Keeping a Victory Log brings a sense of fulfillment and satisfaction into your work day.

UW *says:*
Like it? Log it!

20

Joy Pays Off

**No profit grows where
there is no pleasure ta'en.**

—Shakespeare, *The Taming of the Shrew*

GOING FOR THE GOLD

In order to string together victories, we must constantly question the
rules, roles, and strategies of the "game" we are playing. We also need
to question the goal of the game itself as well as ask "What is winning?"

Over twenty years ago, Dustin Hoffman, in the award-winning film
The Graduate, put on scuba gear and spent the afternoon of his college
graduation party at the bottom of his parents' swimming pool.
Disillusioned by the prospects of a lucrative career in "plastics,"
Hoffman's character was alienated and bewildered, preferring a quest
for meaning and truth.

Twenty years later, a different real-life movie premiers. Where once
college graduates repudiated plastic, now they wear it with pride. The
Harvard University class of 1989 has chosen the winning design for its
official T-shirt. On the front is the motto GOING FOR THE GOLD. As the
graduates walk away, the real meaning becomes clear. Emblazoned on

the shirt's back is a large gold credit card. A lot has changed in two decades.

Nationwide studies, conducted by CollegeTrack, a New York City marketing consulting firm, paint the same picture: In 1980, the primary goal of 53 percent of college was "being very well off financially." A decade later, 93 percent of college seniors surveyed rated "financial security as a major goal in life." In 1980, over 65 percent of college graduates were concerned about a philosophy of life. Only 43 percent of the class of '89 felt this way. "Being very well off financially" has itself become a meaningful philosophy of life. "What you need to make a difference in this world," says a recent graduate, "is money."[1]

"THE MOST TOYS WINS"

Approaching the toll plaza on the Golden Gate Bridge I spotted a sign of our times on the license plate frame of a new BMW: THE ONE WHO DIES WITH THE MOST TOYS WINS.

The rapid-fire accumulation of the "most toys" has become a dominant ethic permeating much of America. The most-toys mind-set wants to have it all *now*—the more the merrier, the sooner the better. Winning is equated with the score at the end of the game, the number of toys you have, or the pot of gold at the end of a rainbow, a career, or simply at the end of a week.

THE HIGH PRICE OF WORKING FOR MONEY

The dues we pay for going for the gold are heavy. Substantial research shows *upward of 70 percent* of all white-collar workers are dissatisfied with their jobs, 40 percent saying that "they would be happier working someplace else." Over one third of 1,100 middle managers surveyed had been in touch with a job-search company in the past six months. More than half said they had recently updated their résumés.

Dissatisfaction strikes at every level and in every profession. A survey of 500 salespeople found that one third of sales reps surveyed were on the verge of quitting their jobs! Another 40 percent said they were only moderately happy with their positions. Furthermore, the American Bar Association found that one fourth of the 3,000 lawyers it surveyed planned to change jobs in the next two years.[2]

A partner at a major investment banking firm told a recent business school graduate that "no one is happy here, and if they say they are, they are lying." He said, "You come in here, make a lot of money and leave as fast as you can."

MOST TOYS–LEAST TIME

The irony is that though a great percentage of people are dissatisfied with what they are doing, they are spending a lot more time doing it. Indeed, the toll in time alone is staggering. The 60-hour week is now "standard"—and many report 70-, 80-, even occasional 90-hour weeks. "A VP at Dean Witter Reynolds told recruits that investment banking demands eighty to one hundred hours of work a week," says Michael Finkel, a recent Wharton School graduate. "I don't see how anyone will ever find time to enjoy the gobs of money they will be making."

The greatest irony in the pursuit of the most toys is that it inevitably requires the most time to get them, leaving the *least* time to use them. Pollster Lou Harris has found that people have an average 32 percent less leisure time than they did a decade ago.[3]

There being only so many hours in the day, something has to give. Consequently, the dream car has been parked so long it's used more air in the tires than gas in the tank. The country house for weekend getaways may as well be in another country. The two-week ski trip to Europe has been delayed for the third winter. And the treasured wooden skiff hasn't touched anything wet in eight months. Blessed are the toys for they shall inherit the . . . dust!

FALLOUT: IS THERE LIFE AFTER WORK?

It's not only material possessions that go untouched; personal lives also suffer as a result of this most toys–least time lifestyle. When someone is working long, stressful days, there is an inevitable fallout into the rest of their lives. No one can spend 60 hours a week as a saber-toothed tiger and walk in their front door as tame as a pussycat. It's very difficult to be burned out for 10 hours a day on the job and still be fired up about life.

The personal price for professional success was dramatically illustrated by the retirement, at age 46, of Peter Lynch, perhaps the best known "stock picker" in the world, who led Fidelity Magellan fund to the highest performance record in the eighties. Lynch stated that he had spent all of his waking hours "poring over company balance sheets and meeting with executives to try to find the next hot stock. I didn't have time to watch sports or look at newspapers and read only about one book a year. Worse still, my family had become strangers."[4]

THE NEWEST GROWTH INDUSTRY

Those driven solely by the desire for big bucks "tend to be negligent of personal relationships," said a *Fortune* magazine report. "The lack of time away from work for falling in love, sitting and talking with a spouse, or answering a child's question" surely contributes to the fact that psychologists, psychiatrists, and counselors are a real "growth industry."[5]

It's no wonder that drug and suicide problems among kids today are serious and mounting. In addition to the enormous pressures on them, there are major problems of self-esteem. Kids today have been "managed"—shipped from preschool to ballet class to language class—and not touched. Parents don't take time with their kids and then wonder why they have become such a problem.

WORKING MOMS AND DADS

One busy executive took two hours off from work to drive her six-year-old son and some classmates on a Valentine's Day field trip. "When I was driving them back, I told Paul, 'That was your Valentine present—the time.'"

Absentee dads—and their children—pay the high price of working for money, too. "It's not that I didn't care about the kids, but I was not like typical fathers," rationalizes one recently divorced executive. "I couldn't be at the Little League games because I had to be in London. My first wife had to make it clear that I had this important job—it wasn't that I didn't want to be with them. . . . It's another price you pay."

Whether it's London or Louisville or Laramie, to a child a miss is as good as a mile. And an "important" parent with an "important" job sends a clear message to the family: You are not as important as my work!

The following research findings, indicating substantial increases in substance abuse, shattered family life, stress-related health problems, and latch-key children left to fend for themselves, shouldn't be surprising.

- Half of all marriages will end in divorce.

- 60 percent of all children born today will spend some time growing up in a single-parent family.

- The incidence of reported child abuse has quadrupled in the last decade.

- The average age of successful suicides is now 40. There has been a 300 percent increase in the suicide rate for 15- to 24-year-olds since 1950.[6]

- Cocaine and/or alcohol abuse actively touches 6 out of 10 American families.

- The average working parent spends only *11 minutes a day* of "quality time" with children.[7]

This "work comes first" attitude seems to change as people realize the high price they are paying for their success. Research indicates that 74 percent of the men responding said, "If I had to do it over again I would spend more time with my family."[8]

WEAK (NOT PEAK) PERFORMANCE

The toll of long hours, family pressures, and increased job dissatisfaction affects business productivity as well, in terms of decreased motivation, creativity, and quality of work. A person who is burned out on the job will be about as good as a surfer who no longer likes the water.

A stressed-out, overwhelmed employee is not going to be a peak performer. He's not going take the risks necessary to keep ahead if he is having trouble keeping up. He won't accept challenge if he feels his job is already more than he can handle. He won't be alert or creative or go the extra mile if he is running on empty.

NECESSARY EVIL

A University of Massachusetts study supports the Conventional Wisdom that work is increasingly seen as a *"necessary evil."*[9] It pays the bills, buys the toys, and in theory enables us to have financial security now and/or later. It doesn't matter if you enjoy your work, since work is expected to be hard, perhaps even unpleasant. The idea of intrinsic pleasure in your work, of enjoyment on the job, of not having a dramatic separation between business and pleasure, is alien to most of the American work force.

John Madden puts it succinctly, "As soon as people hear you say 'business,' they know you're not talking about 'fun.'"[10]

WINNING IS PLAYING

Conventional Wisdom says play to *win.*

UW *says: Play, to win.*

It tells us that work should be fun; that the winning should take place not at the end of the game but every day you are playing.

UW *says: He or she who laughs, lasts.*

"I've come to the realization that entrepreneurs work far too hard," says Chris Whittle. "It's clear to me that I squandered large parts of my twenties and thirties in needless, completely neurotic work. I got tangled up in the myth of the hard-charging, hardworking, we'll-stay-here-till-they-drop entrepreneur. That's a very destructive attitude.

It's unneccessary. It's unhealthy. It's not the best way to live your life and not a good example to set for your company. And you can have entrepreneurial success without it.

"A lot of things feed it. One is that entrepreneurs want to be viewed as indispensable. There's also fear—the fear that if you don't do it you will fail. Inexperience plays a role, too, since a lot of people haven't learned to delegate. Also a kind of macho attitude—'I'm going to be the one to bust my ass.' What bothers me is that this mentality has been celebrated. It should be criticized."[11]

"WORK OUGHT TO BE FUN"

Steeped in the Conventional Wisdom of the business world at PepsiCo, John Sculley ventured out into the unconventional when he took over the silicon reins at Apple Computers.

"I remember I'd been in California a number of months," says Sculley, "and I returned to the East Coast and saw a number of my old friends, and they said, 'Well, how is it out there?' And I said, 'It's great. They've got this idea that work ought to be fun.' And they all looked at me like I'd lost my mind. And they said, 'How can it be fun? Work's supposed to be productive, not fun. You must have been in the California hot tub too long.'"[12]

A NOBEL PRIZE

High school vocational tests indicated that Michael Bishop was best suited to be a reporter, a music teacher, or a forest ranger. There was no mention of science. Going against these "conventional prognoses," Bishop pursued medicine. Highly regarded, he raised eyebrows "when he chose the less prestigious UCSF over top East Coast medical schools" and medical research over practicing medicine. The reason: "I was madly in love with medical research."

In 1989, J. Michael Bishop, along with his partner, Harold Varmus, won the Nobel Prize for medicine. But for Bishop, who had toiled for years in the lab, the "win" wasn't the prize: "The Nobel Prize isn't such a climax for me that everything will be an anticlimax. When someone walks through the door with a new piece of data, that beats the prize any day." Advice Bishop gives to his students: "Loosen up, break all the rules, follow your noses."[13]

The conventional notion that Sculley and others face—that work is supposed to be productive, not fun, drudgery not pleasure—always struck me (as it must have occurred to Whittle and Bishop and other Break-It Thinkers) as illogical, perhaps even absurd. You can't do your best with a terminal case of the blahs or racing around with the Gotta's.

DOING SOMETHING
YOU'D DO FOR NOTHING

In my interviews with over 500 top performers for my last book, *The C Zone: Peak Performance Under Pressure*, I discovered that the most common ingredient for success was that people love what they are doing. Their work brings them not only satisfaction but considerable joy. Doing something you love brings joy, passion, and excitement into your life. It gives you more vitality and makes you *want* to get up in the morning.

"I enjoy [my work] so much," says Tony Tiano, president of KQED-TV, "it doesn't ever seem to be work. I'm surprised every time I get a paycheck!"[14] Tiano is reflecting what I hear whenever I talk to a top performer: making your business a pleasure is necessary.

UW *says: Making your business a pleasure is good business.*

"You can be born with $100 million," observes David Brown, producer of *Jaws, The Sting,* and *The Verdict,* "but unless you find something you really enjoy, money is of no consequence. I always did something I would do for nothing."[15]

DOING WHAT YOU LOVE

The most accurate predictor of success is a strong preference for the work. Aristotle said, "Pleasure in the job puts perfection in the work." But he didn't go far enough! Research reveals that the more you love what you do the better you'll do it and the more money you'll make. One study dramatically illustrates this.

Researchers followed a group of 1,500 people over a period of 20 years. At the outset of the study, the group was divided into Group A, 83 percent of the sample, who were embarking on a career chosen for the prospects of making money now in order to do what they wanted later, and Group B, the other 17 percent of the sample, who had chosen their career path for the reverse reason, they were going to pursue what they wanted to do now and worry about the money later.

The data showed some startling revelations:

- At the end of the 20 years, 101 of the 1,500 had become millionaires.

- Of the millionaires, all but one—100 out of 101—were from Group B, the group that had chosen to pursue what they loved![16]

The key ingredient in most successful projects is loving what you do. Having a goal or a plan is not enough. Academic preparation is not enough. Prior experience is not enough. Pleasure and productivity are Siamese twins in these unconventional times.

TOTAL IMMERSION

Findings such as these shouldn't be surprising, because when you love what you are doing, getting paid for doing it seems like icing on the cake. You are more motivated, you have more energy, you feel more creative and daring, and you end up doing it better.

If you love to play golf, for instance, you immerse yourself in the game. You want to play as much as you can. You go to bookstores for golfing biographies. You talk to people about golf, watch matches on TV, rent how-to tapes. You keep your clubs in the car trunk and a putter in the office. You'll try anything new that might improve your game.

I remember when I first started working in advertising, a group would come to my apartment in the evenings and gather around my TV set to watch the commercials! We would analyze, scrutinize, marvel, and learn from them, trying to figure out the company's marketing and creative strategies. Critiquing them we saw how we could do them better.

We had some fabulous times yakking away while we muted the programming and waited for the next round of commercials. We had caught fire in front of the tube and it hardly seemed like "work" at all. We were having fun and learning a lot. The evenings gave a new twist to the notion of "on-the-job training." When you love something, it tells you all its secrets.

When you are doing what you love, hard work becomes easier, and even the inevitable "drags" don't take you down with them.

THE NINJAS OF JOY

Paul Hawken, best-selling author, businessman, and entrepreneur par excellence, says, "I don't believe there is a business in America that would not benefit by loosening up and having fun with its customers." Using the analogy of coal miners bringing birds into the shafts for early warnings of danger, Hawken says, "Laughter and good humor are the canaries in the mine of commerce—when the laughter dies, it's an early warning that life is ebbing from the enterprise."[17]

Jerry Greenfield of phenomenally successful Ben & Jerry's Ice Cream concurs. "There was pretty much an agreement that things at work are tough, and that with all the tasks we have to perform, and the stress people are under, it would be a good idea to try to infuse a little more joy."[18]

So they established a "joy gang" whose charge was to put more joy into the workday. One of the more memorable of the many "Joy" events was an Elvis Day. Everyone came dressed as Elvis or in fifties costumes. There were a few "hounddogs," lots of blue suede shoes, a group of "Elvis lives" cheerleaders, an Elvis impersonator, and even an Elvis snarl contest. The president, Fred "Chico" Lager, came to work with black magic-marker sideburns and a white jumpsuit as he conducted "business as usual."

The company also has a group of 20 active "joy ninjas" whose role is to spread happiness throughout the company. One evening they served a "joy breakfast" at 10 P.M. for the second and third shift. Another time they made the world's largest milkshake. Ben & Jerry's has also started a "spontaneous performance" program in which any group or individual in the company can make a suggestion for bringing more joy to work—and get a grant to do it.

Also, anyone can create a fun title to describe their otherwise serious job. For instance, Jerry Greenfield is known as the "minister of joy." Peter Lind, the ice cream idea facilitator who is the head of the "alchemy lab," has dubbed himself "the "Primal I scream therapist."[19]

As you might expect, employees enjoy working at Ben & Jerry's, there is little absenteeism, and they are a very productive work force.

VARIETY ADDS SPICE

Another way to make work a pleasure is to add variety. At work, as at play, variety does add spice to life. Companies are now beginning to understand the benefits, to both employees and to the company's bottom line, that accrue from building diversity into the workday. The conventional "one person, one job" is being replaced by the unconventional "one person, three or four jobs."

The retail chain of Lechmere Sales, a Dayton Hudson subsidiary, recently was forced to find new ways to deal with labor shortages. At their Sarasota, Florida, store they offered pay raises to their employees on the basis of the number of jobs they learned to perform. Cashiers drove forklifts, sold records and tapes, and worked the warehouse. Lechmere can now quickly adjust to shifts in staffing needs simply by redeploying existing workers.

"The pay incentives, along with the prospects of a more varied and interesting workday, proved substantial lures in recruiting," says Paul Chandler, senior vice president of personnel. "What's more, the Sarasota store is substantially more productive than the others."[20]

"REPOTTING" EXECUTIVES

Both executives and staff in corporations like General Motors, National Steel, and Motorola have reached similar conclusions: "A flexible work force increases speed, efficiency, quality, productivity and job satisfaction."[21]

"Today, most people gain expertise through their working lives by doing a variety of things, sometimes simultaneously," says Harvard professor of management Robert Reich. "I teach, write, lecture, consult, and pontificate on TV. Some days I do all five."[22]

RJR Nabisco's CEO, Louis V. Gerstner, Jr., likes the variety that comes with a change of jobs. "Executives should be repotted from time to time. Having different episodes in your career keeps you fresh and running hard."[23]

CHANGING THE JOB YOU HAVE INTO THE JOB YOU WANT

Don't jump ship if you're having some rough sailing—you might only have to patch up a leak or two. Don't blame the job, the company, or the boss. That will only create frustration, disappointment, and anger, and it makes us feel helpless and hopeless. Blame alleviates our responsibility for situations but at the same time make us feel powerless. There are many steps we can take to regain our personal power and recapture a sense of control and direction, no matter how bad things seem.

• The first step is to determine what specifically *isn't* working. Maybe what's bothering you is a demanding, disgruntled boss, or that you aren't learning anything new, or that you don't have any free time or are stuck in a rut.

• The second step is to see how you could make the job work for you. Visualize yourself changing the job you *have* into the job you *want*. What would you be doing differently to make you really enjoy what you are doing? How would you change your role or the rules of your job? What "sacred cows" would you have to kill? Picture yourself happy in your work, learning, growing, communicating, being appreciated. See yourself doing it, and don't Firehose it.

• The third step is to write yourself a new job description and give yourself a new title.

• The fourth step is to take action. What is one small step you could do tomorrow to begin to turn your new job description into a reality? What strength could you build on to add pleasure to your work?

BALANCE

For many people the issue these days is balancing work and the rest of life. Sandy Mobley, while a director of training at Wyatt, an independent benefits and compensation consulting firm, was working 70 to 80 hours a week (including weekends) with lots of travel. "I never had time for myself. I had no social life to speak of and was quickly reaching the point of burnout. I was tired all the time and feeling sluggish and putting on weight because I had no time to work out."

Over a period of time and with a job change she cut back to 40- or 45-hour weeks with minimal travel. The change is dramatic. "I am feeling great. Everything has picked up. I have time for friends, exercise, little projects of my own. And I am actually getting more work done with more quality and creativity."

It's not that hard to believe Mobley's experience. When you are tired, you work slower, don't think as clearly, are less creative, and make more mistakes, and the quality of work drops. You get home exhausted, but it's difficult to sleep because your mind is still racing. You wake up the next morning tired, and the cycle continues. Obviously, all of us have to work late sometime. But a steady diet of long hours kills creativity, enthusiasm, and energy, and the resulting stress may eventually kill you.

WORKAHOLISM

"If someone tells me they are working ninety-hour weeks" says GE chief Jack Welch, "I say you're doing something terribly wrong. I go skiing on the weekend, I go out with my buddies on Friday and party. You've got to do the same or you've got a bad deal. Put down a list of the twenty things you are doing that make you work ninety hours, and ten of them have to be nonsense . . ."[24]

Echoing Welch, former Time Warner co-chairman Dick Munro says, "I'm dead against workaholics. Working like that causes you to lose enthusiasm and vitality and inhibits creativity." To confirm this,

Munro told me that throughout his long career at Time Inc., starting as a college graduate, he very rarely took a train home later than 6:00 P.M.[25]

DOING MORE IN LESS TIME

As a reward to their employees, many organizations institute a policy of working half days on Friday during summer months. In itself that's not so surprising as companies these days try to find ways to rejuvenate a hard-working staff. The surprising thing is that many employees are discovering that they are getting as much done in half a day as they do during a regular workday!

"I always walk out on Friday feeling I have done a full day's work," an editor of a major publishing house told me, "something I don't always feel on other days." The reason? "I am more focused and have more energy. One o'clock is like a firm deadline that I *want* to keep. I prioritize my work better. I know exactly what has to be done and do it. I waste less time."

We all know the tendency to create work to fill up any amount of time we have. As I described earlier, I have observed that people will accomplish the same amount of work in a 45-minute meeting that they will in one that is an hour and a half long. A finish time set in advance, whether it's a meeting, a workday, or a work week, makes you mentally aim for it. You prioritize better, do what has to be done, and waste less time out in the hall, on the phone, or doing jobs that can wait. You do what you do with more energy and concentration.

Conversely, when working late is the habit, you tend to slack off a little. You know there's no rush, you're not as focused and don't push yourself or prioritize as well. You also waste time on things that don't need to be done or you socialize in the hall. And though you work later, it's not necessarily because of the amount of work but because you had it in your mind that you were going to do so. The result is that we often convince ourselves that we need to work all those hours, and the routine becomes a rut.

It used to be that working late was considered heroic and the sign of a person on their way up. But this has shifted. "In the last two and a half to three years we've seen a dramatic change," says Dan Stamp, a time-management specialist. "Now it is mainstream thinking that there has to be more to life than just work. . . . I think the people who reject long hours will be the real leaders in the years to come—they're the brightest, the innovators. The guys logging really long hours aren't seen as heroes anymore. They're seen as turkeys."[26]

Starting next week, leave work an hour earlier than usual. I guarantee that you will get the same amount of work done as when you worked the extra hour. And you'll have added an extra hour to your outside life.

RIGHT LIVELIHOOD

If you have tried changing your job description, if you've tried adjusting your hours, and your work is no more enjoyable or meaningful than before, then you have to look elsewhere. The key is to trust that there's something out there that's right for you. Beware of the Firehosers who tell you you can't do what you love, that those who really enjoy what they are doing are few and far between.

You can bypass the roadblocks of the Firehosers by resisting the temptation of looking in the same field. A headhunter or career counselor looking at your résumé will probably advise you that the best move would be to another company in your field or doing the same type of work for a different company. Sure, that is where you have the most experience, and therefore the temptation is to hedge, to stay with what is familiar and financially the best deal. But if you no longer enjoy that type of work and nevertheless continue it, you will soon find yourself in the same predicament you are in now.

To find your "right livelihood" and determine the "perfect" work for you, don't look in the classifieds, look in the mirror. What do *you* love to do? What in your current work do you really enjoy doing? Is it the "people" or the creativity or the problem solving? What experience are you seeking in your work?

What do you enjoy doing in your spare time? And what is the quality you are expressing during these times?

Answering the following questions will also give you some clues as to where to look and what to seek:

Wouldn't it be great if I could . . .

If I had my druthers I would . . .

If I didn't have to make a living I would . . .

SMALL CHANGE, BIG REWARDS

Sometimes a dramatic change is necessary. But examples like that of my old friend Jim Hayes, the lawyer who became a potter in Northern California, are the exceptions rather than the rules. Changes don't have to be earth-shaking. Small ones, if made in the right direction, can yield big rewards and make a substantial difference in your outlook. the following are three areas to look at when considering a new choice:

1. What to do

2. Where to do it

3. How to do it

CHANGING *WHAT* YOU DO

Susan Lawley was playing on the fast track and, by every conventional measure, was winning handily. As VP of Goldman-Sachs, she was earning $250,000 a year, the same salary as her husband, Robert, a VP at Bankers Trust. Card-carrying members of the "most toys" club, they owned a four-bedroom house, drove to their offices in Mercedes-Benz and a Lincoln Continental, had a beachhouse and a motorboat, and took an annual trip to Europe with their 11-year-old son, Greg.[27]

But one night Susan realized where the fast track was leading. "I was driving home from work at ten P.M. . . . and . . . I suddenly burst into tears," she recalled. "I couldn't see the road, I was crying so hard. I had realized that that night, like almost every night, I would miss seeing my son because he was already in bed."

To make up for her lack of time with Greg, "he got every toy and went to every movie," she said. "I wanted to make him happy." But that night she had realized, "he was turning into a demanding brat. His teachers had called me from school to say he was disruptive and doing badly in class [because] we didn't give him a value system—no one was there to teach him at home. . . . I realized that life is too short to live like that."[28]

As a result of this late-night revelation, *everything* changed. She and her husband *both* quit their jobs and set up small consulting firms with flexible hours—at one fifth their former combined income. They have offices in the same building and see each other for lunch. They are home for dinner to see Greg every day. He is now an A, not a C, student and gets a small weekly allowance, which he has to earn by doing chores around the house. And Susan Lawley feels that what she has earned in pride, self-respect, and family values far exceeds the loss of monetary rewards.

COMBINING WHAT YOU DO WITH WHAT YOU LOVE

• Paul Marston was a computer professional in Sydney, Australia, whose hobby was bridge. A proficient player, he won many tournaments around Australia and New Zealand. He then began being invited to play in large international tournaments, for which he was paid. After several years of doing this, he quit programming to play bridge full time; he has now become a key member of the Australian bridge team and plays around the world. But Marston didn't stop there. He has written several successful books on bridge, owns the "Grand Slam" bridge clubs throughout Australia, developed a computer system that makes bridge more attractive to club players, and publishes a bridge magazine.

On the surface the change from a computer programmer to a bridge champion and entrepreneur seems like a giant step. Marston made the change, however, by taking a series of many small steps to get there. By the time he was ready to quit programming, he already knew the people in the bridge world and had made many of the contacts that enabled him to make his first step a successful one.

• Signe Hanson was a manager of social service programs, but, she says, "I woke up in the morning yawning. I would go to the mall [at lunchbreak] and drop some money on a dress because I was depressed." Now her old job (and her old wardrobe) are gone and she is pursuing a career in horticulture. Her old business suits line her closet. "I might as well give them to the Smithsonian," she says. Clad in overalls and boots to dig in the dirt all day, she comes home physically tired, but emotionally very satisfied, one of the perks of doing something she loves.[29]

• At 33 years of age, Tom Simpson became president and CEO of Norwegian Caribbean Lines. After doubling NCL's income within a short period of time, Simpson's career was on a roll. But after a few years he was no longer getting the same satisfaction from his work. He eventually took a leave of absence, which turned into a master's degree in counseling. Tom is now working happily as a counselor in the Southwest.

I have known many lawyers who have changed their environment but not their work. Using their existing skills in an arena that is more meaningful, they have become lobbyists, legal advisers, and even CEO's for nonprofit agencies.

Susie's choir

Another way of combining what you do with what you love is to do it at night! Often loving something you are doing outside of work will help to give you more energy at work. It's important to have something in your life that you love to do. Many people do volunteer work for nonprofit agencies in their spare time. Others find pleasure pursuing sports, hobbies, music, or the arts.

Susan Harris was a counselor for the state unemployment agency. To cool out at the end of the day she would turn on the radio and do backup vocals, "accompanying" her favorite rock 'n' roll stars. She felt so good doing this that it occurred to her that there must be other people with good voices who also loved to sing rock 'n' roll.

Thus, the Marin County Rock and Roll Choir was born. She organized and selected material, produced tapes for friends, and is having a ball doing it. She looks and feels great, and recently got a terrific new job.

CHANGING *WHERE* YOU DO IT

Sometimes the problem is not *what* you do, but *where* you do it. Often a change in atmosphere can convert a seemingly dull job into a rewarding one. If you love skiing, working in a bookstore in Vail can be a lot more fun than working in one in a big city far from the snow. A friend of mine managed a resort hotel in the Southeast but was miserable. She dreamed of living in southern California. Eventually she found a job managing a big hotel in San Diego and now loves her work.

CHANGING *HOW* YOU DO IT

Often a mundane career can be made exciting by its proximity to something you love. Consider the story of Dave and Jim Warsaw. Dave and Jim's dad, Bob, loved sports, and as a boy growing up in Chicago, Bob Warsaw dreamed of playing second base for the Cubs. He hung around Wrigley Field; then, one day in the thirties, he baked a "cute but lifeless" ceramic baseball player. He added one moving part—a small spring attaching the head and the body—and the bobble-head doll with a Cubs logo was born.

His sons inherited their love of sports from their dad. They also inherited his commitment to making a living by being around sports. In their case it wasn't dolls but hats. They decided that players and fans have one thing very much in common, they both need hats. They started a company that makes all kinds of sports hats, 5 million of which were sold last year, some in the $17 to $20 range.

"We take our caps very seriously," says Jim, president of Sports Specialities, during a break from a business trip to the Super Bowl and the NBA All-Star Game, "but making them gives us an excuse to have fun."[30]

A new wrinkle

You can also add a new wrinkle to the same work you are doing and make it more exciting and fulfilling. A travel agent friend of mine originally chose the travel industry because he loved going to new places. But he was bored with sitting in an office spending his days behind a computer, making reservations, and sending out brochures. So he decided to specialize on adventure tours to Africa, South America, and Australia, places he loved to visit. He started out by doing a lot of research on the different destinations, which he found fascinating. He then sent letters of inquiry to hotels, resorts, and national wildlife parks in these areas and actually got invited to visit many of them free. His next step was to prepare a special brochure for a select few of these trips. The first trip filled up in three weeks. He still books trips, but he also goes on them and explores many new areas as well. "It's like I am living my dream," he told me.

Doug Shaffer was a barber and half partner in a chain of salons in Indiana. Shaffer, whose passion in life was playing *and* talking about sports, was getting bored with cutting hair, so he added a new wrinkle. He founded Doug's Sports Cuts—part barber shop, part sports gossip center, and part giftshop for sports memorabilia.

The shop's floorplan includes a tiny basketball court with parquet floor, a dugout for customers waiting for their appointments, and a scaled-down baseball field with the barber chair squarely on home plate. Doug cleans up snipped locks of hair with an umpire's broom. And the only topic of conversation allowed is, of course . . . sports, as customers watch the progress of their trim in an enormous round mirror resembling a baseball.[31]

IN NATURE, NOTHING "RETIRES"

What, where, and how you do what you do is something well within your control, whether you're 20 or 70. It is never too late to find your passion, inject more variety into your daily round, and enjoy life. Nothing in nature retires. As a nation caught up in what Ken Dychtwald calls *The Age Wave*,[32] more and more Americans can now expect to live longer, more productive lives.

As Break-It Thinkers join the age wave, they know that just because you're good at something doesn't mean that you have to do it for the rest of your life. People change. Times change. What you felt passionate about in one phase of your life may not be what turns you on 15 or 20 years later. It's important to gravitate toward those things that infuse your life with gusto, whether you are 28 or 48 or 88.

WINNING IS *PLAYING*

Conventional Wisdom says that you must play to win and winning comes at the end of the game. Not so! Break-It Thinkers know that winning is playing the game. Wins occur every day for the Break-It Thinker. Winning can mean different things to different people. For some it may be working with all kinds of people, for others it can be feeling challenged, learning and growing, doing different things every day, or tackling new challenges, doing creative problem solving or helping the homeless or the environment.

Winning to the Break-It Thinker is *loving what you are doing and doing what you love.*

UW *says:*
Play, to win.

21
Breaking Out

A SIGH OF RELIEF

Although I still run into corporations that limit their thinking to "the way we always do it around here," most are trying to grow beyond this attitude. That is probably why the "unconventional" message of this book is so well received as I speak around the country.

I frequently hear an audible sigh of relief for having confirmed what people's instincts were telling them all along.

People *intuitively* understand that they need to try something new, to take a bold step. They know they must break out of their old way of thinking and responding.

BEYOND WORK

Break-It Thinking is not limited to the world of work but is a style of thinking that will enable anyone to excel in a rapidly changing environment. And since our whole world—not just work, but education, government, the law, athletics not to mention lifestyles and the family—is undergoing radical change, there is an opportunity to apply Break-It Thinking everywhere, in everything we do.

BREAK-IT LEADERSHIP—CREATING THE FUTURE

Conventional wisdom tells us we must respond quickly to change. But the leaders of the future must be creators, not responders. Break-It Thinkers know that the future isn't found; it is invented. It is shaped by people with the vision, courage, and wisdom to think beyond the boundaries of the known.

In our conflict-riddled world, governments have a tough challenge. "Let's face it, it was easier to govern a hundred years ago. The pace of change was slower, and our societies were more coherent. Now even within one country we have more diverse opinions and, naturally, more contention. Becoming a cabinet minister today means a very different set of challenges," says the Honorable Elaine McCoy, Minister of Labour, Alberta, Canada.

"They don't have schools for cabinet ministers—we have to get new ideas wherever we can. And then we have to get our departments to break out of their old thinking and try some new ways to do things. To create a bridge to the future we need to lose our fear of challenging the traditional wisdom," says McCoy.

For our organizations, institutions, and systems to succeed, leaders must, like McCoy, provide guidance, direction, and inspiration, especially in tough times.

Those who will lead us into tomorrow can't be playing it safe or resting on their laurels but must be bold and daring and have fire in their hearts, constantly looking outside to the horizon, seeing beyond the present.

These individuals are proactive thinkers and doers with the courage to take risks and challenge the status quo. They know that the ability to invent a desired future is directly dependant upon the willingness to break with the past.

BREAK-IT SCHOOLS

You can teach people to think in new ways—even in government—but first there is something to unlearn. And that is the belief that we should already have all the answers.

As a consultant for several big-city school districts and a spokesman for Bristol-Myers, speaking to college students throughout the country, I have recently had firsthand experience with our educational system. And nowhere do we need Break-It Thinkers more than in our schools and universities.

One of the reasons for this is that our educational system, as it looks now, was originally designed for the industrial age, when people had predictable jobs, at predictable times, requiring predictable skills since they were going to be employed in predictable places. Now we know that the high point of this industrial society was the mid-fifties. For the past 40 years our economy has been changing into something else—but our educational system has not.

As the problems in education become more alarming, the reaction is very much the same as in business. The tougher things get, the more people play it safe and rely on the old tried and true. The result is an educational system that is literally bound and gagged by tradition.

INFORMATION CHOKE

One of the ironies of our information society is that its students are choking on the amount of information that has to be digested. An education based on the ability to remember and regurgitate information is an education that is outdated long before graduation.

In a culture where the information that is relevant today is obsolete tomorrow, students need to learn *how* to learn, not what to learn. They need to be taught *how* to think, not what to think. Learning how to learn and learning how to embrace change are the critical skills that will enable an individual to thrive in any situation.

We need an educational system run by people who have the courage to challenge tradition, who are not bound by the old ways and limited by conventional thinking. We need individuals with vision, passion, and daring, who are willing to take risks, break old rules, and innovate. And we need to teach our students to be doing the same thing. In short, we need an educational system that is run by Break-It Thinkers for Break-It Thinkers.

BREAK-IT SPORTS

Athletics, the most visible high-pressure arena in the world, have a great influence on many of our structures, strategies, and thinking. Its jargon is used commonly as a metaphor in business: "I struck out" "Don't drop the ball" "When in doubt . . . punt." Athletes can have an equally powerful effect on how to handle pressure.

The breakthroughs in sports have come from Break-It Thinkers, like Jean-Claude Killy, Dick Fosbury, and John Wooden, mentioned earlier. Bill Walsh, who won three Super Bowls as coach of the SF 49ers, was a Break-It Thinker who turned the traditional thinking about offensive football on its head. So was Sonja Heinie, who won the gold medal in figure skating in 1928 by daring to introduce ballet into her routine. And Pancho Segura, who was the first to challenge tradition and use a double-fisted backhand.

These people, like the risk takers who keep pushing the envelope, expand our vistas about what is possible both physically and mentally. These Break-It Thinkers model what it takes for anyone to succeed in any highly competitive, pressure-filled environment.

BREAK-IT RELATIONSHIPS

I once read that when people over 85 were asked about the most meaningful memories of their lives, none mentioned anything about business. They all talked about family, people they loved, and relationships.

Many of the Break-It Thinking tips and techniques discussed throughout this book will enable you to spend more quality time with your family.

But when we do spend time with loved ones we often fall into old, familiar habits and patterns. We go to the same places, see the same people, eat at the same restaurants, talk about the same subjects. The result is that our relationships become predictable, safe, and comfortable. We have lost the connection, the spark.

My wife and I use a Break-It Thinking technique to recapture the excitement. Each month one of us takes responsibility for planning an event that is out of our usual pattern. We treat it like a blind date, not telling the other anything other than when to be ready and what type of clothes to wear. The result is anticipation and delight.

There is another rule in this game. We don't talk about the usual maintenance and logistic issues such as kids, school, work, schedules, house repairs.

We have had some fabulous times. Recently Marilyn took me for a full-moon sea kayak trip on San Francisco Bay. We've also had some faux pas—but even those, because they were out of the ordinary, were refreshing and revitalizing.

IGNITING THE SPARK

Break-It Thinking rekindles a spark, touching something in many of us that has been trapped and submerged too long. We all have dreams tucked away. We all want to feel passionate about what we are doing and how we are living our lives. We all want to "break free" and live life to the fullest.

No one wants to look in the mirror late in his life and feel he didn't give it his best shot. We don't want to give in to our fears. We all want to stand out, to "go for it," to live life as an exciting adventure—with flair, boldness, depth, and daring.

One of the most important realizations I have had in my 25 years of work as a performance psychologist is that there is a Break-It Thinker in each of us. If you reflect on your life you will see that when you were at your best you were experiencing and expressing many of the qualities discussed in this book. You had fire in your heart, were taking risks, chasing dreams . . .

BREAK-IT!

As you close the book, open your Victory Log and reflect on a Break-It Thinking experience you have had. Experience the creativity, passion, and boldness that already exists within you. And remind yourself that it is always there, waiting to be expressed in whatever you are doing, and wherever you go.

Live your life as a Break-It Thinker and you will continually surprise yourself. You'll *do* more than you ever thought you could, *be* more than you ever thought you were, and live a more rewarding, fulfilling, and exciting life.

> **UW** *says:*
> *Break Out—Spread Your Wings*

Source Notes

INTRODUCTION

1. From speech by Walter E. Hoadley, Senior Research Fellow, Hoover Institution, speech to Commonwealth Club, *The Commonwealth* (January 26, 1989): p. 20; Wm. Van Duesen, *Boardroom Reports* (March 15, 1990): p. 5.
2. *Business Week* (September 19, 1988): p. 141.
3. *Inc.* (May 1989): p. 41.

CHAPTER ONE

1. Tuttle, "Maintaining Competitiveness," *Vital Speeches* (January 19, 1989): p. 598.
2. U.S. Congress Office of Technology.
3. Rosabeth Kanter, *When Giants Learn to Dance* (New York: Simon & Schuster, 1990), p. 19–20
4. *Time* (April 14, 1989): p. 59.
5. MIT's Commission on Industrial Productivity, *Fortune* (May 22, 1989): pp. 92–97.
6. Stanley M. Davis, *Future Perfect* (Reading, Mass.: Addison Wesley, 1987).
7. *Fortune* (March 26, 1990): p. 30.
8. Lee Iacocca, *San Francisco Sunday Examiner* (June 22, 1986), p. D2.
9. Bank of America senior v.p. K. Shelly Porges, *Interview* (September 1989).
10. *Forbes* (October 2, 1989): p. 31.

CHAPTER TWO

1. Innovation, *Business Week* (1989): p. 74.
2. *Scanorama* (April 1990): p. 92.
3. *American Way* (January 15, 1990): p. 64–65.
4. *Walt Frazier* (New York: Times Books, 1988), p. 47.
5. *Success* (June 1989): p. 44.
6. James M. Kouzes and Barry Z. Posner, *The Leadership Challenge* (San Francisco: Jossey-Bass, 1987), pp. 5, 6.
7. *Success* (July/August 1989): p. 18.
8. Edward Beauvais, *America West*, letter (November 20, 1990).
9. "King of the Hill," by Rick Reilly. *Sports Illustrated* (June 26, 1989): p. 22.
10. *Esquire* (May 1987): p. 132.
11. Gifford Pinchot III, *Intrapreneuring* (New York: Harper & Row, 1985), p. 42.
12. *Dallas Times Herald*, March 15, 1985, p. 4D.
13. *Vital Speeches of the Day* (September 14, 1988).
14. *Success* (December 1988): p. 32.

CHAPTER THREE

1. *New York Times Magazine*, September 6, 1987, p. 14.
2. *New York Times Magazine*, September 6, 1987, p. 14.
3. *Independent Journal Marin*, KRTN News Wire, July 4, 1989.
4. Richard Thalheimer, *The Sharper Image*, letter (September 21, 1990).
5. *Fortune* (August 18, 1986), p. 27.
6. *New York Times*, May 14, 1989, p. 2, business section.
7. *Healthy Companies* (1989): p. 17.
8. Eddie Murphy to Arsenio Hall, November 16, 1989.

CHAPTER FOUR

1. *San Francisco Examiner*, May 27, 1990, p. D3.
2. K. Shelly Porges, Bank of America, Senior V.P., *Interview* (September, 1989).
3. Peter Block, *The Empowered Manager* (San Francisco: Jossey-Bass, 1988), p. 103.
4. *Inc.* (April 1989): p. 42.
5. *Fortune* (April 24, 1989).
6. *Sports Illustrated* (January 30, 1989), p. 76.
7. *Spirit* (December 1987): p. 36.
8. Tony Tiano, president, KQED.
9. Phone interview, Yvon Chouinard, March 12, 1990.
10. John Sculley, *Odyssey* (New York: Harper & Row, 1987), pp. 220, 320–21, 370.
11. *Success* (December 1988): p. 32.
12. *Esquire* (December 1987): p. 102.
13. *Vis a Vis* (July 1988): p. 58.
14. K. Shelly Porges, Bank of America.
15. *Ibid.*
16. Mike Stanley, *Interview*.

CHAPTER FIVE

1. *USA Weekend* (February 2–4, 1990): p. 6.
2. Dr. Ken Pelletier, *The C Zone* (New York: Fawcett, 1984).
3. *San Francisco Chronicle,* March 20, 1990, p. A15.
4. *San Francisco Sunday Examiner,* July 22, 1990, p. D1.
5. *Fortune* (April 9, 1990): p. 42.

CHAPTER SIX

1. A speech to the American Electronics Association, *Vital Speeches* (September 28, 1988): p. 112.
2. *Forbes* (January 8, 1990).
3. *Forbes* (October 2, 1989): p. 72.
4. *Business Week* (March 30, 1987): pp. 86–87.
5. Ibid.
6. *Forbes* (February 8, 1988): p. 130.
7. *Success* (December 1988): p. 35.
8. *Fortune* (November 19, 1990): p. 67.
9. 1989 Annual Report, PepsiCo., p. 30.
10. *Boardroom* (September 1, 1989): p. 6, and *Boardroom* (July 15, 1987): p. 1.
11. *Marin Independent Journal,* November 13, 1989, p. B5.
12. *Success* (December 1989): p. 51.
13. *Vis a Vis* (March 1990): p. 80.
14. *Esquire* (December 1987): p. 110.
15. Ibid.
16. *Vis a Vis* (March 1990): p. 72.
17. *Sports Illustrated* (April 14, 1986): p. 52.
18. *On Your Behalf* (November 1989): p. 1.
19. *Sports Illustrated* (June 29, 1987): p. 41.
20. *Esquire* (May 1987): p. 122.
21. *Sports Illustrated* (June 29, 1987): p. 41.
22. *Esquire* (December 1987): p. 106.
23. Robert H. Waterman, *The Renewal Factor* (New York: Bantam Books, 1987), p. 154.
24. *Continental Profiles* (January 1990): p. 29.
25. Waterman, p. 216.
26. Paul Viviano, *Interview* (November 15, 1988).
27. *They Call Me Coach* (New York:Comtemporary Books, 1988), p. 114.

CHAPTER SEVEN

1. *San Francisco Chronicle,* July 4, 1990, p. D4.
2. *Fortune* (August 31, 1987): p. 29.
3. *Fortune* (April 10, 1989): p. 86.
4. *Fortune* (June 4, 1990): p. 179, 186.
5. *Fortune* (June 4, 1990): p. 179.
6. *Fortune* (April 9, 1990): p. 40.
7. *Fortune* (May 23, 1988): p. 42.

8. *The Executive Speaker* (August 1989): pp. 5–6.
9. *New York Times Magazine,* October 29, 1989, pp. 43–44.
10. *Inc.* (May 1989): p. 36.
11. *Fortune* (January 15, 1990): p. 97.
12. *Fortune* (January 15, 1990): p. 81.
13. *San Francisco Chronicle,* September 4, 1990, p. D5.

CHAPTER EIGHT

1. Phone interview, Bob Siegel, June 28, 1990.
2. Phone interview, Yvon Chouinard, March 12, 1990.
3. *Fortune* (February 12, 1990): p. 96.
4. Mat Roush, *USA Today* (June 4, 1990): p. D1.
5. C. V. Prahalad, *Vital Speeches* (April 1, 1990): p. 355.
6. *Fortune* (August 13, 1990): p. 48.
7. *Success* (September 1990): p. 12.
8. Interview with Sarah Nolan, March 1990.
9. *Success* (June 1989): p. 45.
10. *Inc.* (April 1989): p. 77.
11. Anita Roddick, speech, Lost Arrow meeting, January 15, 1990.
12. *Esquire* (December 1987): pp. 29, 30, 65.
13. Ibid.
14. *Sports Illustrated* (September 4, 1989): pp. 118–24.

CHAPTER NINE

1. *Success* (November 1989): p. 18.
2. *Boardroom Reports* (August 1, 1990): p. 3.
3. *Vital Speeches* (January 19, 1989): pp. 598–99.
4. *New York Times,* June 3, 1990, section 3, part 2, p. 25.
5. Stanley M. Davis, *Future Perfect* (Reading, Mass.: Addison-Wesley, 1987).
6. *Fortune* (February 15, 1988): p. 48.
7. Innovation, *Business Week* (1989): p. 128.
8. *Success* (June 1988): p. 8.
9. *Fortune* (April 9, 1990): p. 41.
10. Ibid.
11. Ibid.
12. Phone interview, February 15, 1990.
13. K. Shelly Porges *Interview.*
14. *New York Times,* March 25, 1990, section 3, p. 6.
15. *Fortune* (May 7, 1990), p. 52.
16. *Boardroom Reports* (February 15, 1990): p. 2.
17. *Success* magazine.
18. *San Francisco Chronicle,* November 9, 1987, p. C1.
19. *New York Times,* February 5, 1990, p. D6.
20. *Speakout* (November 1989): p. 7.
21. *Fortune* (January 1, 1990): p. 14.

CHAPTER TEN

1. Richard Tamm, *Interview* (October 1989).
2. The Honorable Elaine McCoy, *Interview* (August 1990).
3. *Vis a vis* (February 1989): p. 100.
4. *Business Week* (December 1989): p. 107.
5. *San Francisco Chronicle*, November 9, 1987, pp. C1, C7.
6. Ibid.

CHAPTER ELEVEN

1. *Success* (January/February, 1989): p. 16.
2. *House and Garden* (February 1990): p. 168.
3. *Fortune* (May 23, 1988): p. 30.
4. *Business Week* (March 23, 1987): p. 93.
5. Phone interview, Jack Wilborn, December 5, 1989.
6. *Fortune* (September 12, 1988): p. 156.
7. *Fortune* (February 12, 1990): p. 100.
8. *Success* (January/February, 1989): pp. 72–73.
9. *Business Week* (December 15, 1986): p. 65.
10. *New York Times*, June 11, 1989, p. 65.
11. *Fortune* (July 17, 1989): p. 115.
12. *Success* (December 1989): p. 31.
13. Joe Robinson, *You're the Boss* (New York: St. Martin's Press, 1987), p. 78.
14. *San Francisco Chronicle*, July 18, 1990, pp. 1, 16.
15. KCBS news, March 14, 1990.
16. *Fortune* (June 6, 1988): p. 56.
17. Ibid.
18. Ibid.
19. Charles Panati, *Extraordinary Origins of Everyday Things* (New York: Harper & Row, 1987).
20. *Inc.* (November 1989): p. 66.

CHAPTER TWELVE

1. *San Francisco Sunday Examiner*, June 22, 1986, p. D2.
2. *Time* (August 29, 1983): p. 52.
3. Gifford Pinchot III, *Intraprenuring* (New York: Harper & Row, 1985), p. 68.
4. *Fortune* (January 15, 1990): p. 144.
5. *Walt Frazier* (New York: Times Books, 1988), p. 178.
6. CBS Morning, July 23, 1990.
7. *United Airlines Mainliner* (January 1986): p. 56.
8. *Sound Management Newsletter*, vol 1, no. 1 (1989): pp. 6–8.
9. *Independent Journal* (February 20, 1990): p. A7.
10. *Vital Speeches of the Day* (March 29, 1989): pp. 531, 533.
11. *Time* (August 29, 1983): p. 56.
12. *Esquire* (September 1985): p. 42.
13. *USAIR* (December 1989): p. 65.
14. *Fortune* (November 19, 1990): p. 34.
15. *Think*, no. 1 (1989): p. 1.

CHAPTER THIRTEEN

1. *Sports Illustrated* (October 17, 1988): p. 34.
2. *Success* (December 1987): p. 52.
3. Robert J. Kriegel and Marilyn Harris Kriegel, *The C Zone* (New York: Anchor Press/Doubleday, 1984), p. 71.
4. Ibid, p. 92.

CHAPTER FOURTEEN

1. *Success* (September 1988): p. 30.
2. James M. Kouzes and Barry Z. Posner, *Leadership Challenge* (San Francisco: Jossey-Bass, 1987), p. 63.
3. *Boardroom Reports* (July 1, 1990): p. 8.
4. *Inc.* (January 1989): p. 60.
5. John Sculley, *Odyssey* (New York: Harper & Row, 1987), pp. 264, 420.
6. Kouzes and Posner, p. 64.
7. *U.S. News & World Report* (nd).
8. Jim Tunney *Speak Out* (June 6, 1987): p. 3.
9. *New York Times*, December 1, 1985, section 3, p. 1.
10. Phone interview, Phillip Moffitt, August 2, 1990.
11. *New York Times*, December 1, 1985, section 3, p. 1.
12. *Sports Illustrated* (December 2, 1985): p. 91–92.
13. *Sports Illustrated* (June 23, 1986): p. 78.
14. *Footwear News* magazine (February 1989): p. 49.
15. *Inc.* (May 1989): p. 36.
16. *Fortune* (August 31, 1987): p. 28.
17. *Fortune* (June 6, 1988): p. 60.
18. *Sound Management Newsletter* (February 1990): p. 4.

CHAPTER FIFTEEN

1. Walter Wriston speaking to Washington Business Group on Health, Washington, D.C. (September 18, 1981).
2. *Boardroom Reports* (April 1, 1990): p. 13.
3. *Creative Living* (1990): p. 23.
4. *Success* (April 1990): p. 47.
5. *New York Times Magazine*, January 31, 1988, p. 37.
6. *Wall Street Journal*, May 2, 1988, p. 25.

CHAPTER SIXTEEN

1. *Success* (September 1988): p. 54.
2. *Esquire* (October 1986): p. 73.

CHAPTER SEVENTEEN

1. *Boardroom Reports* (July 1, 1990): p. 13
2. *Inc.* (May 1989): p. 35.

CHAPTER EIGHTEEN

1. *Pacific Sun,* April 26–May 2, 1985, p. 1.
2. Robert J. Kriegel and Marilyn Harris Kriegel, *The C Zone* (New York: Anchor Press/Doubleday, 1984), p. 98.
3. Ibid, pp. 100, 150.
4. *TRiPs* (September/October 1989): pp. 8–9.
5. Kriegel and Kriegel, p. 101.
6. *San Francisco Chronicle,* August 3, 1990, p. D3.
7. Kriegel and Kriegel, p. 110.

CHAPTER TWENTY

1. *Fortune* (June 5, 1989): pp. 202, 210.
2. *Boardroom Reports* (April 1, 1990): p. 16.
3. *Fortune* (June 5, 1989).
4. *San Francisco Chronicle,* March 29, 1990, p. C1.
5. *Fortune* (April 10, 1989): p. 58.
6. *Bottom Line* (January 30, 1989): p. 1.
7. *Fortune* (April 10, 1989): p. 62.
8. *San Francisco Chronicle,* November 12, 1989, p. 7.
9. *San Francisco Chronicle,* January 12, 1990, p. C1.
10. KYA radio, September 4, 1989.
11. *Inc.* (November 1989): p. 52.
12. *Inc.* (April 1989): p. 45.
13. *San Francisco Chronicle,* December 6, 1989, p. B5.
14. Robert J. Kriegel and Marilyn Harris Kriegel, *The C Zone* (New York: Anchor Press/Doubleday, 1984), p. 48.
15. *Success* (June 1985): p. 43.
16. Srully Blotnick, *Getting Rich Your Own Way* (New York: Playboy Paperbacks, 1982), p. 3.
17. Paul Hawken, *Growing a Business* (New York: A Fireside Book, Simon & Schuster, 1988), pp. 81–82.
18. *Inc.* (July 1989): p. 53.
19. Phone interview, Peter Lind, July 26, 1990.
20. *Inc.* (July 1989): p. 53.
21. *Fortune* (February 13, 1989): p. 62.
22. *Inc.* (April 1989): p. 49.
23. *Fortune* (April 10, 1989): p. 18.
24. *Fortune* (March 27, 1989).
25. Kriegel and Kriegel, p. 126.
26. *Fortune* (July 16, 1990): p. 118.
27. *New York Times,* June 24, 1990, section 3, part 2, p. 25.
28. *New York Times,* June 24, 1990, section 3, part 2, p. 25.
29. *New York Times,* April 15, 1990, section 1, page 18.
30. *Sports Illustrated* (June 2, 1989), design column, np.
31. *Sports Illustrated* (June 18, 1990): p. 10.
32. Ken Dychtwald, *The Age Wave* (New York: Bantam Books, 1990), p. 108.

ROBERT J. KRIEGEL, PH.D., is the co-author of *The C Zone: Peak Performance Under Pressure* and co-author of the *New York Times* bestseller *Inner Skiing*. A former all-American athlete and pioneer in the field of performance psychology, Kriegel has been the mental coach for many Olympic and professional athletes and has been called by *U.S. News and World Report*, "One of the leading authorities in the field of human performance." The *New York Times* said his work "created a revolution in performance practices." He has also been a marketing and advertising executive with a major New York advertising agency, has taught at Stanford University's Executive Management Program, and is a commentator on "Marketplace" on National Public Radio.

A former member of the California Governor's Council and a national spokesman for Bristol-Meyers Squibb, Kriegel currently gives speeches and programs for major corporations and associations around the world and is on the advisory board of the Green Century Project. He lives and works in Muir Beach, California.

LOUIS PATLER, PH.D., is president of the B.I.T. Group, an international training and consulting company based in Marin County, California, that brings "Break-It!" Thinking technologies to corporations, associations, and governments. Dr. Patler, award-winning author, speaker, and former editor of the *American Trend Report*, lives with his family in Mill Valley, California.